Frommer's™

Philadelphia day BY day™

1st Edition

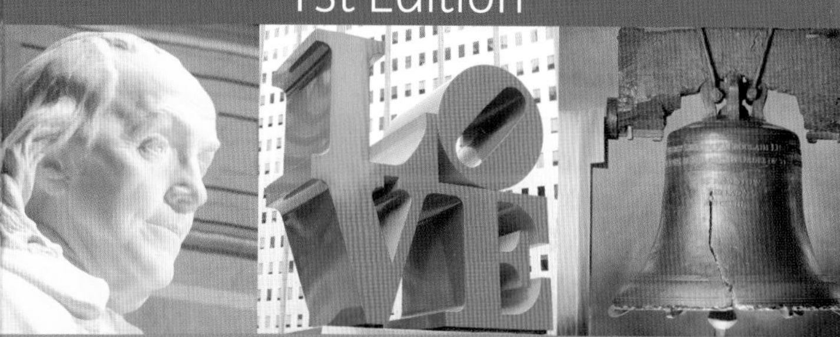

by Lauren McCutcheon

WILEY

John Wiley & Sons Canada, Ltd.

Contents

Published by:

John Wiley & Sons Canada, Ltd.

6045 Freemont Blvd.
Mississauga, ON L5R 4J3

ISBN 978-0-470-73767-5
Editor: Gene Shannon
Developmental Editor: Melissa Klurman
Production Editor: Pamela Vokey
Project Coordinator: Lynsey Stanford
Editorial Assistant: Katie Wolsley
Photo Editor: Photo Affairs Inc.
Cartographer: Lohnes + Wright
Vice President, Publishing Services: Karen Bryan
Production by Wiley Indianapolis Composition Services

For information on our other products and services or to obtain technical support, please contact our Customer Care Department within the U.S. at 877/762-2974, outside the U.S. at 317/572-3993 or fax 317/572-4002.

Wiley also publishes its books in a variety of electronic formats. Some content that appears in print may not be available in electronic formats.

Manufactured in China

5 4 3 2 1

A Note from the Editorial Director

Organizing your time. That's what this guide is all about.

Other guides give you long lists of things to see and do and then expect you to fit the pieces together. The Day by Day guides are different. These guides tell you the best of everything, and then they show you how to see it *in the smartest, most time-efficient way*. Our authors have designed detailed itineraries organized by time, neighborhood, or special interest. And each tour comes with a bulleted map that takes you from stop to stop.

Hoping to immerse yourself in American history or delve into the amazing art treasures of the Barnes collection? Planning to eat your way through Philly's top culinary hotspots, or tour the iconic Rocky Balboa sites? Whatever your interest or schedule, the Day by Days give you the smartest routes to follow. Not only do we take you to the top attractions, hotels, and restaurants, but we also help you access those special moments that locals get to experience—those "finds" that turn tourists into travelers.

The Day by Days are also your top choice if you're looking for one complete guide for all your travel needs. The best hotels and restaurants for every budget, the greatest shopping values, the wildest nightlife—it's all here.

Why should you trust our judgment? Because our authors personally visit each place they write about. They're an independent lot who say what they think and would never include places they wouldn't recommend to their best friends. They're also open to suggestions from readers. If you'd like to contact them, please send your comments our way at feedback@frommers.com, and we'll pass them on.

Enjoy your Day by Day guide—the most helpful travel companion you can buy. And have the trip of a lifetime.

Warm regards,

Kelly Regan

Kelly Regan, Editorial Director
Frommer's Travel Guides

About the Author

Lauren McCutcheon grew up outside Philadelphia in Jenkintown and has lived in the city for 10 years. She writes for *Philadelphia Magazine* and has contributed to *Philadelphia Weekly, Philadelphia Daily News, Mademoiselle,* and others, and she was an editor for Philadelphia.Citysearch.com. She has written two modern etiquette guides, *A Virgin's Guide to Everything* (Warner Books) and *The Right Way* (F + W Publications). She is also the co-author of *Frommer's Philadelphia & the Amish Country*.

An Additional Note

Please be advised that travel information is subject to change at any time—and this is especially true of prices. We therefore suggest that you write or call ahead for confirmation when making your travel plans. The authors, editors, and publisher cannot be held responsible for the experiences of readers while traveling. Your safety is important to us, however, so we encourage you to stay alert and be aware of your surroundings.

Star Ratings, Icons & Abbreviations

Every hotel, restaurant, and attraction listing in this guide has been ranked for quality, value, service, amenities, and special features using a **star-rating system.** Hotels, restaurants, attractions, shopping, and nightlife are rated on a scale of zero stars (recommended) to three stars (exceptional). In addition to the star-rating system, we also use a kids **icon** to point out the best bets for families. Within each tour, we recommend cafes, bars, or restaurants where you can take a break. Each of these stops appears in a shaded box marked with a coffee-cup-shaped bullet.

The following **abbreviations** are used for credit cards:

AE	American Express	DISC	Discover	V	Visa
DC	Diners Club	MC	MasterCard		

Frommers.com

Now that you have this guidebook to help you plan a great trip, visit our website at **www.frommers.com** for additional travel information on more than 4,000 destinations. We update features regularly to give you instant access to the most current trip-planning information available. At Frommers.com, you'll find scoops on the best airfares, lodging rates, and car rental bargains. You can even book your travel online through our reliable travel booking partners. Other popular features include:

- Online updates of our most popular guidebooks
- Vacation sweepstakes and contest giveaways
- Newsletters highlighting the hottest travel trends
- Podcasts, interactive maps, and up-to-the-minute events listings
- Opinionated blog entries by Arthur Frommer himself
- Online travel message boards with featured travel discussions

A Note on Prices

In the "Take a Break" and "Best Bets" sections of this book, we have used a system of dollar signs to show a range of costs for 1 night in a hotel (the price of a double-occupancy room) or the cost of an entree at a restaurant. Use the following table to decipher the dollar signs:

Cost	Hotels	Restaurants
$	under $100	under $10
$$	$100–$200	$10–$20
$$$	$200–$300	$20–$30
$$$$	$300–$400	$30–$40
$$$$$	over $400	over $40

An Invitation to the Reader

In researching this book, we discovered many wonderful places—hotels, restaurants, shops, and more. We're sure you'll find others. Please tell us about them, so we can share the information with your fellow travelers in upcoming editions. If you were disappointed with a recommendation, we'd love to know that, too. Please write to:

Frommer's Philadelphia Day by Day, 1st Edition
John Wiley & Sons Canada, Ltd. • 6045 Freemont Blvd. •
Mississauga, ON L5R 4J3

excelleRx

16 Favorite **Moments**

16 Favorite **Moments**

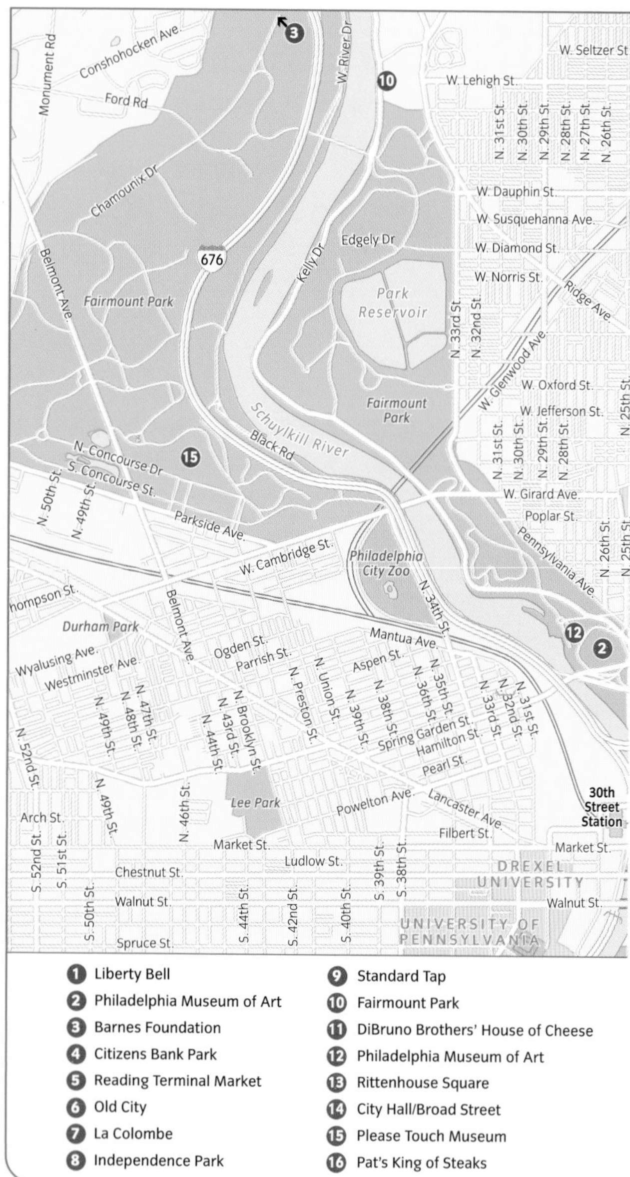

1. Liberty Bell
2. Philadelphia Museum of Art
3. Barnes Foundation
4. Citizens Bank Park
5. Reading Terminal Market
6. Old City
7. La Colombe
8. Independence Park
9. Standard Tap
10. Fairmount Park
11. DiBruno Brothers' House of Cheese
12. Philadelphia Museum of Art
13. Rittenhouse Square
14. City Hall/Broad Street
15. Please Touch Museum
16. Pat's King of Steaks

Previous Page: Children play in a fountain at Logan Circle.

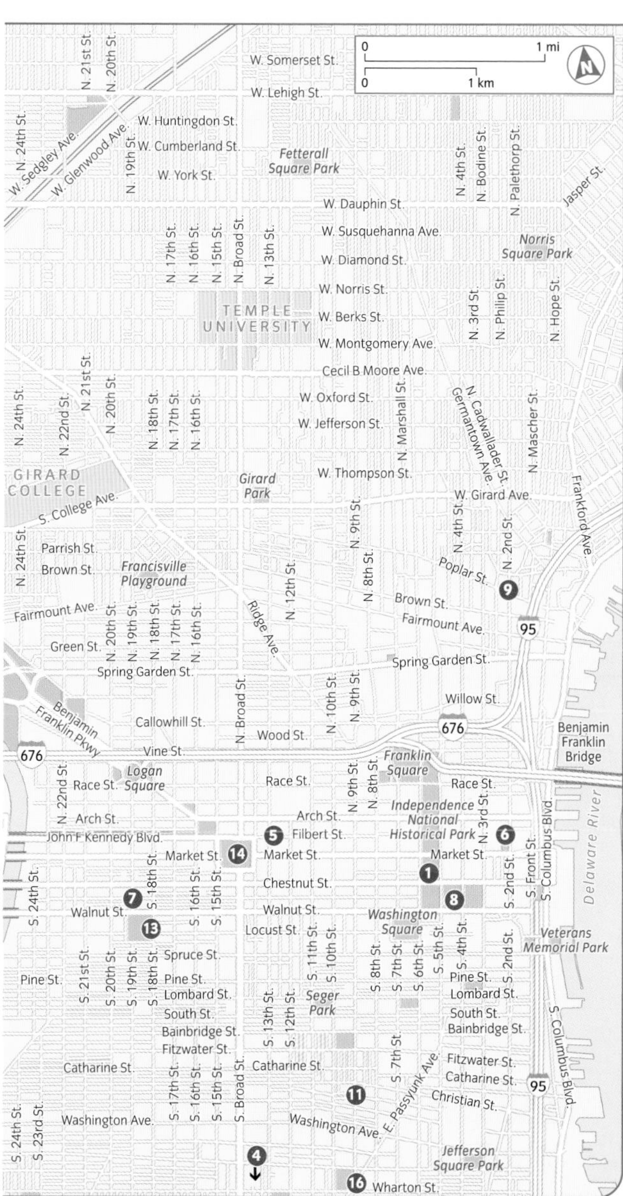
0
1 mi
0
1 km
N
W. Somerset St.
W. Lehigh St.
N. 21st St.
N. 20th St.
N. 24th St.
W. Sedgley Ave.
W. Glenwood Ave.
W. Huntingdon St.
W. Cumberland St.
N. 19th St.
W. York St.
Fetterall Square Park
N. 4th St.
N. Bodine St.
N. Palethorp St.
Jasper St.
W. Dauphin St.
W. Susquehanna Ave.
W. Diamond St.
N. 17th St.
N. 16th St.
N. 15th St.
N. Broad St.
N. 13th St.
Norris Square Park
W. Norris St.
W. Berks St.
W. Montgomery Ave.
TEMPLE UNIVERSITY
N. 3rd St.
N. Philip St.
N. Hope St.
Cecil B Moore Ave.
W. Oxford St.
W. Jefferson St.
N. 21st St.
N. 20th St.
N. 24th St.
N. 22nd St.
N. 18th St.
N. 17th St.
N. 16th St.
N. Marshall St.
N. Cadwallader St.
Germantown Ave.
N. Mascher St.
GIRARD COLLEGE
Girard Park
W. Thompson St.
W. Girard Ave.
Frankford Ave.
S. College Ave.
N. 9th St.
N. 4th St.
N. 2nd St.
N. 24th St.
Parrish St.
Brown St.
Francisville Playground
N. 12th St.
N. 8th St.
Poplar St.
9
Fairmount Ave.
N. 20th St.
N. 19th St.
N. 18th St.
N. 17th St.
N. 16th St.
Ridge Ave.
Brown St.
Fairmount Ave.
95
Green St.
Spring Garden St.
Spring Garden St.
N. Broad St.
N. 10th St.
N. 9th St.
Willow St.
Benjamin Franklin Pkwy
Callowhill St.
Wood St.
676
Benjamin Franklin Bridge
676
Vine St.
Franklin Square
N. 22nd St.
Race St.
Logan Square
Race St.
N. 9th St.
N. 8th St.
Race St.
Arch St.
Arch St.
Independence National Historical Park
N. 3rd St.
John F Kennedy Blvd.
5
Filbert St.
6
S. Columbus Blvd.
Delaware River
Market St.
14
Market St.
Market St.
S. 18th St.
S. 16th St.
S. 15th St.
1
S. 2nd St.
S. Front St.
S. 24th St.
Chestnut St.
7
8
Walnut St.
Walnut St.
Washington Square
13
Locust St.
S. 11th St.
S. 10th St.
S. 5th St.
S. 4th St.
Veterans Memorial Park
S. 21st St.
S. 20th St.
S. 19th St.
S. 18th St.
Spruce St.
S. 8th St.
S. 7th St.
S. 6th St.
S. 2nd St.
Pine St.
Pine St.
Pine St.
Lombard St.
S. 13th St.
S. 12th St.
Seger Park
Lombard St.
South St.
South St.
Bainbridge St.
Bainbridge St.
S. Columbus Blvd.
Fitzwater St.
S. 7th St.
Fitzwater St.
Catharine St.
S. 17th St.
S. 16th St.
S. 15th St.
S. Broad St.
Catharine St.
E. Passyunk Ave.
Catharine St.
95
11
Christian St.
S. 24th St.
S. 23rd St.
Washington Ave.
Washington Ave.
4
Jefferson Square Park
16
Wharton St.

Getting a true feeling for all that is Philadelphia means being willing to embrace extremes. One minute, you're immersed in American history. The next, you're elbow-to-elbow in a crowd of modern-day foodies. You'll be able to embrace nature at the country's largest city park, glimpse the city's unique brand of chic at Rittenhouse Square, see cutting-edge art in Old City—and, of course, have your fill of that one particular sandwich which many Philadelphians think is as important as Benjamin Franklin (well, almost).

1 Visit the Liberty Bell. The cracked bell that no longer tolls seems to top every tourist's to-do list. Go see it early, but also walk by it again after dusk, when its bronze cast seems to glow inside its modern glass-and-steel house. *See p 9.*

2 Run like Rocky up the steps of the Philadelphia Museum of Art. When you get to the top, turn around, pump your fists in the air, and belt out a few bars of "Gonna Fly Now" (or just play it in the soundtrack in your head). Then, get your photo taken with the boxer's statue at the foot of the museum. *See p 13.*

3 Soak in Albert Barnes' amazingly eclectic collection. You'll find an amazing array of Matisses (1869–1954), Renoirs (1841–1919), Picassos (1881–1973), Cézannes (1839–1906), African sculpture, Pennsylvania Dutch furniture, and more just outside the city limits in Barnes' suburban Merion manse, while it's still there. (In 2012, the collection moves to a new space along Ben Franklin Pkwy.) For now, however, reserve well in advance. *See p 34.*

4 Take in a Phillies game. Don't tell, but the Phillies are my favorite of all of the local teams, and not just because they brought home the Series in 2008 and went all the way in 2009. Led by soft-spoken sage Charlie Manuel, the Phils have a special vibe that's spirited and modest. (Plus, you gotta admit: Those fellas are easy on the eyes.) Go catch a game at Citizens Bank Park, and when that ball soars "outta here," watch—and hear—the ballpark's giant Liberty Bell ring. *See p 167.*

5 Get a taste—literally—of Reading Terminal Market. You'll find dozens of local vendors here,

The Barnes has an unparalleled collection of work by Impressionist painters and others.

The Philadelphia Phillies always attract an energetic crowd to Citizens Bank Park.

boasting every sort of fare Philadelphia has to offer, from oysters to cheesesteaks, cannoli to shoofly pie. Even though it's crazy-packed on Saturday mornings, that's when I like to go, to soak in the hustle and bustle—and to see what everyone else is buying. *See p 83.*

6 **Friday gallery hop in Old City.** Go on the first Friday of each month, and you'll be treated to edgy art, welcoming crowds, and free wine and beer—if you can snag it—mostly along North 2nd and 3rd streets. *See p 33.*

7 **Order a "cappuccino for here" at La Colombe.** At this popular cafe, for less than $3, you can enjoy a silky-foamed coffee in a handsome Fima Deruta cup and discover why *Food and Wine* rated this spot the best cafe in the country. *See p 63.*

8 **Meet the Colonials.** Go ahead. Strike up a chat with the 18th-century characters roaming Independence Park and Old City. Each tricorn-hatted soldier and full-skirted seamstress and fresh-faced page and dead-ringer for Ben Franklin has an engaging personal story to tell about the birth of the nation. (Plus, they give the best directions.) *See p 26.*

9 **Drink a pint of hand-pumped ale at Northern Liberties' Standard Tap.** You'll be participating in an age-old tradition. Before Prohibition, Philadelphia was the beer-brewing capital of the Western Hemisphere. Today, local microbrewers such as the Philadelphia Brewing Company, Yards, and Victory are reviving that legacy via delicious stouts, lagers, ambers, pilsners, and more. *See p 122.*

10 **Take a long walk in Fairmount Park.** It's the country's largest city park; my favorite place to roam there is called Valley Green, with its wide pathways, historic bridges, and free admission. The area is especially pretty in fall when the leaves change colors and in winter when you can just imagine the horse-and-carriages of yesteryear

La Colombe has been rated the best cafe in the country.

DiBruno Brothers' House of Cheese boasts outstanding cheeses from around the world.

jingle-belling through the snow. *See p 89.*

⑪ Cram yourself into the DiBruno Brothers' House of Cheese. The impossibly narrow space in the Italian Market is full of charming cheesemongers who talk you into blowing all your money on an herb-coated raw sheep's milk concoction from the wilds of Provence, or an extra-sharp Provolone aged for two years in Italy. *See p 19.*

⑫ Don't walk: Ride. A Segway i2 Glider, specifically. These futuristically goofy "personal transporters" really are the best way to roam the larger-than-it-looks area around the Philadelphia Museum of Art. Who cares that you'll look kinda goofy? You've got the best ride in town! *See p 166.*

⑬ Go high-brow along Rittenhouse Square. The time to go is late afternoon to late evening, when a seat at a sidewalk table at one of the seen-and-be-seen watering holes will ensure you a view of the most stylish impromptu parade in town. *See p 93.*

⑭ Catch the Mummers. What Mardi Gras is to New Orleans, this oddly engaging, entirely debauched New Year's Day parade is to Philadelphia, only much chillier and much less organized, if you can picture that. (Imagine a bunch of contractors dressed in sequins, feathers, and face paint, stopping along Broad Street to dance and march to loud pop tunes, and you've got an idea of Mummery.) *See p 18.*

⑮ Let the kids go nuts at Memorial Hall. It may look like an imposing venue, but ever since the Please Touch Museum moved in, it's as welcoming as a playground—besides reversing the "no touching" rule, it has hundreds of exhibits encouraging kids to play and explore, ride and create, and play some more. *See p 37.*

⑯ Eat a cheesesteak. Preferably at a red picnic table beneath the neon lights at Pat's King of Steaks in South Philly. At 2:30am, just after the bars have all let out. (You didn't think I'd leave this off the list, did you?) *See p 44.* ●

1 The Best **Full-Day Tours**

The Best in One Day

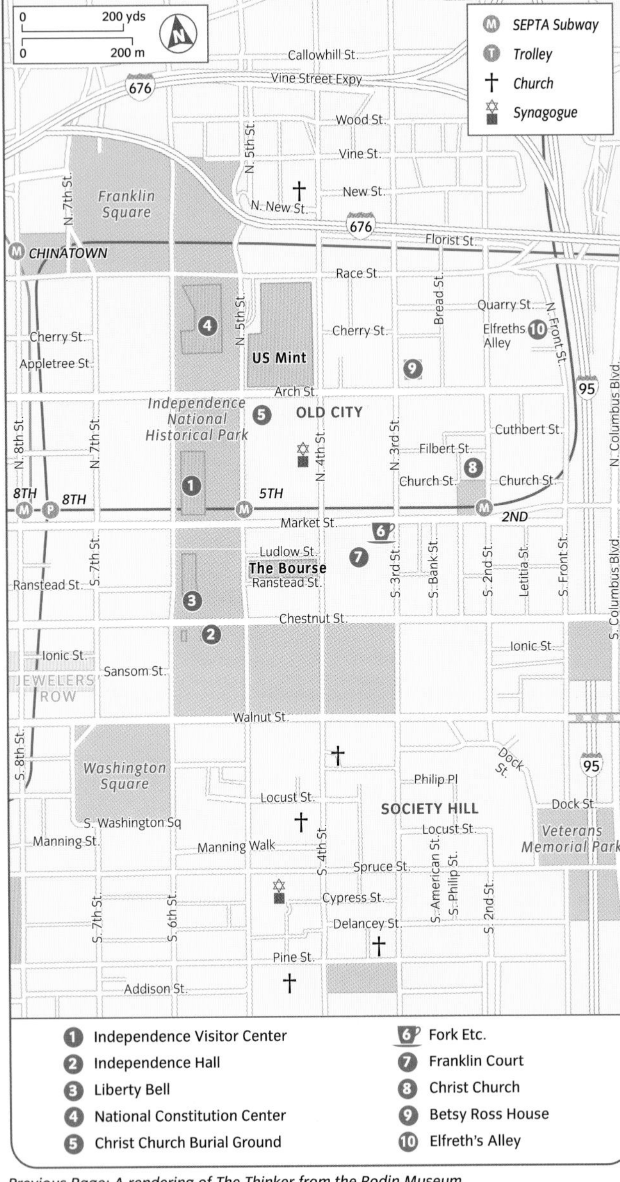

1. Independence Visitor Center
2. Independence Hall
3. Liberty Bell
4. National Constitution Center
5. Christ Church Burial Ground
6. Fork Etc.
7. Franklin Court
8. Christ Church
9. Betsy Ross House
10. Elfreth's Alley

Previous Page: A rendering of The Thinker from the Rodin Museum.

This 1-day tour offers a glimpse of early Philadelphia, and, therefore, insight into early America—starting with the Revolution. For the next few days, the country's "most historic square mile" will be your stomping grounds: Wear comfortable shoes, and don't be afraid to chat up the costumed Colonials. START: **Independence Visitor Center, 6th & Market sts.**

1 ★★ Independence Visitor Center. This welcome center, with its self-service kiosks, concierge services, umpteen maps and brochures, and box office for tickets to Independence Hall and historic homes isn't just a great first stop for a tour of historic Philadelphia, it's a great first stop for *any* tour of Philadelphia. ½ *hr. 6th & Market sts.* ☎ *800/537-7676. www.independencevisitorcenter.com. Daily from 8:30am.*

2 ★★★ Independence Hall. Where it all went down: the Declaration of Independence, the Articles of Confederation, and the U.S. Constitution. Squeeze into the stately spaces where George Washington (1732–1799), Thomas Jefferson (1743–1826), John Adams (1735–1826), Benjamin Franklin (1706–1790), and their Colonial brethren conceived of a country affording its citizens "life, liberty and the pursuit of happiness." Don't miss Washington's "Rising Sun Chair," rare maps of the 13 colonies, and the tipstaff (a wooden and brass instrument used to subdue rowdy onlookers in the courtroom). Half-hour tours are guided. *1 hr.; includes wait in line. Chestnut St., btw. 5th & 6th sts.* ☎ *215/965-2305. www.nps.gov/inde. Mar 1–Dec 31, tickets are required (free at Visitor Center or $1.50 in advance online: pick up at least one hour before tour). Daily 9am–5pm.*

3 ★★★ Liberty Bell. The cracked, one-ton symbol of American independence and equality resides in a $12.6-million glass gazebo across Chestnut Street from Independence Hall. Interactive exhibits aim to keep you from reaching out and ringing the bell. (Don't even think about it.) ½ *hr. Free admission (tickets not required; mandatory security check). Daily 9am–5pm.*

Guided tours of Independence Hall leave every half-hour.

The National Constitution Center has performances and interactive exhibits dedicated to the U.S. Constitution.

❹ ★★ kids **National Constitution Center.** The newest addition to Independence Park is the world's only museum devoted to the U.S. Constitution—which is way more fun than it sounds. There are live performances-in-the-round that explain the document's history, as well as interactive exhibits that let you take the Presidential Oath of Office, don a Supreme Court robe, stand next to a Declaration signer, and examine hanging chads from the 2000 election. ⌚ *1½ hr. 525 Arch St. ☎ 215/409-6600. www.constitutioncenter.org. Admission $12 adults, $11 seniors, $8 children 4–12. Buy tickets in advance; arrive 20 minutes early for timed theater show. Mon–Fri 9:30am–5pm, Sat 9:30am–6pm, Sun noon–5pm.*

❺ ★ **Christ Church Burial Ground.** The 1719 expansion of Christ Church *(see p 11, bullet ❽)*, includes the graves of signers of the Declaration of Independence, including, most notably, that of Benjamin Franklin. Join the throngs who have tossed a penny on it (through the fence) for good luck. ⌚ *¼ hr. SE corner of 5th & Arch sts. www.oldchristchurch.org. Closed to the public.*

❻ ★★ **Fork Etc.** Step back, momentarily, into modern times for a tasty salad, light sandwich, natural soda, cappuccino, and the day's papers at this quick-stop gourmet cafe. For a longer lunch, try Etc.'s slightly-more-formal sister restaurant, Fork, next door (see p 106). *308 Market St. ☎ 215/625-9425. www.forkrestaurant.com. $–$$.*

❼ ★★ kids **Franklin Court.** Brick arches disguise Ben Franklin's former home, which, since it was long ago demolished, is now represented by a steel frame girder. Nearby is a museum that pays tribute to Franklin's many

The museum at Franklin Court pays tribute to the man's many careers.

Elfreth's Alley is the oldest continually inhabited street in the United States.

careers, shows a 22-minute film about *The Real Ben Franklin,* and operates a post office that hand-stamps postcards. ⌚ ***1 hr. 314–322 Market St. ☎ 215/965-2305. Free admission. Daily 11am–5pm. Post office closed Sun.***

8 ★★ Christ Church. Old City might be proudest of this English Palladian landmark, oft regarded as the neighborhood's most important Colonial building. George Washington had his own pew here. William Penn (1644–1718) received his baptism in the font, a gift from London's All Hallows' Church. Although plaques and memorial markers abound, keep in mind that person seated beneath the circa 1744 chandelier could be one of the active church's congregants. A volunteer guide in the nave will gladly offer an impromptu tour—and hush you, if necessary. ⌚ ***½ hr. 2nd & Market sts. ☎ 215/922-1695. www.christchurchphila.org. Free admission; donations accepted. Mon–Sat 9am–5pm; Sun 12:30–5pm. Closed Mon–Tues in Jan–Feb.***

9 ★ kids Betsy Ross House. The jury's out on whether Betsy Ross (1752–1836), the seamstress of the Stars and Stripes, actually lived in this teensy abode (or, actually, if she really sewed the first flag). No matter: This restored dwelling remains a minute joy to explore, from cellar kitchen to wee bedrooms to flag-filled gift shop. ⌚ ***½ hr. 239 Arch St. ☎ 215/686-1252. www.betsyrosshouse.org. Suggested donation $3 adults, $2 students; audio tour $5. Apr–Sept daily 10am–5pm; Oct–Mar Tues–Sun 10am–5pm.***

10 ★★★ Elfreth's Alley. The oldest continuously inhabited street in the States could teach you a thing or two about getting along with the neighbors. Small, two-story row houses line the narrow cobblestone lane, the original homes of tradesmen, artisans, and urbanites of varied religions and ethnicities. Number 126, the Mantua Maker's House (cape maker) is the alley's museum, complete with 18th-century garden and dressmaker's shop. ⌚ ***1 hr. Off 2nd St., toward Front St., btw. Arch & Race sts. ☎ 215/574-0560. www.elfrethsalley.org. Free admission to visitor center & gift shop; Mantua Maker's House $5 adults, $1 children (includes 20-minute tour). Mar–Oct Tues noon–5pm, Wed–Sat 10am–5pm, Sun noon–5pm; Nov–Feb Thurs–Sat 10am–5pm, Sun noon–5pm.***

The Best **in Two Days**

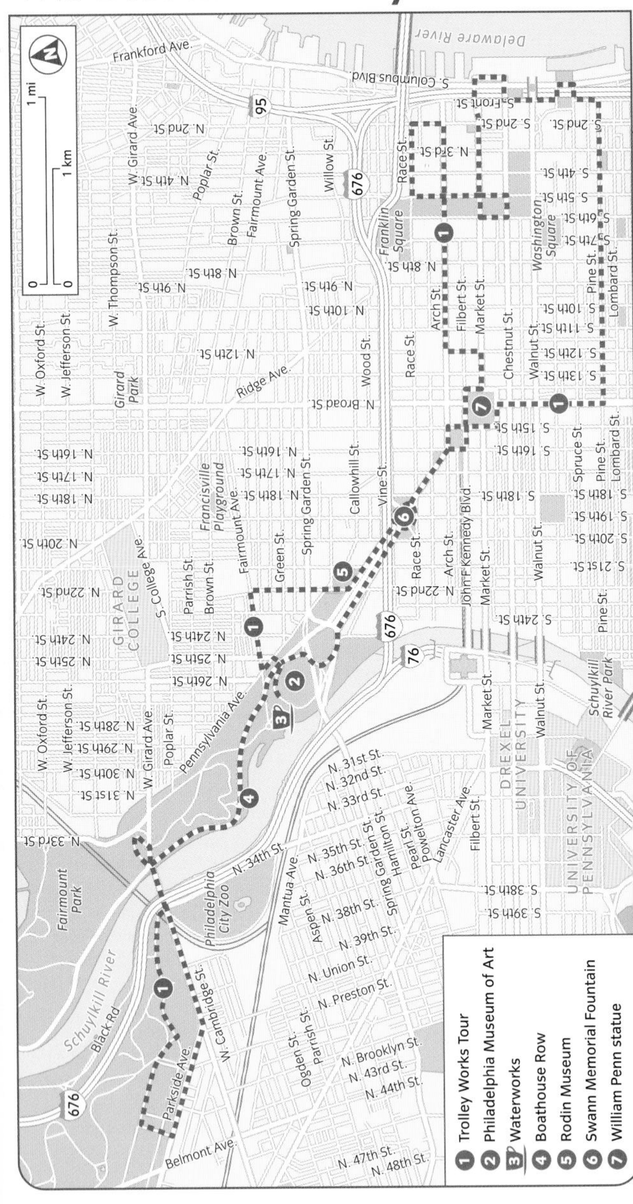

You've done enough walking. On day two, it's time to take a load off (at least, for the morning) and get the lay of the land. Of all of Philadelphia's touring methods—amphibious landing vehicles, horses-and-carriages—the Victorian-style trolleys are my favorites. START: **5th & Market sts, or any of the 20 stops along the trolley's route.**

❶ ★★ kids **Trolley Works Tour.** A 24-hour pass for the surprisingly speedy rail-less trolleys and double-decker buses gets you the most comprehensive tour of downtown. On-and-off privileges and unlimited rides mean if Junior wants to see the fortress-like Eastern State Penitentiary *(see p 48, bullet ❽)* again, or if you regret not picking up those vintage earbobs on Antique Row, a second chance at satisfaction is just a short ride away. ◷ *1½ hr. 5th & Market sts., 19 more stops along route, plus shuttles from hotels. ☎ 215/389-TOUR. www.phillytour.com. 24-hour pass: $27 adults, $25 seniors, $18 children. Apr–Nov Mon–Fri 9:30am–5:30pm, Sat–Sun 9:30am–6pm; Dec–Mar daily 10am–4pm.*

❷ ★★ **Philadelphia Museum of Art.** Hop off at this Greco-Roman temple on a hill, jog up the steps à la *Rocky,* and get lost in 80-some galleries of art and *objets,* even a medieval cloister. Cézanne's (1839–1906) monumental *Bathers* is here, as are works by native Philadelphian Thomas Eakins (1844–1916), classics from Van Gogh (1853–1890), Poussin (1594–1665), Rubens (1577–1640), Duchamp (1887–1968), and Monet (1840–1926). Recent special exhibitions include Cézanne and Renoir (1841–1919), and across the street at the newer Perelman Building, Marcel Wanders (1963–) and Frank Gehry (1929–). ◷ *2 hrs. 26th St. & Ben Franklin Pkwy. ☎ 215/763-1000. www.philamuseum.org. Admission $16 adults,*

The Philadelphia Museum of Art features more than 80 galleries.

$14 seniors, $12 students (does not include special exhibits); first Sunday of the month, pay what you wish. *Tue–Sun 10am–5pm (Fri until 8:45pm).*

Philadelphia Museum of Art

SECOND FLOOR

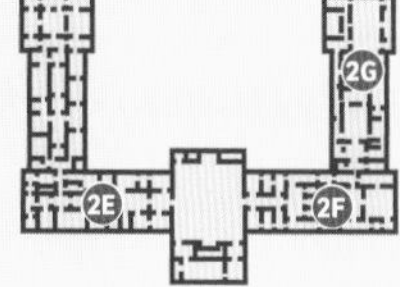

FIRST FLOOR

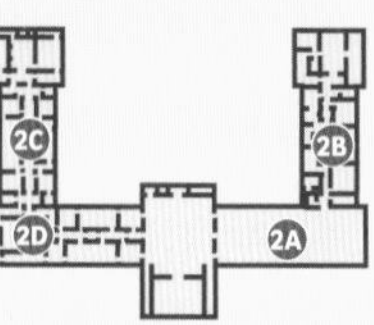

GROUND FLOOR

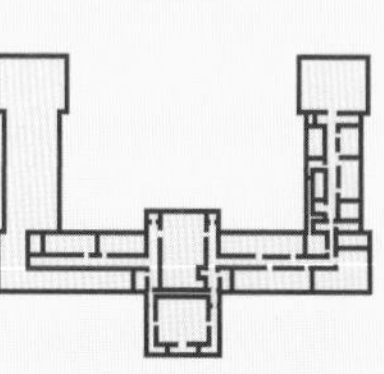

You'll spend most of your time on the first and second floors of this U-shaped museum. Begin where your interests lie—especially at 2A **Special Exhibitions,** which are almost always world-class, usually require advance reservations, and charge additional admission. Next, explore works by Thomas Eakins, as well as Shaker and Pennsylvania Dutch furnishings in the 2B **American Collection.** Cross the grand stair (looking up to see Alexander Calder's [1898–1976] "Ghost" mobile) to 2C **Modern and Contemporary Art,** where you can find iconoclastic pieces by Jasper Johns (1930–), Marcel Duchamp, Cy Twombly (1928–), and Constantin Brancusi (1876–1957). Before you head upstairs, 2D **European Art 1850–1900** deserves your perusal: Review your art history lessons with works representative of the Impressionist, Symbolist, Naturalist, and Art Nouveau styles—including Cézannes, Cassatts (1844–1926), Monets, Van Goghs, and amazing period *objets.* The second floor shows earlier pieces from Europe: 2E **1500–1850 French and English period** rooms, Poussins and Rubenses, and 2F **1100–1500: Renaissance works,** a 15th-century Venetian bedroom, a French Gothic chapel, and an 2G **Asian gallery** that includes an interesting mix: a Japanese teahouse, Persian carpets, and a 16th-century Indian temple hall.

3 ★ **Waterworks.** Just behind the museum, a 200-year-old municipal water system has been cleverly restored as an elegant river-top restaurant. Try the grilled haloumi cheese, the lobster BLT, and a bottle from the water list. ***640 Water Works Dr. ☎ 215/236-9000. www.thewaterworksrestaurant.com. $–$$$.***

4 ★★ **Boathouse Row.** From the restaurant, head toward the river, along Kelly Drive, to this iconic row of 10 antique (circa 1850s–1870s) clubhouses belonging to collegiate and other amateur crew groups and teams. You'll likely glimpse some oarsmen sculling along the river. Come back, if you can, after dark to see the houses lit up. *½ hr.*

The clubhouses along Boathouse Row date back to the mid-19th century.

5 ★★★ **Rodin Museum.** Farther up the Parkway, stop by this Paul Cret–designed mini-museum (on the street's north side). Here, a rendering of *The Thinker* and the *Gates of Hell* will greet you to the largest collection of Rodin's (1840–1917) works outside of Paris. It's a lovely spot, really, replete with major sculpture, plaster models, and original sketchbooks. ***1 hr. 22nd St. & Ben Franklin Pkwy. ☎ 215/568-6026. www.rodinmuseum.org. Suggested admission $5. Tues–Sun 10am–5pm.***

6 ★★ **Swann Memorial Fountain.** A few more blocks, and you'll run into Logan Circle and its classical centerpiece fountain, a creation of Alexander Stirling Calder (1870–1945), the son of City Hall sculptor Alexander. Also known as "The Fountain of the Three Rivers," the aquatic sculpture represents the region's three major waterways: the Schuylkill, Delaware, and Wissahickon rivers. ***20 min. 1 Logan Sq., at 18th St. & Ben Franklin Pkwy.***

7 ★★★ **William Penn statue.** Finally, go a few blocks more to reach City Hall and Philadelphia's biggest statue of all. Created by Alexander Milne Calder (1846–1923), father to Alexander Stirling, this enormous topper represents Philadelphia's original city planner and Pennsylvania's namesake. ***20 min. Broad & Market sts.***

The Best in Three Days

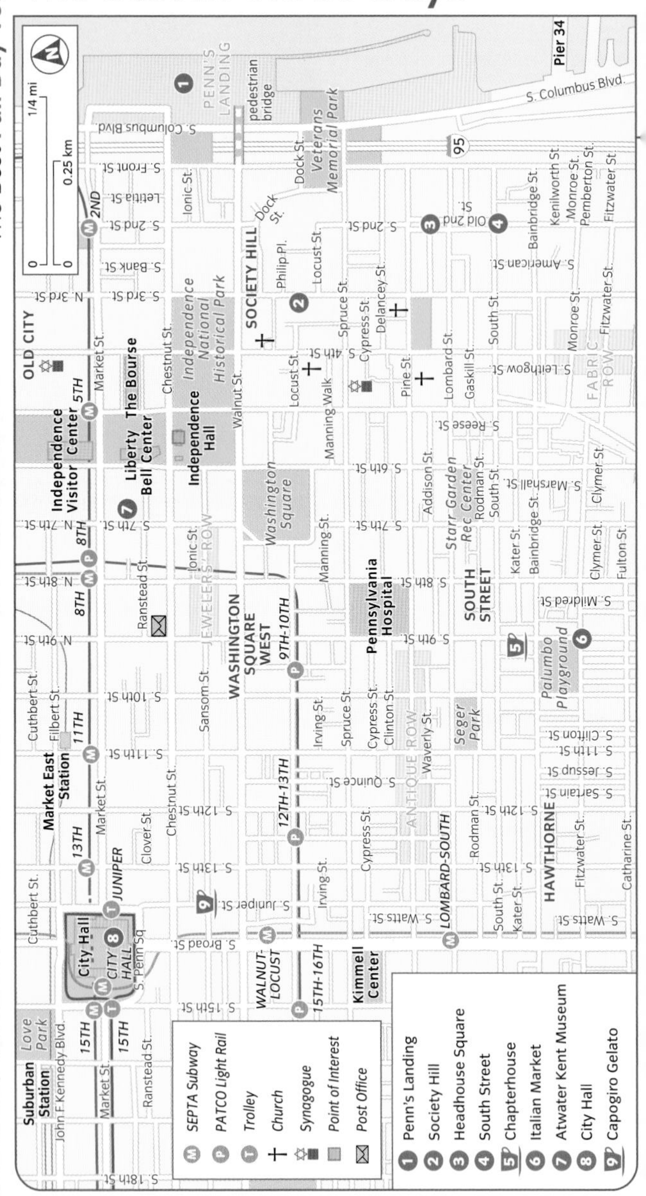

So, you've done high-brow culture and big-time history. On day three, it's time to get to know the city's inimitable blend of gorgeous, gritty, and gourmet—the essential components that make Philadelphia . . . ***Philly***. Start with a brisk walk. (You'll need the exercise: Soon, you'll be eating your way through 9th Street's Italian Market.) START: **Columbus Blvd. at Walnut St.**

1 Penn's Landing. The nicest time of day to visit the pedestrian-friendly Delaware Riverfront is morning, with the seagulls and joggers. No longer the bustling port it once was, the area is nonetheless a decent place to stroll, to gaze across the river at Camden, New Jersey, and if you're into shipbuilding and seafaring, to return to later, to visit the Independence Seaport Museum, USS *Becuna*, USS *Olympia*, and the four-mast-tall ship the Moshulu, converted into a restaurant *(see p 96)*. For now, however, walk south along the water, past the Art Deco–inspired Hyatt Regency, then cross back over Columbus Boulevard at Spruce Street. ½ ***hr. Columbus Blvd at Walnut St. www.delawareriverwaterfrontcorp.com.***

2 ★★ Society Hill. Back on the "mainland," you can find the very Philly dichotomy of living styles. To the north: I.M. Pei's (1917–) circa 1963 modernist Society Hill Towers. To the west and south: Historic brick Colonial-, Georgian-, and Federal-style townhouses, some of the city's first. Society Hill, a neighborhood loosely bound by Walnut and South streets, the river, and 8th Street, gets its name from the Free Society of Traders, a wealthy 18th-century group of Quaker financiers who footed some of William Penn's bills and who resided here. Today, the area is considered the city's second-most sought-after real estate, after Rittenhouse Square. (I think Society Hill is infinitely more charming.) To really get a flavor for the blend of history here, explore a few blocks and be sure to seek out details such as "busybody" mirrors in upper-floor windows, invented by Ben Franklin, used by residents to see who's at the door without having to descend the stairs; original wrought-iron boot scrapers; and sidewalks that bear antique hitching

Penn's Landing is home to the four-masted tall ship Moshulu, now a restaurant.

South Street is a beacon to the city's adolescents.

posts and marble steps, relics of horse-and-buggy days. To explore the inside of a residence-turned-museum, call ahead to see the Powel House. ⏲ *½ hr. 244 S. 3rd St.* *(See p 55.)*

❸ **Headhouse Square.** This all-brick replica of the original "New Market" or "Shambles" was once—and is again—an open-air market in continuous, English-style sheds. And it's attached to the nation's oldest surviving volunteer firehouse. Weekends in the spring through fall, shop or browse Headhouse's bustling farmer's market. ⏲ *15 min. 2nd St., btw. Pine & Lombard sts.*

❹ **South Street.** To skip this colorful strip of sneaker stores, costume jewelers, rustic cafes, and neon-lit food stands would be to miss out on the city's beating adolescent heart. For decades, this one-way boulevard has been a sort of Mecca for the under-21 set. Notice the gum stuck to the tree trunks. Darn kids. ⏲ *15 min.*

5 ★★ **Chapterhouse.** This airy and art-dappled converted storefront serves great espresso, fresh fruit smoothies, and breakfast pastries to a crowd of serious medical students and laid-back neighborhood types. *620 S. 9th St. (btw. South & Bainbridge sts.). ☎ 215/238-2626. $.*

Keeping Mum

If you thought the Italian Market was gritty, you ain't seen nothing 'til you've seen the **Mummers' Museum.** This unintentionally oddball homage to Philly's New Year's Day parade (think Mardi Gras with more feathers, fewer beads, less organization) encapsulates a local tradition that's virtually ineffable, but here goes . . . Every January 1, hundreds of locals who've spent the previous year rehearsing routines, concocting opulently clownish costumes and over-the-top sets, and spray-painting shoes gold, "perform" (dance, play instruments, stumble intoxicatedly) up Broad Street. The parade descends, apparently, from an old wassailing-style tradition. But this spot, with its strange decor and old-to-quite-old memorabilia, feels more eccentric than historic—in a good way, of course. ⏲ *½ hr. 2nd St. (referred to as "Two" St.) & Washington Ave. ☎ 215/336-3050. www.mummersmuseum.com. Admission $3.50 adults, $2.50 seniors & children.*

6 ★★ **Italian Market.** The "oldest outdoor market in America" may not be the city's best-kept thoroughfare—nor is it uniquely Italian—but it sure is fun to explore. The mix of old-school Italian vendors of meats, cheeses, pastry, and produce—along with Mexican bodegas and *tacquerias,* and junk shops galore—is nothing if not vibrant.

Circa 1918, 6A **Sarcone's** turns out crusty sesame-seed loaves, garlicky tomato pies, and pepperoni stuffed breads. 6B **Isgro's Pastry** bakes amazing pine-nut cookies and cannoli. 6C **Mew Gallery** offers cool local art and crafts. 6D **Fiorella's** makes sausage, right in front of you. 6E **D'Angelo Bros:** This butcher has seriously wild game. 6F **The Spice Corner** offers bargain flavorings. This 6G **mural of former mayor Frank Rizzo** is Philly's most defaced public art. Head to 6H **Claudio's** for olives, charcuterie, and house-made mozzarella. 6I **DiBruno Brothers' House of Cheese** is the market's most vaunted kiosk for amazing cheeses. 6J **Fante's** offers a cook- and bake-ware bonanza. 6K **Giordano's** has cheap produce out front, cheap parmesan and provolone in back. 6L **Geno's** is the neon half of the city's famed cheesesteak duel. 6M **Pat's King of Steaks** is the duel's other half, claiming original sandwich cred. Order one "wid" or "widout" onions and/or (Cheez) "Whiz." ⌚ *2–3 hrs. www.9thstreetitalianmarket.com. 9th St. btwn. Fitzwater & Federal sts. Mon–Sat 9am–4pm; Sun 9am–noon.*

Visitors to City Hall can ride the elevator up into the statue of William Penn at the top of the building.

7 ★ Atwater Kent Museum. The only venue offering homage to history, that's specifically Philadelphia, lays out the birth (and continuing life) of the city via sublime art and amazing objects spanning early Quaker fashions to Norman Rockwell works to 2008 Phillies memorabilia. On the first floor you can't — and shouldn't — miss the giant, walk-upon floor map detailing Philly's every natural and man-made nook and cranny. ⌚ *1 hr. 15 S. 7th St. (between Chestnut and Market sts.) ☎ 215/685-4830. www.philadelphiahistory.org. Admission $5 adults; $3 seniors and students 13–17; free children 12 and under. Weds–Sun 1–5pm. (Museum closed for renovations until mid 2010.)*

8 ★★ City Hall. Ready to walk again? Head toward the elaborate, all-masonry crux of Philadelphia government, home to the mayor's office, courtrooms, and other dubiously functional functionaries. Visitors may peek into an ornate reception room (no. 202) and Council Chambers (no. 400), and if City Hall's whims permit, take a tour, too. (Call ahead to find out.) If you can, ride the elevator up into the statue of William Penn for an amazing view. ⌚ *1–2 hrs. Broad & Market sts. www.phila.gov/. Admission $5 observation deck; $10 tour, including observation deck. Mon–Fri 9:30am–4:15pm.*

9 ★★★ kids Capogiro Gelato. The most delicious gelato and sorbets reside at this popular spot, where samples are free, scoops are pricey, and flavors include sublime *fior di latte* (milk), classic *baccio* (hazelnut), and offbeat-but-delish pineapple with Lancaster mint. *13th & Sansom sts. ☎ 215/351-0900. www.capogirogelato.com. $.* ●

Capogiro Gelato features free samples and several outstanding flavors.

2 The Best Special Interest Tours

Philadelphia Early America

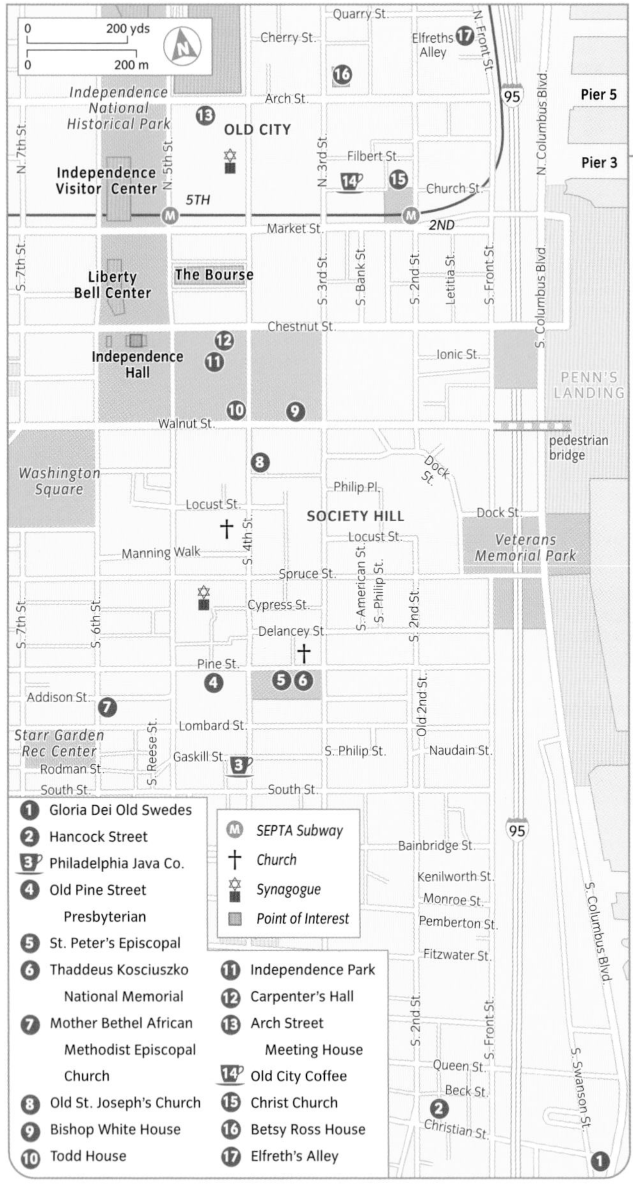

Previous page: Kids enjoy the goat sculpture at Rittenhouse Square.

It can be easy to forget that the quest for religious freedom inspired the founding of the United States. To early Americans, churches were more than places to worship: They were symbols of liberation. This tour includes some of the city's oldest churches and houses-turned-museums—as vibrant today as they were more than 200 years ago. START: **Gloria Dei Old Swedes, Columbus Blvd. & Christian St.**

Gloria Dei Old Swedes is the oldest church in Pennsylvania (and still active).

1 ★★ Gloria Dei Old Swedes. Established in 1700, this still-active Episcopal parish is the oldest church in Pennsylvania. Step inside here to enter an 18th-century microcosm, complete with mini parish hall, rectory, and graveyard. Two models of ships that carried the first Swedish settlers to these shores in 1638 hang inside the church. In the vestry is a silver crown that any woman married here may wear to her wedding. Old maps star in the one-room museum. *½ hr. 916 Swanson St. ☎ 215/389-1513. www.old-swedes.org. Free admission. Memorial Day–Labor Day daily 9am–4pm; Labor Day–Memorial Day Tues–Sun 9am–4pm.*

2 ★ Hancock Street. One of the many dozens of Center City's pretty little tree-lined alleys, this street is bordered by tiny houses called "trinities"—one floor each for faith, hope, and charity. While walking around the city, take small streets like this one, and you'll escape traffic and feel like a local—or maybe even a Colonial. *10 min.*

3 ★ Philadelphia Java Co. Always busy, this eclectic neighborhood cafe has yummy coffee drinks, simple salads, French pastry, and sandwiches, including marvelous labneh and green olives on soft white bread. *518 S. 4th St. (btw. South & Lombard sts.). ☎ 215/928-1811. $.*

4 ★ Old Pine Street Presbyterian. The city's oldest standing (circa 1768) Presbyterian church offers a glimpse of Colonial design—the hand-painted stencils

The Thaddeus Kosciuszko National Memorial pays tribute to a Polish hero of the American Revolution.

are particularly lovely—and an idea of how John Adams (1735–1826) spent his Sundays. In 1774, pastor George Duffield (1732–1790) was chaplain to the First Continental Congress. In 1776 and 1777, he served under George Washington (1732–1799) during the harsh winter at Valley Forge, making Old Pine known as the "church of the patriots." Buried in the churchyard are 50-some Revolutionary War soldiers, a signer of the Constitution, and a ringer of the Liberty Bell.

Old Pine Street Presbyterian is known as "the church of the patriots."

½ hr. 412 Pine St. ☎ 215/925-8051. www.oldpine.org. Free admission.

5 ★ St. Peter's Episcopal. If you've just left Old Pine and are hearing church bells, look west to see the William Strickland–designed (1788–1854) steeple of this ornate structure, built by the hand that built Carpenter's Hall, and attended by George Washington, who sat in pew 41. *½ hr. 3rd & Pine sts. ☎ 215/925-5968. www.stpetersphila.org. Free admission.*

6 ★★ Thaddeus Kosciuszko National Memorial. One of the great foreign heroes of the Revolution, Thaddeus Kosciuszko (1746–1817), a son of Poland, came to Philadelphia in 1776, just in time to read the Declaration, befriend Thomas Jefferson (1743–1826), and fortify the city. (After the Revolution, he returned home to lead an uprising against Imperial Russia and the Kingdom of Prussia.) But before all that glory, he occupied a room in this Georgian-style boardinghouse, a dwelling he'd requested to be "as small, as remote, and as cheap" as possible. *½ hr. 310 Pine St. ☎ 215/597-9618. Free admission. Wed–Sun noon–4pm.*

7 ★ Mother Bethel African Methodist Episcopal Church. On the oldest piece of American soil continuously owned by African-Americans is the mother church of African Methodist Episcopalism, a faith practiced by 2.5 million believers. Originally dedicated in 1794 by pastor Richard Allen (1760–1831), who bought his freedom from slavery in 1782, the handsome current version of this church was built in 1890. Still home to an active congregation, Mother Bethel houses Allen's tomb, his Bible, and his hand-hewn pulpit—all downstairs and available for view by appointment only. ½ *hr. 419 S. 6th St. (btw. Pine & Lombard sts.). 215/925-0616. Free admission.*

8 ★ Old St. Joseph's Church. When St. Joseph's was founded in 1733, it was the only place in the English-speaking world where Roman Catholics could celebrate Mass publicly. Among its worshippers were French allies, including General Lafayette (1757–1834). The building's unassuming facade is intentional: Ben Franklin (1706–1790) advised Founding Father John Greaton (1741–1783) to do what he could to protect the church against acts of religious intolerance. Although the structure incurred damage during anti-Catholic riots in the 1830s, late-20th-century restorations have returned the interior to its Colonial glory—a style especially unusual for a Catholic church. *20 min. 321 Willings Alley (4th St., near Walnut St.). 215/923-1733. www.oldstjoseph.org. Free admission.*

9 ★★ Bishop White House. The founder of the breakaway Episcopal Church; rector of both St. Peter's and Christ Church; chaplain to the Second Continental Congress; and a pal to Franklin, Washington, and Adams, Dr. William White (1783–1815) was a community pillar in Federal America. His elegant, circa 1786 house is decidedly upper-class, from its painted cloth floor to its unusually-stocked second-floor library and, highlight of highlights, its indoor "necessary," a novelty in its time. Visits are for 1-hour tours only. Tours include the

The elegant Bishop White House is circa 1786.

Todd House was home to a young Quaker lawyer whose widow married President James Madison.

Todd House. Day-of-only tickets available at the Independence Visitor Center. ½ hr. *309 Walnut St. ☎ 215/965-2305. Free admission. Daily 10am–4pm.*

⑩ ★ **Todd House.** John Todd, Jr. was a young Quaker lawyer of moderate means. In his circa-1775 Georgian dwelling, the first floor was his office, and his family lived and entertained on the second floor. Todd died in the 1793 yellow fever epidemic. His widow Dolley married future President James Madison (1751–1836). ½ hr. *4th & Walnut sts. Free admission. Daily 10am–4pm.*

⑪ ★★★ kids **Independence Park.** You've already visited portions of "America's most historic square mile," also home to must-visits Independence Hall and the Liberty Bell. *(See p 9, bullet ③.)* Now, take a load off—and meet a Colonial or two. Every summer, actors in 18th-century costumes roam this area, performing as rabble rousers, muster leaders, and passersby. Some give speeches. Others teach kids to march or roll hoops. Check online for scheduling details or grab a bench and see what happens. One tip: If you ask for the nearest Wi-Fi hotspot, you might be greeted with a blank stare. These actors stay in character. *1 hr. www.onceuponanation.org.*

⑫ ★ **Carpenter's Hall.** In 1774, one year after the Boston Tea Party, delegates from 12 of the 13 colonies gathered at this neutral meeting spot, home to the trade guild that erected Independence Hall and Christ Church, to spend seven weeks adopting 10 resolutions that declared the rights of colonists to the British King and Parliament. This meeting was called the First Continental Congress, and its resolutions formed the precedent to the Declaration of Independence. Today, Carpenter's Hall remains the meeting place for a club of architects, builders, and structural engineers. ½ hr. *320 Chestnut St. ☎ 215/925-0167. Free admission. Daily 10am–4pm.*

Independence Park often features actors in 18th-century garb.

The resolutions decided on in 1774 at Carpenter's Hall formed the precedent to the Declaration of Independence.

13 ★ Arch Street Meeting House. This plain brick building dates from 1804, but William Penn (1644–1718) gave the land to his Religious Society of Friends—a.k.a. Quakers—in 1693. Quakers, not to be confused with Shakers, believe in a plain and hierarchy-free style of worship referred to as "meeting." Weekly meeting includes much silent meditation, until a "Friend" is moved to stand and speak. ⌚ *20 min. 4th & Arch sts.* ☎ *215/627-2667. www.archstreetfriends.org. Free admission. Guided tours Mon–Sat 10am–4pm.*

14 ★ Old City Coffee. This charming cafe (on yet another side street) is the perfect spot to rev back up with a double espresso, chill out with an iced green tea, or treat yourself to homemade coffee cake. *221 Church St.* ☎ *215/629-9292. $.*

15 ★★ Christ Church. Another church, but likely the most prominent on the list, this landmark Colonial structure—one of the country's finest examples of ethereally symmetric Georgian architecture—is a quick visit, where you'll learn that many a Signer had membership in more than one church. *(See p 11, bullet 8.)* ⌚ *½ hr. 2nd & Market sts. Free admission.*

16 ★ kids Betsy Ross House. After all, one of these houses ought to be best known for its female resident. This twee residence may have belonged to Betsy Ross (1752–1836), the woman who may have designed and sewn the nation's first flag (the jury's still out on both questions). *(See p 11, bullet 9.)* ⌚ *½ hr. 239 Arch St. Free admission.*

17 ★★★ Elfreth's Alley. A sweet little street with some seriously big history. In the shadow of the Ben Franklin Bridge, Elfreth's Alley remains the longest continuously inhabited street in America. Along the lane are a house that's now a museum and garden—Number 126—and sun-dappled cobblestones for quiet wandering. *(See p 11, bullet 10.)* ⌚ *½ hr. Off 2nd St., toward Front St., btw. Arch & Race sts.*

Art Philly-Style

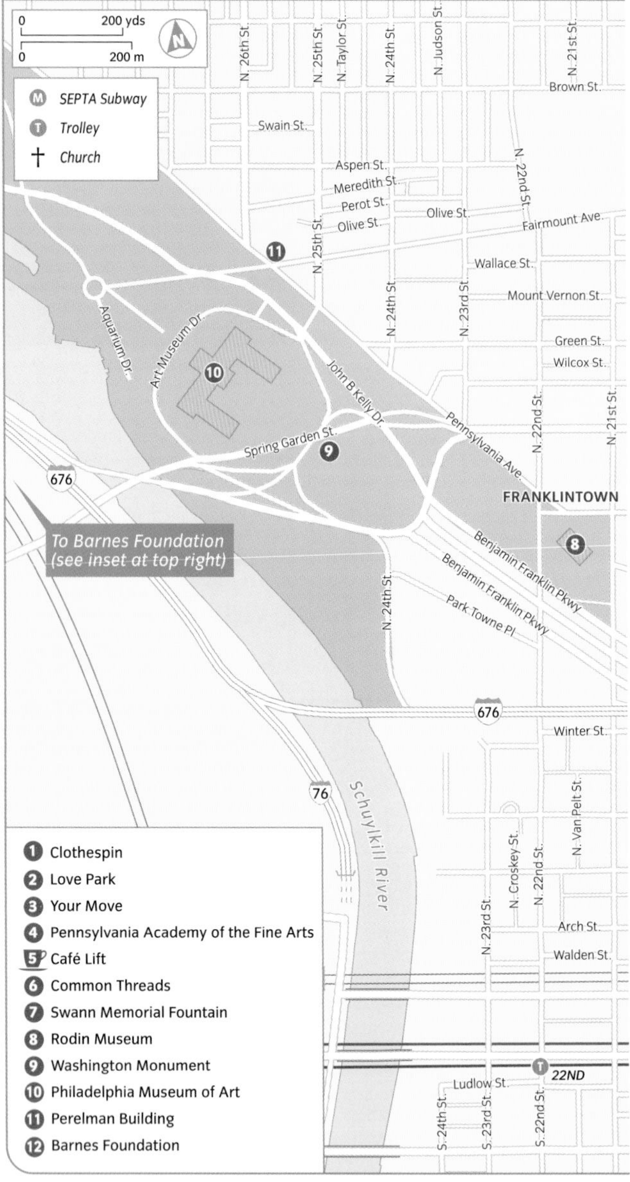

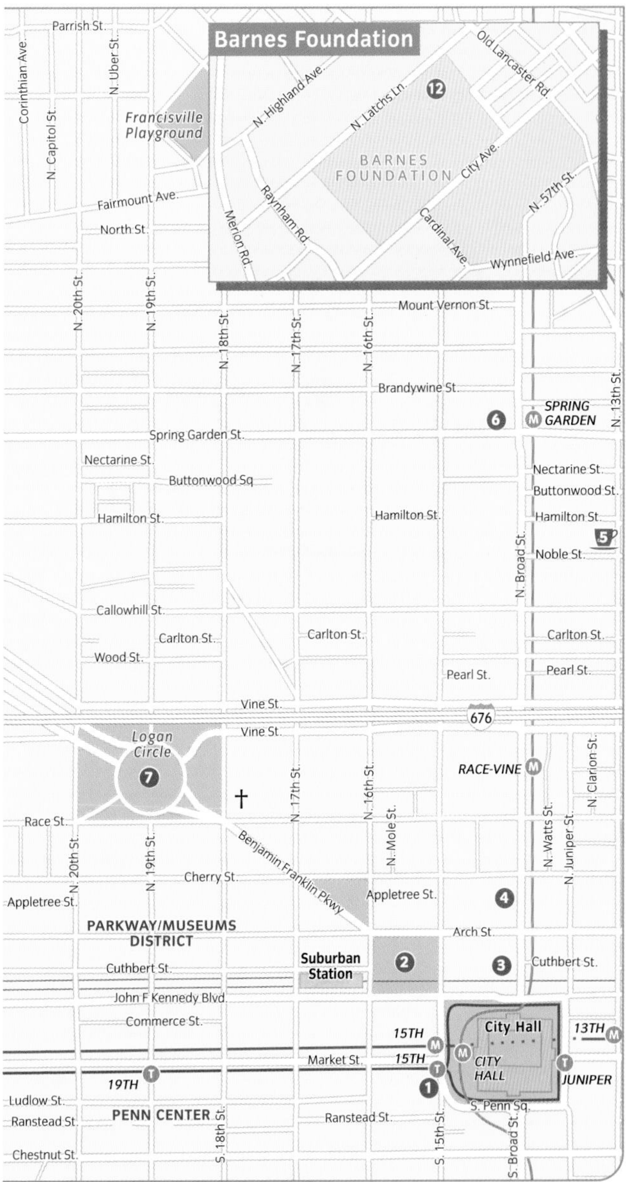
Barnes Foundation
BARNES FOUNDATION
N. Highland Ave.
N. Latchs Ln.
Old Lancaster Rd.
City Ave.
N. 57th St.
Raynham Rd.
Merion Rd.
Cardinal Ave.
Wynnefield Ave.
Parrish St.
Corinthian Ave.
N. Uber St.
N. Capitol St.
Francisville Playground
Fairmount Ave.
North St.
N. 20th St.
N. 19th St.
N. 18th St.
N. 17th St.
N. 16th St.
Mount Vernon St.
Brandywine St.
SPRING GARDEN
N. 13th St.
Spring Garden St.
Nectarine St.
Buttonwood Sq
Buttonwood St.
Hamilton St.
Noble St.
N. Broad St.
Callowhill St.
Carlton St.
Wood St.
Pearl St.
Vine St.
676
Logan Circle
RACE-VINE
N. Clarion St.
Race St.
N. Mole St.
N. Watts St.
N. Juniper St.
Benjamin Franklin Pkwy
Cherry St.
Appletree St.
PARKWAY/MUSEUMS DISTRICT
Arch St.
Suburban Station
Cuthbert St.
John F Kennedy Blvd.
Commerce St.
City Hall
15TH
13TH
Market St.
CITY HALL
JUNIPER
19TH
Ludlow St.
Ranstead St.
PENN CENTER
S. Penn Sq.
S. 18th St.
S. 15th St.
S. Broad St.
Chestnut St.

The grand Philadelphia Museum of Art and the rich, eclectic Barnes are the stars of the local art scene. Still, any tour of the city is an art tour, thanks to a 1959 mandate that all new building projects dedicate 1% of construction costs to public art. Consider such serendipitous finds PDAs—public displays of art-fection. **START: City Hall, 15th & Market sts.**

1 ★ Clothespin. One of Philadelphia's many public displays of art is Claes Oldenburg's (1929–) 10-ton, 45-foot-tall, circa-1976 tribute to, yes, laundry, but also to Brancusi's (1876–1957) *The Kiss.* Across from City Hall *(see p 30, bullet 1)*, this sculpture is a feat of imagination and engineering—notice how the *Clothespin* isn't quite closed—and not without its critics. ⌚ *10 min. 15th & Market sts.*

Claes Oldenburg's famous "Clothespin" statue.

2 ★★ Love Park. Robert Indiana's (1928–) bright red, font-based work is one of the most iconic monuments in the City of Brotherly Love, even though duplicates exist throughout the world. Still, as centerpiece of this lovingly planted park (a former haven for urban skateboarders), it serves as a gentle reminder of all we need. ⌚ *15 min. 15th St. & JFK Blvd.*

3 ★ kids Your Move. It's no coincidence that Daniel Martinez's (1957–) colossal game pieces—an iron from Monopoly; dominoes; and "men" from Parcheesi, checkers, and chess—are located directly across from City Hall. The hodgepodge juxtaposes childhood pastimes and adult responsibilities—and offers a nice spot for a photo. ⌚ *10 min. Broad St & JFK Blvd.*

4 ★★★ Pennsylvania Academy of the Fine Arts. Two blocks north of City Hall stands the country's first art museum, which also happens to be the country's first fine arts school. Known by its acronym, PAFA occupies a beautifully restored, circa-1876 High Victorian Gothic building designed by architects Frank Furness (1839–1912) and George W. Hewitt (1841–1916). Presidential portraitist Charles Willson Peale (1741–1827) and early American sculptor William Rush (1756–1833) founded the Academy in 1805. American realist Thomas Eakins (1844–1916) studied and taught here. All three artists were Philadelphians, and all are well represented among the gallery's thousands of all-American works. Of special note: Furness' splendid red, gold, and blue staircase; an elegant rotunda where Walt Whitman (1819–1892) attended concerts; Benjamin West's (1738–1820) *Penn's Treaty with the Indians*;

Peale's paintings of Franklin and Washington; rare works by Rush; and pieces by more modern American artists such as Mark Rothko (1903–1970), Robert Motherwell (1915–1991), Georgia O'Keefe (1887–1986), Edward Hopper (1882–1967), Andrew Wyeth (1917–2009), and Robert Rauschenberg (1925–2008). *2 hr. 118 N. Broad St. 215/972-7600. www.pafa.org. Admission to permanent collection $10 adults, $8 seniors & students with ID, $6 children 5–18. (Free admission to ground-floor gallery). Tues–Sat 10am–5pm, Sun 11am–5pm. Free tours Tues, Thurs–Fri 11:30am & 12:30pm, Wed, Sat–Sun 1pm & 2pm.*

This bright red statue is the centerpiece of Love Park.

5 ★ **Café Lift.** In the bottom of converted warehouse condos, this favorite locals' spot displays student art and serves a creative little menu of frittatas (veggie or sausage), panini (grilled chicken, Cuban, tuna, and artichoke) and salads (Caprese, Caesar, spinach). *428 N. 13th St. (btw. Callowhill & Spring Garden sts). 215/922-3031. www.cafelift.com. $–$$.*

6 ★ **Common Threads.** One of the city's proudest modern achievements is its Mural Arts Program, an artist-community collaboration that started in the '80s as an anti-graffiti program, and continues today to transform neighborhoods, engage kids, employ artists, and attract thousands of onlookers. At the northwest corner of Broad and

Daniel Martinez's "Your Move" is located directly across from City Hall.

The Pennsylvania Academy of the Fine Arts is the country's first art museum and its first arts school.

Spring Garden streets is one of nearly 3,000 homes to these giant artworks. Meg Saligman's (1965–) eight-story-tall *Common Threads* depicts contemporary high school students alongside historic figures. ⌚ *10 min.* ☎ ***215/389-8687. www.muralarts.org. Mural trolley tours are available from the Independence Visitor Center. $25 adults, $23 seniors, $15 children. Apr–Nov Wed 10am–noon, Sat–Sun 12:30–2:30pm.***

Meg Saligman's "Common Threads" is part of the city's Mural Arts program.

7 ★★ kids Swann Memorial Fountain. Back along Ben Franklin Parkway—occasionally referred to as Philly's Champs-Élysées—are more examples of public artwork, especially sculpture. This grand, classical fountain, with ornate horses and mile-high water, represents the city's three major waterways. It is the work of Philadelphian Alexander Stirling Calder (1870–1945), son of Alexander Milne Calder (1846–1923), creator of City Hall's bronze, 27-ton likeness of William Penn, and father of Alexander Calder (1898–1976), who made the ethereal *Ghost* mobile in the PMA. The fountain serves as a warm-weather splashing spot for many local kids. The surrounding formal garden is a leafy refuge for weary grown-ups. ⌚ ***½ hr. Logan Sq. (19th & Race sts).***

8 ★★★ Rodin Museum. Nearby up the Parkway, this hidden gem of a museum houses the largest collection of works by Pierre August Rodin (1840–1917) outside the Musée Rodin in Paris. You'll recognize the artist's iconic works such as *The Thinker* and the *Gates of Hell*, but don't miss the smaller, more process-oriented exhibits of bronze castings, plaster studies, original sketchbooks, letters, and books. *1 hr. 22nd St. & Ben Franklin Pkwy. ☎ 215/568-6026. Suggested admission of $5. www.rodinmuseum.org. Tues–Sun 10am–5pm.*

9 ★ Washington Monument. Alike in name alone to the capitol city's famed obelisk, this fountain no longer spouts water but does represent the entry to the Philadelphia Museum of Art. Little-known sculptor Rudolf Siemering (1835–1905) completed the work in 1897. A proud General Washington, in tricorn hat and cape, and mounted on a fine steed, once stood at the entrance to Fairmount Park. Today, he faces City Hall, inside Eakins Oval, named for the beloved Philadelphia painter. *15 min. Eakins Oval (26th St. & Ben Franklin Pkwy.).*

10 ★★ Philadelphia Museum of Art. This Greco-Roman temple on a hill has 200,000 works for your not-so-quick perusal. Among the masterpieces: Cézanne's (1839–1906) monumental *Bathers;* regionally-themed works by Eakins; classics from Van Gogh (1853–1890), Rubens (1577–1640), Duchamp (1877–1968), and Monet (1840–1926); plus, stunning collections of furniture, jewelry, ceramics, and armor. The permanent installations of a medieval cloister and a Japanese teahouse are especially restful and lovely. *1½ hrs.* *(For more information, see p 13.) 2600 Ben Franklin Pkwy. ☎ 215/763-8100. Admission $16 adults, $14 seniors, $12 students (does not include special exhibits); first Sunday of the month, pay what you wish. www.philamuseum.org. Tue–Sun 10am–5pm (Fri until 8:45pm).*

The Swann Memorial Fountain was created by local sculptor Alexander Stirling Calder.

A Night of Art

Every "First Friday" of the month, the independent art galleries of Old City stay open late to debut exhibits and to serve wine in little plastic cups to enthused, mostly youthful, crowds. If you happen to be in town on a First Friday, get to Old City early (gallery hr. are usually 5–9pm for the event), start your exploration north of Market Street along 2nd or 3rd, and have at it. Also, if you're planning to dine after you wine, and if you'd like to remain in the neighborhood, be sure to make dinner reservations. On a typical Friday night, Old City is the busiest spot in town. On a First Friday, it's busier still.

The Rodin Museum houses the largest collection of the artist's work outside of Paris.

⑪ ★★ **Perelman Building.** This recently opened, thoroughly gorgeous Art Deco building just across the street also belongs to the PMA. The Perelman offers marvelously tactile collections in textile and design, along with special exhibits in the same realms; has a distinguished art reference library; and serves as a satellite for smaller PMA exhibits, including Andrew Wyeth (1917–2009), Matisse (1869–1954), and Renoir (1841–1919). Until the planned Frank Gehry–designed (1929–) tunnel connects this building to the PMA, a shuttle operates between them. 🕘 *1 hr. Fairmount & Pennsylvania aves.* ☎ *215/763-8100. www.philamuseum.org. Admission $8 adults, $7 seniors, $6 students (free with admission to PMA). Tues–Sun 10am–5pm.*

⑫ ★★★ **Barnes Foundation.** Just outside city limits (for now), this world-renowned museum was the life's work of prescient collector Albert Barnes (1872–1951), a pharmaceutical tycoon who amassed 8,000 works, including 181 Renoirs, 69 Cézannes, 59 Matisses, 46 Picassos (1881–1973), Pennsylvania "Dutch" furniture, primitive sculpture, and forged ironwork. Currently housed in a circa-1925 Provincial gallery, the Barnes is scheduled to move to the 2000 block of the Parkway in 2012.

The Perelman Building offers collections of textiles and design.

Barnes Foundation

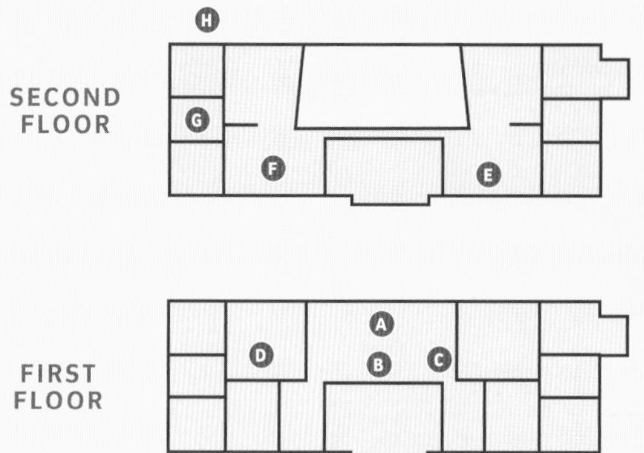

Just in the front door, you'll see friezes inspired by primitive African sculpture: Albert Barnes had this building designed especially for his artwork, which he personally arranged in eclectic montages. Matisse painted the mural **A** ***The Dance II*** to fit precisely beneath these arches. The largest room is on the first floor. It has **B** ***Card Players,*** one of Cézanne's favorite subjects, and **C** ***Models,*** Seurat's (1859–1891) meta study for *Ile de la Grande Jatte.* Nearby, Van Gogh's **D** ***Postman,*** a portrait of Joseph Roulin, the artist's own mailman. To the right: **E** ***Scout Attacked by a Tiger,*** one of Rousseau's (1844–1910) signature jungle scenes. Left: Picasso's paternal, symbolist painting, **F** ***Harlequins.*** Among the *objets,* don't miss **G** ***Seated Couple,*** one of Barnes' 200 African sculptures. Outdoors, a 12-acre **H** **Arboretum** offers woodland, formal rose and perennial gardens, a pond, a greenhouse, and hundreds of rare plant species and varieties. *3 hrs. 300 N. Latches Lane, Merion. 610/667-0290. www.barnesfoundation.org. Reservations required, recommended at least 30 days in advance. Admission $15 adults; parking $15 vehicles. Sept–May Fri–Sun 9:30am–5pm; June–Aug Wed–Sun 9:30am–5pm.*

Philly With Kids

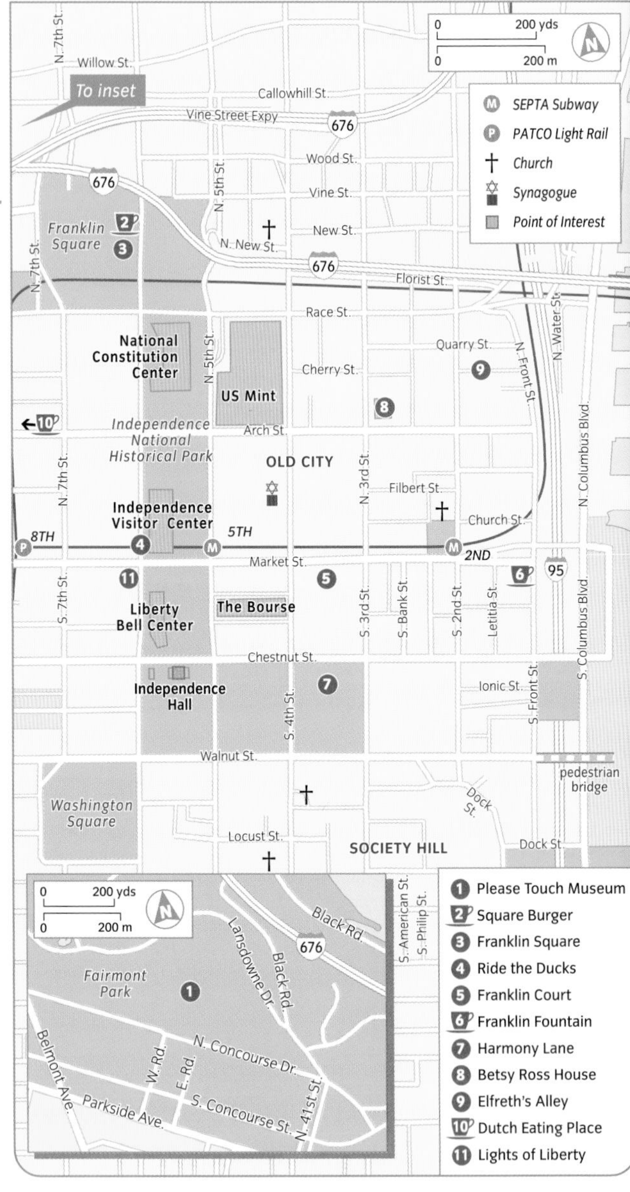

In a big city that feels small, small people feel big. A fuss-free day of the kid-centric calls for frequent breaks, comfortable footwear, and knowing which activities to save for another day, such as the Philadelphia Zoo (see p 45, bullet 8), Adventure Aquarium (see p 96, bullet 6), and Franklin Institute (see p 47, bullet 4). Even without these three biggies, there's still a great day's worth of fun to be had for little people in the City of Brotherly Love. START: **Please Touch Museum, 4231 Ave. of the Republic.**

The Please Touch Museum encourages a hands-on experience.

❶ ★★ **Please Touch Museum.** Start off by getting a pass for the purple PHLASH bus *(see p 161)* and take it to Fairmount Park's Memorial Hall. Here, at the serious-looking site of the 1876 Centennial Exhibition (a.k.a. the first World's Fair) is this least-serious of museums, a bright, educational mega-playground for the Gymboree set. As its name suggests, the Please Touch's number one rule is opposite that of its adult-centric counterparts. Climbing, throwing, splashing, honking, jumping, riding, and playing are both permitted *and* encouraged. Little ones will love the waist-high water tables of River Adventure, the faux shopping at a low-shelved supermarket, the "work" of a safety-first construction zone, a magically rendered *Alice in Wonderland* maze, regular story times, and a mint-condition circa-1824 carousel. Philly-inspired exhibits of a once-beloved kids' TV show, *Captain Noah,* and the monorail from the old toy department of the historic John Wanamaker store offer a glimpse of local childhoods of yore. There's also a busy cafe for juice and pizza. The staff here is marvelous, but they are not babysitters. Guardians must accompany children at all times. *3 hr. 4231 Ave. of the Republic. ☎ 215/581-3181. www.pleasetouchmuseum.org. Admission $15 adults & children (free for children 1 & under). Mon–Sat 9am–5pm; Sun 11am–5pm. Automobile & stroller parking available.*

Franklin Square dates to 1682 and has recently added child-friendly attractions like mini-golf.

2 ★★ Square Burger. Stephen Starr, Philly's biggest-deal restaurateur, is responsible for the inexpensive and delicious hamburgers, salami-wrapped kosher hotdogs, hand-cut fries, and milkshakes made with Butterscotch Tastykake Krimpets (a local, er, delicacy) at this super-fun walk-up stand, named for the location (see below), not the shape of the burger. *200 S. 6th St. (btw. 6th & 7th sts. on Race St.) No phone. $–$$.*

3 ★★★ Franklin Square. One of William Penn's five original squares, this 7½-acre plot dates to 1682 and has recently been reincarnated as a low-key, amusement park-like haven for families. Among the attractions: an 18-hole, Philadelphia-theme mini-golf; a slew of jungle gyms; a giant sand sculpture; a merry-go-round with seats that resemble animals; and benches where "Once Upon A Nation" performers tell entertaining historical stories and make balloon animals. *1½ hr. Btw. 6th & 7th sts. on Race St. Carousel: $3 adults, $2 children 3–12, free children 2 & under. Mini-golf: $8 adults, $6 children 3–12. Apr 1–Oct 31 10am–dusk. Storytelling 11am–4pm, Apr 1–Oct 31.*

4 ★ Ride the Ducks. One of the best things about exploring with kids is getting to act like a kid yourself. On these land-to-water touring vehicles, delightfully immature behavior is practically *de rigueur*. Though you won't get the most erudite rundown of local history, you

The amphibious Ride the Ducks vehicles provide a kid-friendly environment for touring Old City and Society Hill.

Old-fashioned Franklin Fountain boasts several varieties of homemade ice cream.

will see a nice bit of Old City and Society Hill, make ridiculous noises with plastic "duckbills," and giggle at the joke-cracking, oldies-blaring guides. If your child is brave enough to take the wheel once you reach the Delaware River, it'll be his or her day's highlight. ⌚ *1½ hr. Independence Visitor Center, 6th & Market sts.* ☎ *877/887-8225. www.phillyducks.com. Admission $26 adults, $24 seniors, $16 children 3–12.*

5 ★★ **Franklin Court.** Beyond an unassuming brick archway on Market Street is the site, if not the structure, of Ben Franklin's Philadelphia home. The original dwelling was razed in 1812. All that's left is an archeological dig–looking foundation and the modern steel frame "ghost" girder meant to represent the original house—neither of which might impress the kids. What they will love are a museum that cleverly outlines Franklin's irrepressible ingenuity and Colonials that seem to live and work around the court. In the museum: Some of Franklin's lesser-known, more offbeat inventions, such as bowls for a glass armonica (played like water glasses at the dinner table) and swim fins (Franklin was a champion swimmer). There's a 22-minute film, *The Real Ben Franklin,* but better yet are the storytellers (even "Ben" appears regularly beneath his beloved mulberry tree) to enliven the court with true tales and craft projects. The gift shop here is especially nice; have the kids buy a postcard and get the instant satisfaction they crave by mailing it at the still-active post office where Franklin served as the nation's first Postmaster General, and where all mail is still hand-cancelled. ⌚ *1½ hr. 314–322 Market St.* ☎ *215/965-2305. Free admission. Daily 11am–5pm. (Post office closed Sun.)*

6 ★★★ **Franklin Fountain.** Homemade ice cream in flavors both familiar (vanilla bean, mint chip, peach) and throwback (teaberry gum, licorice) come by the scoop, in parfaits, banana splits, floats, milkshakes, and more at this old-fashioned fountain. *116 Market St.* ☎ *215/627-1899. $.*

7 ★★★ **Harmony Lane.** Older kids appreciate important sights like Independence Hall and the Liberty

Tiny Betsy Ross House recreates the life of an average Colonial family.

Bell, *(see p 9, bullet 3)* but littler ones may get more out of this simple green plot, where "Once Upon a Nation's" characters engage small-fries in tricky Colonial games like graces and quoits. *1 hr. Chestnut St. btw. 3rd & 4th sts. Free admission. Memorial Day to Labor Day 11am–4pm.*

8 ★ **Betsy Ross House.** Flag-making lore aside, this tiny house seems just the right fit for pint-sized explorers, who'll marvel at the absolute compactness of life for the average Colonial family. Although Quaker seamstress Elizabeth (Betsy) Ross may not have even lived here, the house's preservers sure have made it look like she did, what with careful placement of reusable ivory tablets, pinecones to help start hearth fires, and a handy kitchen hourglass. The courtyard park separating the house from the street isn't just the burial ground for Ross and her last husband—it's the place where you're most likely to meet "Betsy" herself, and to hear her stories. *(See p 11, bullet 9.)* *1 hr. 239 Arch St. Free admission.*

9 ★★★ **Elfreth's Alley.** No need to do the full-tour of the museum at the oldest continuously inhabited street in the United States. It's enough to walk down this narrow cobblestone stretch, look up at the centuries-old row houses, think with your child of your own dwelling, and offer a gentle lesson about getting along with the neighbors. *(See p 11, bullet*

Harmony Lane's "Once Upon a Nation" uses games to keep younger kids engaged.

Come An' Play

Up I-95 about 27 miles (43.4km), Sesame Place is theme-park paradise for the post-toddler set. The 14-acre outdoor "neighborhood" of recreation—and nothing but recreation—offers a dizzying array of splashy water-park-style rides (bring bathing suits), kiddie coasters, a carousel, and hundreds of ways to experience Elmo and his ilk, including a twice-daily parade, and regular staged performances. The park is consistently crowded, so arrive early. *100 Sesame Rd., Langhorne. ☎ 866/GO-4-ELMO; 215/752-7070. www.sesameplace.com. $54.95 adults and children 2 and over; $49.95 55+; free children under 23 months. First 3 weeks in May, Fri and Sun 10am–6pm, Sat 10am–8pm; last week in May, first week in June, Sun–Fri 10am–6pm and Sat 10am–8pm; second week June–first week Sept 10am–8pm; Sept–Oct Sat–Sun 10am–6pm, last weekend Oct until 4pm.*

⑩.) 🕘 *20 min. Off 2nd St., toward Front St., btw. Arch & Race sts.*

10 ★★ **Dutch Eating Place.** Use your PHLASH pass to get to this Mennonite-run Reading Terminal Market luncheonette. Spin your kids up to a counter seat for a hearty chicken-pot-pie late lunch (or check out their breakfasts: blueberry pancakes, apple toast, and oddly yummy scrapple). They're open 8 to 6 Monday to Saturday. Note to latte-loving parents: Head to Old City Coffee's nearby kiosk. *12th & Arch sts. ☎ 215/922-0425. Closed Sun. $.*

⑪ **Lights of Liberty.** Thought the Duck Boats were too mild-mannered? Then join this flashy after-dark tour of Independence Park, narrated by celebrities who speak via surround sound technology into your headset while rifles crackle, cannons burst, and the Philadelphia Orchestra plays, and you, charged with adrenaline, walk past flamboyantly lit historic buildings, amid smoke machines simulating mist and exploded gunpowder. 🕘 *1 hr. PECO Energy Center, 6th & Chestnut sts. ☎ 877/462-1776. www.lightsofliberty.org. Admission $20 adults, $17 seniors & students, $13 children 12 & under. Mid-Apr to mid-June Fri–Sat at dusk; mid-June to mid-Aug Thurs–Sat at dusk; mid-Aug to mid-Sept Sat at dusk.*

Lights of Liberty is an adrenaline-packed nighttime tour of Independence Park.

What Would Rocky Do?

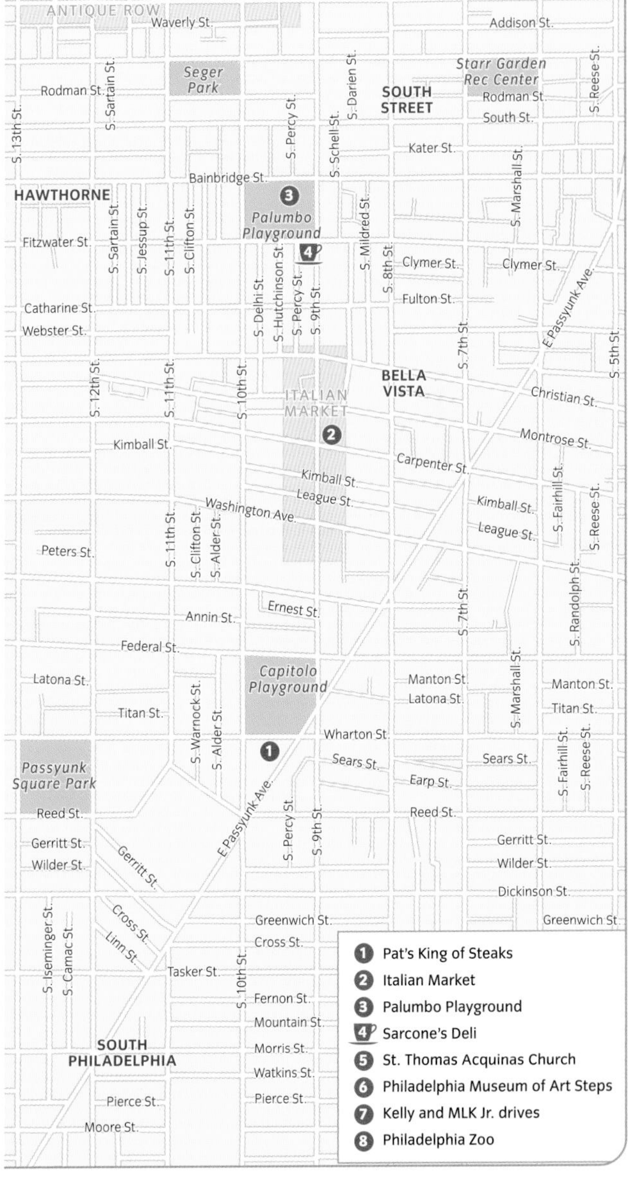
ANTIQUE ROW
Waverly St.
Addison St.
Seger Park
Starr Garden Rec Center
Rodman St.
SOUTH STREET
South St.
Kater St.
Bainbridge St.
HAWTHORNE
Palumbo Playground
Fitzwater St.
Clymer St.
Fulton St.
Catharine St.
Webster St.
BELLA VISTA
ITALIAN MARKET
Christian St.
Montrose St.
Kimball St.
Carpenter St.
League St.
Washington Ave.
Peters St.
Ernest St.
Annin St.
Federal St.
Capitolo Playground
Latona St.
Manton St.
Titan St.
Wharton St.
Sears St.
Earp St.
Passyunk Square Park
Reed St.
Gerritt St.
Wilder St.
Dickinson St.
Greenwich St.
Cross St.
Linn St.
Tasker St.
Fernon St.
Mountain St.
Morris St.
Watkins St.
Pierce St.
Moore St.
SOUTH PHILADELPHIA
E. Passyunk Ave.
S. 13th St.
S. 12th St.
S. 11th St.
S. 10th St.
S. 9th St.
S. 8th St.
S. 7th St.
S. 5th St.
S. Sartain St.
S. Jessup St.
S. Clifton St.
S. Alder St.
S. Warnock St.
S. Delhi St.
S. Hutchinson St.
S. Percy St.
S. Schell St.
S. Darien St.
S. Mildred St.
S. Marshall St.
S. Fairhill St.
S. Reese St.
S. Randolph St.
S. Iseminger St.
S. Camac St.
1 Pat's King of Steaks
2 Italian Market
3 Palumbo Playground
4 Sarcone's Deli
5 St. Thomas Acquinas Church
6 Philadelphia Museum of Art Steps
7 Kelly and MLK Jr. drives
8 Philadelphia Zoo

In 1976, a rags-to-riches film about a hardscrabble pugilist from Philly's Kensington neighborhood captured America's heart—and, as far as Philadelphians are concerned, never let go. Below are highlights of Rocky Balboa's favorite spots. (One tip: Don't attempt a literal version of the "Rocky Run:" You'll be dashing across town for days.) START: **Pat's King of Steaks—in South Philly, yo.**

The Italian Market is America's oldest outdoor market.

1 ★★ Pat's King of Steaks. Balboa started his day with a glass of raw eggs. Only slightly less off-putting is breakfast of bread-swaddled steak topped "wid" fried onions and "Whiz." But, heck; if you're gonna do it once in your life, do it where, in 1930, a hot-dog seller invented Philly's most famous sandwich, and 46 years later, Rocky ate it (for lunch). ½ *hr. 1237 E. Passyunk Ave. (at Wharton St.). ☎ 215/468-1546. www.patskingofsteaks.com. Open 24 hrs.*

2 ★★ Italian Market. America's oldest outdoor market apparently welcomes guys in gray sweat suits who run in traffic. Filmed here: The scene where a vendor tosses Balboa an apple. How the boxer ate the fruit while jogging past flaming 55-gallon drums of trash is anyone's guess. Our advice: Don't run. Stroll. Shop. *2 hr. S 9th St., btw. Christian & Federal sts. www.9thstreetitalianmarket.com.* *(See p 19, bullet 6.)*

3 kids Palumbo Playground. There's no proof Stallone ever set foot in this South Philly neighborhood park, but it's a great spot for the kids to enjoy the jungle gym and swing set, and for you to engage in a few outdoor exercises without ever having to punch a frozen carcass. Squat thrusts, anyone? ½ *hr. Btw. 9th & 10th sts., Fitzwater & Bainbridge sts.*

4 ★★ Sarcone's Deli. Amazing Italian hoagies loaded up with prosciutto, capacola, hard salami, sharp provolone, roasted red peppers, and broccoli rabe, served on Italian bread baked a few doors down at the family's circa-1918 bakery. *734 S. 9th St. (at Fitzwater St.) ☎ 215/922-1717. $.*

5 ★ St. Thomas Acquinas Church. The little parish where Rocky and Adrienne got hitched isn't exactly set up to host tourists, but you can pop in for a look-see. The gilded, chandeliered, Italian baroque-style 1904 St. Thomas has been called the loveliest Catholic Church in South Philadelphia. ½ hr. *17th & Morris sts. ☎ 215/334-2312. Free admission.*

6 ★★ kids Philadelphia Museum of Art Steps. If you don't know what happened here, consider re-renting the movie. The scene of Balboa running up the 72 steps, turning around, and pumping his fists in the air was an instant American film classic. Each year, thousands of visitors decide they're "Gonna Fly Now" (many never set foot in the museum itself). At the top of the steps is an imprint of Stallone's Converse sneakers. At the foot of the steps, a bronze Rocky statue. ½ hr. *(See p 13, bullet 2.)*

7 ★★ Kelly and MLK Jr. drives. Stretching from Boathouse Row along the Schuylkill River, these winding drives have a wide, sculpture-studded, tree-lined pedestrian path. It's a handsome spot, as crew teams skim along the river. It's also your best bet for attempting a Rocky-like jog. A loop from the Art Museum over Strawberry Mansion Bridge and back is 6¼ miles. *1½ hr.*

8 ★★ kids Philadelphia Zoo. The country's first zoo dates back to 1874 and consists of 42 acres on the west side of Fairmount Park. Nearly 1,800 animals dwell here. A few not-to-be-missed spots: The new **McNeil Avian Center,** with walk-through jungle-like habitats, a 4-D Migration Theater, and extinct-in-the-wild Guam Rail and Micronesian Kingfisher; **Carnivore Kingdom's** snow leopards, red pandas, and family of giant otters; **African Plains** for warthogs, antelope, gazelle, giraffes, hippos, and zebras. There's also a petting zoo and, for an extra fee, a ride 400 feet above the city via the tiger-striped **Zooballoon.** Best bet for transportation: Take a PHLASH or SEPTA bus, since parking is sparse and traffic gets heavy. (As for the Rocky connection: In *Rocky II,* our hero proposed to his sweetheart Adrienne, played by Talia Shire, on a winter's day at what is now **Big Cat Falls.**) *2 hrs. 34th St. & Girard Ave. ☎ 215/243-1100. www.philadelphiazoo.org. Admission Mar–Nov $17 adults, $14 children 2–11; Dec–Feb $14 adults & children. Zooballoon Mon–Fri additional $10, Sat–Sun $15. Feb–Nov daily 9:30am–5pm; Dec–Jan daily 9:30am–4pm.*

The original Rocky statue.

Romantic Philadelphia

Touring Philly à deux can be twice the fun—provided you know where to go. Lucky for couples, Center City's laid-back sidewalks are wide enough for ample hand-holding, and its park benches were custom made for snuggling. (It didn't earn the name "City of Brotherly Love" for nothing.) START: **Rittenhouse Square, 18th & Locust sts.**

1 ★★ Rittenhouse Square. Designed by French architect Paul Philippe Cret in 1913, this park is the leafy heart of Philly's fanciest neighborhood. Start your day here, when the grass is dewy and everyone else is rushing off to work. *1 hr. Btw. 18th & 19th sts., Walnut & Rittenhouse sts.*

2 ★★ Parc. Come nighttime, this glittery Parisian brasserie absolutely bursts with the see-and-be-seen crowd. At breakfast, however, the light is naturally dim and the vibe is delightfully low-key. Order espresso, eggs in cocotte, or a chocolate croissant—and linger. *18th & Locust sts. ☎ 215/545-2262. $$-$$$.*

3 ★ Rosenbach Museum. A quiet, elegant old townhouse filled with 30,000 rare books and three times that number of precious documents, including James Joyce's original *Ulysses*, Herman Melville first editions, Maurice Sendak art—perfect for old-fashioned flirting. *1 hr. 2010 Delancey Place. ☎ 215/732-1600. www.rosenbach.org. Admission $10 adults, $8 seniors, $5 students. Tues & Thurs–Sun 10am–5pm; Wed 10am–8pm.*

4 ★★★ Franklin Institute. Although this science museum is a bit kids-centric, it also boasts arguably the best spot in town to steal a kiss, a giant-but-cramped, continuously beating, walk-through *heart*. If that doesn't work, there's also the drama of an IMAX theater (additional fee to enter) for innocuous cuddling and eight interactive exhibits that feel straight out of a one-on-one date on *The Bachelor*, including "Skybike," which lets you ride atop the atrium on a 1-inch cable. There's also a certain romance to discovering the drama of traveling exhibits: Recent shows have included Galileo's (1564–1642) original telescope and sets

The giant walk-through heart at the Franklin Institute.

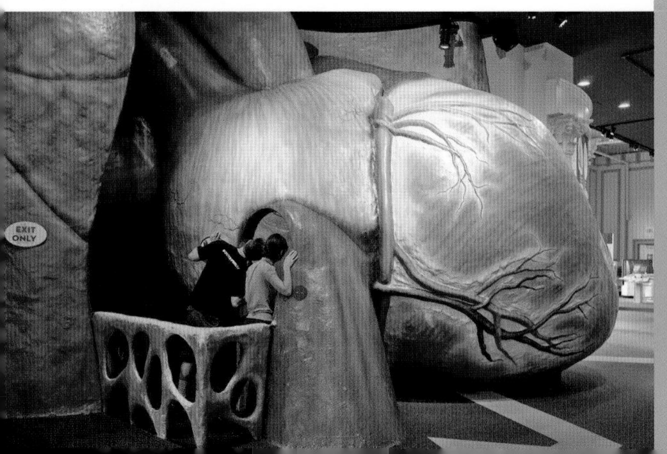

from *Star Trek.* Then, just outside the museum, an adults-allowed playground offers a high-wire version of a bicycle built for two. ⏲ *2 hr. 20th St. & Ben Franklin Pkwy.* ☎ *215/448-1200. www.fi.edu. Admission $14 adults, $13 seniors, $12 children 4–11; additional $5–$6 adults for IMAX Theater. Museum daily 9:30am–5pm; IMAX Sun–Thurs 10am–6pm, Fri–Sat 10am–9pm.*

5 ★★ **Tinto.** Sipping white sangria while tucked into a cozy booth feels downright clandestine in midday. This Basque tapas bar offers great, grown-up noshes, too. Try the Spanish meats and cheeses, a rich sandwich, or salad. *116 S. 20th St. (btw. Chestnut & Sansom sts.)* ☎ *215/665-9150. $–$$$.*

6 ★★ **Love Park.** If you haven't felt compelled to say those three little words yet, you'll certainly feel the mood when you take a seat in this charming urban park, where you won't be able to miss Robert Indiana's bright red, font-based LOVE sculpture. (If that's not a sign, nothing is.) ⏲ *½ hr. 15th St. & JFK Blvd.*

7 ★★★ **Rodin Museum.** Is there an artist more romantic than Auguste Rodin (1840–1917)? Perhaps, but there's not a Philadelphia art museum more romantic than this petite space, with its leafy overhangs and serene sculpture. Plus, if you recently bought, say, a circular piece of diamond jewelry, you won't be put off by the admission, a suggested donation of $5. *(See p 32, bullet 8).* ⏲ *1 hr. 22nd St. & Ben Franklin Pkwy. Suggested donation of $5.*

8 ★ **Eastern State Penitentiary.** Back when it opened in 1829, a visit to this medieval fortress–looking prison was no fun at all. These days, however, a stroll through Eastern State's decrepit cell blocks is perversely beautiful. An hour-long audio tour offers a glimpse into solitary confinement "rehabilitation" cells (in use until 1971) and into the lives of its inmates, including robber Willie Sutton (1901–1980), gangster Al Capone (1899–1947), and one very naughty dog. The weeks leading up to Halloween, ESP hosts the city's scariest haunted house—a perfect excuse for some extended hand-holding. ⏲ *1 hr. 2124 Fairmount Ave. (btw. 21 & 22 sts.).* ☎ *215/236-3300. www.easternstate.org. Admission $12 adults, $10 seniors, $8 students. Sept–May daily 10am–5pm; June–Aug Thurs–Tues 10am–5pm, Wed 10am–8pm.*

9 ★★ **Mercury Pavilion.** Got a ring in your pocket? Keep it there until you reach this cliff-top overlook between the Philadelphia Museum of Art and the Waterworks/Boathouse Row, the prettiest neoclassical gazebo in town for watching a sunset and declaring your undying affection. ⏲ *Whatever it takes. Behind Philadelphia Museum of Art (see p 13).*

A cell from Eastern State Penitentiary, first opened in 1829.

3 The Best Neighborhood Tours

Old City

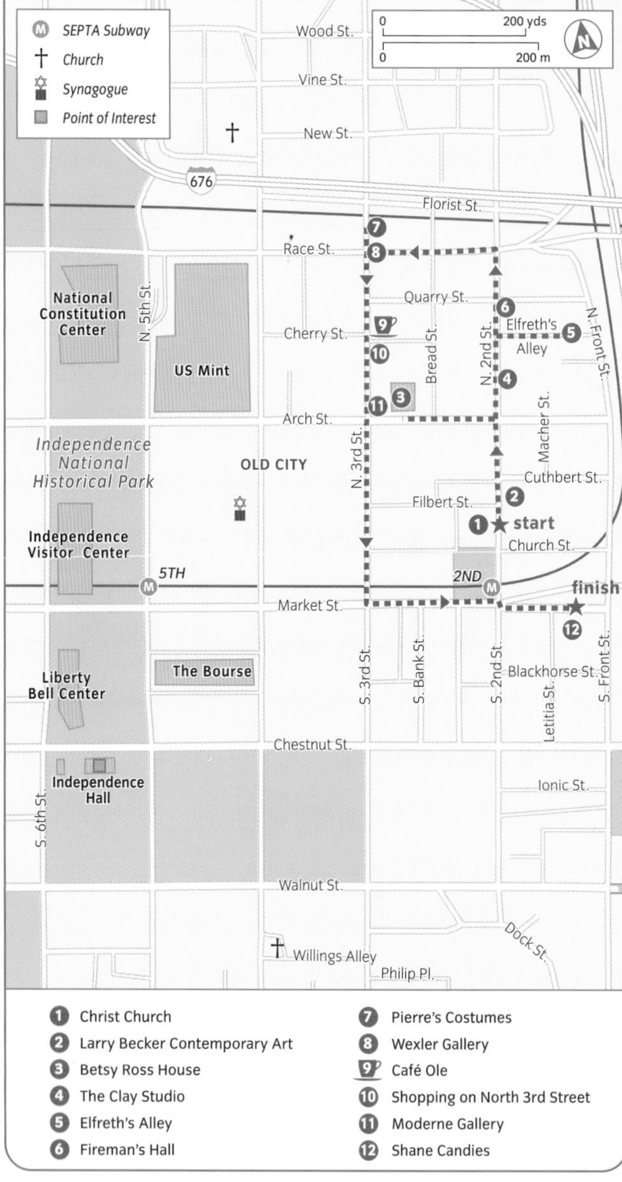

1. Christ Church
2. Larry Becker Contemporary Art
3. Betsy Ross House
4. The Clay Studio
5. Elfreth's Alley
6. Fireman's Hall
7. Pierre's Costumes
8. Wexler Gallery
9. Café Ole
10. Shopping on North 3rd Street
11. Moderne Gallery
12. Shane Candies

Previous page: Students stroll along the Locust Walk at the University of Pennsylvania.

The tree-lined streets of Philadelphia's most landmark-laden neighborhood are perfect for exploring by foot. What's loveliest about Old City is the seamless urban melding of old and new, Colonial and contemporary, classical and artful, and the excellent (and often eccentric) discoveries that pop up where you least expect them. **START: Old City Coffee, 221 Church St.**

1 ★★ Christ Church. To Old City residents, the gleaming white spire of this most Colonial of churches is as iconic to their neighborhood as City Hall's statue of William Penn (1644–1718) is to the whole of Philadelphia. A few facts worth-noting about this built-in-1727–1754, but-still-well-attended-today landmark: The massive Palladian window behind the altar was the inspiration for that of Independence Hall. Assigned seating was by pew rather than open benches (note Washington's [1732–1799] spot). William Penn was baptized in the font, a gift from All Hallows' Church in London. It's perfectly fine to walk on the floor-level tomb markers in the nave. And the shaded churchyard benches are great places to catch up on your people watching. (See p 11, 8.) *½ hr. 2nd & Market sts. Free admission.*

Mass at the 18th-century Christ Church is still well attended.

2 ★ Larry Becker Contemporary Art. Your first example of the newer half of Old City, this minimalist, modern gallery displays the mostly spare and always modern work of international artists such as Robert Ryman (1930–), Rebecca Salter (1977–), and native son Quentin Morris (1945–). *20 min. 43 N. 2nd St. ☎ 215/925-5389. Free admission. Fri–Sat 11am–5pm; Tues–Thurs by appointment.*

3 ★ kids Betsy Ross House. Another architectural emblem, this American seamstress' apparent dwelling is a brilliant example of the absolute compactness of life for the average Colonial family. Elizabeth (Betsy) Ross (1752–1836) was a Quaker needlewoman who, newly widowed in 1776, worked as a seamstress and upholsterer out of the space that is now the gift shop. According to lore, General Washington asked Ross to sew the original flag, 13 stars set in a field of 13 red and white stripes. According to recorded history, Ross at the very least sewed such flags for the American fleet. A courtyard park separates the house from the street; here Ross and her last husband are buried. The best day in the year to visit: June 14, Flag Day. (See p 11, 9.) *½ hr. Free admission. 239 Arch St.*

4 ★ The Clay Studio. This center for ceramics is one of the busiest artist spaces in this always-busy artist community. The Studio—which started as just that, an affordable workspace—now includes a two-floor gallery for new exhibits by international and up-and-coming ceramicists. Behind the scenes: workshops and classrooms. *20 min. 137–139 N. 2nd St. 215/925-3453. www.theclaystudio.org. Free admission. Tues–Sat 11am–7pm, Sun noon–6pm.*

5 ★★ Elfreth's Alley. From a small house to a small street of small houses. In 1700, this cobblestone lane was the address of a melting pot of artisans and tradesmen who worked in shipping. Fifty years later, the street was occupied by haberdashers, bakers, printers, and carpenters. In the late 18th through 19th centuries, Jewish, African-American, Welsh, and German residents lived along Elfreth's Alley. Number 126, the circa-1755 Mantua (cape) Maker's House belonged to blacksmith Jeremiah Elfreth (1723–1765). It's now the street's museum, with restored back garden and an interior that includes a dressmaker's shop and bedroom. Best time to visit: The first weekend in June, when all the alley's houses are open for touring. (See p 11, 10.) *1 hr. Off 2nd St., toward Front St., btw. Arch & Race sts. Free admission.*

6 kids Fireman's Hall. Run by the Philadelphia Fire Department, this restored 1902 firehouse traces its history back to Ben Franklin (1706–1790), the country's first fire marshal. On display: A circa-1730 hand pumper, the nation's oldest steam fire engine, modern-day fire safety displays, and artifacts from Ground Zero. *½ hr. 147 N. 2nd St. 215/923-1438. www.firemanshall.org. Free admission. Tues–Sat 10am–4:30pm.*

7 kids Pierre's Costumes. More than a million costumes reside at this 50-something-year-old store, a truly fun place to browse—or, if the occasion calls for it, to buy an Uncle Sam top hat, George Washington wig, or just about any Halloween outfit imaginable. *20 min. 211 N. 3rd St. 215/925-7121. www.costumers.com. Mon–Fri 10am–5:30pm, Sat 10am–4pm.*

8 ★ Wexler Gallery. This serene corner space hosts a marvelous variety of cutting-edge art exhibits of fine crafts, exquisite furniture, art glass, studio jewelry, and more. Like most of the galleries in Old City, on the first Friday of each month, Wexler stays open late to welcome art-fueled revelers. *½ hr. 205 N. 3rd St. (at Race St.). 215/923-7030. www.wexlergallery.com. Free admission. Tues–Sat 10am–6pm.*

The restored 1902 Fireman's Hall.

Wexler Gallery hosts a variety of cutting-edge exhibits.

9 **Café Ole.** If you haven't yet noticed why Old City has earned its nickname, the "Hipstoric District," you will once you set foot in this laid-back cafe. Stand in line for truly cool fresh-mint iced tea, creative grilled paninis, and tasty hummus plates and Mediterranean salads that won't break the bank. *147 N. 3rd St. ☎ 215/627-2140. $.*

⑩ ★★ **Shopping.** We may be pointing out the obvious, but this stretch of North 3rd Street between Race and Market streets is sublimely studded with great boutiques—and the occasional bargain. Read more about what's in stores in Chapter 4 *(see p 73)* or just take our word for it and pop into Sugarcube, Art in the Age, Vagabond, J. Karma, Third Street Habit, Reward, Lost & Found—or whatever latest vintage or new shop may catch your eye. (We promise you'll come out dressed like you totally belong in the Hipstoric District!) *Take all the time you need.*

⑪ ★ **Moderne Gallery.** Among the handful of really great furnishings shops in this area is Bob Aibel's 20,000-square-foot space, gently stocked with decorative arts from the last century. Look for rare French Art Deco, vintage George Nakashima (1905–1990), Wharton Esherick (1887–1970) pieces, and more artistic gems, all on display and for sale. *½ hr. 111 N. 3rd St. ☎ 215/923-8536. www.modernegallery.com. Free admission.*

⑫ ★ kids **Shane Candies.** Sure, you could head to Franklin Court *(see p 39)* for more history, but wouldn't you rather *taste* the history of the country's oldest candy store? For 130 years, the Shane family has stocked their shop with their famous buttercreams, almond butter crunch, cherry bark, and confections galore. *20 min. 110 Market St. ☎ 215/922-1048.*

Many great boutiques, like Vagabond, line North 3rd Street.

Society Hill

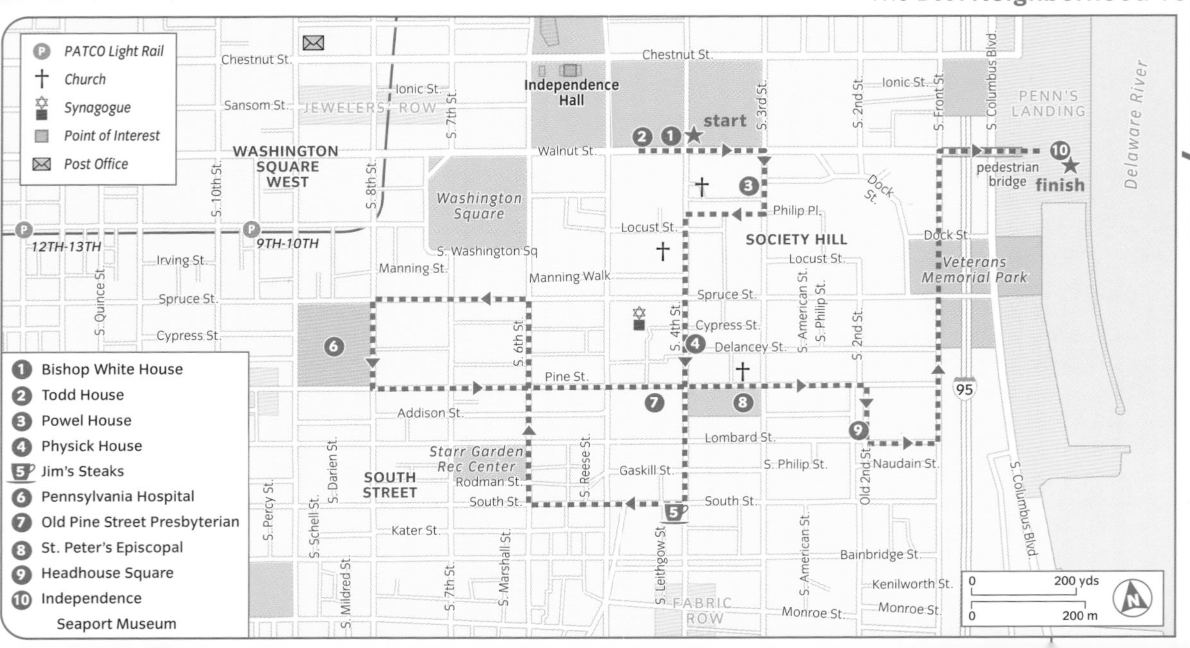

Society Hill has the largest concentration of 18th- and early-19th-century architecture in the city—and the country. It also has some of Philly's most modern houses, intended at one point to improve the caliber of the neighborhood. Before you go, pick up tickets for the first two stops at the Independence Visitor Center *(see p 9, ❶)*. START: **3rd & Walnut sts.**

❶ ★★ **Bishop White House.** This elegant circa-1786 home exemplifies gracious upper-class life in early America. Owner William White was quite a worldly fellow: Notice his library, with *Encyclopedia Britannica,* Sir Walter Scott's novels, the Koran—and, a luxury for any reader, an indoor "necessary." ◷ *½ hr. (See p 25, ❾.)*

❷ ★ **Todd House.** A much more modest (but far from small) dwelling belonged to John Todd, Jr. This solid, circa-1775 Georgian had a Colonial version of the family storefront, with a first-floor office and a large upstairs parlor, where Todd's widow Dolley (1768–1849) is said to have met one Mr. James Madison (1751–1836). ◷ *½ hr. (See p 26, ❿.)*

❸ ★★ **Powel House.** Built in 1765 by a wealthy merchant, this gorgeous Colonial Georgian became the home of Philadelphia mayor Samuel Powel (1738–1793) and his wife, Elizabeth Willing (1743–1830), in 1769. The gentle couple were major party throwers: Anyone who was anyone—Lafayette (1757–1834), Washington, Rush (1756–1833), Franklin—feasted and danced here. (Adams [1735–1826] dubbed the Powels' parties "sinful dinners.") Note the entryway's bas-relief plasterwork, mahogany wainscoting, ballroom chandelier, and formal garden. Since the house is still available for private parties, call before visiting. ◷ *½ hr. 224 S. 3rd St. (btw. Walnut & Locust sts).* ☎ *215/627-0364. Admission $5 adults, $4 seniors & students; $12 families. Thurs–Sat noon–4pm; Sun 1–4pm.*

❹ ★ **Physick House.** Freestanding, with a walled garden, this home diverges from its conjoined peers. Madeira wine importer Henry Hill

Physick House was home to "the father of American surgery."

The azalea gardens of Pennsylvania Hospital, the first hospital in the American Colonies.

built the place in 1786; subsequent owner Philip Syng Physick (1768–1837) added Federal flourishes, an inkstand (with Ben Franklin's fingerprints), and 18th century Italian art. Known as "the father of American surgery," Physick invented the stomach pump, created new ways to repair fractures, designed needle forceps, pioneered catgut sutures, removed thousands of bladder stones from Supreme Court Chief Justice John Marshall (1755–1835), was doctor to Dolley Madison and Andrew Jackson (1767–1845)—oh, and he invented soda, too. ***321 S. 4th St. (btw. Spruce & Pine sts). ☎ 215/925-7866. Admission $5 adults, $4 seniors & students. Thurs–Sat noon–4pm; Sun 1–4pm.***

5 ★ Jim's Steaks. If it's past 11am, there's a line at this corner steak stand, a pioneer in the field of cheesesteaks since 1939. To enjoy the real deal, order "with onions, with (Cheez) Whiz," (or, if you must, provolone). Bonus: Unlike its competitors, Jim's serves beer. ***4th & South sts. ☎ 215/928-1911. $.***

6 ★ Pennsylvania Hospital. The Colonies' first hospital was founded by—you guessed it—one Benjamin Franklin. Back in 1755, it seemed to its contemporaries like a strange venture in social welfare. Today, it's as vibrant as ever—and welcomes visitors who sign in and stay in non-patient areas. The hospital consists of two wings connected by a grand Center Building, the highlight of which was a sky-lit surgical amphitheater. As you might imagine, the hospital's interiors have much altered since those days, but the lovely azalea garden (facing Pine St.) remains, as does a carefully tended apothecary garden of medicinal herbs. ***½ hr. 8th & Spruce sts. ☎ 215/829-5439. www.pennhealth.com/pahosp. Free admission to historic sections of the hospital. Mon–Fri 8:30am–4:30pm.***

7 ★ Old Pine Street Presbyterian. When John Adams wasn't grumbling about fancy parties, he might have been sitting in a pew inside the city's oldest standing (ca. 1768) Presbyterian church. The Colonial nave and the old churchyard are both worth a visit. Old Pine's congregants are very welcoming. ***½ hr.*** ***(See p 23, 4.)***

8 ★ St. Peter's Episcopal. When Washington wasn't feasting on potpie and dancing jigs in the Powels' ballroom, he and Martha (1731–1802) were participating in more solemn occasions as members of this circa-1761 house of worship, part of the "breakaway" from England's Anglican church in 1784. ***½ hr.*** ***(See p 24, 5.)***

9 Headhouse Square. Although this all-brick, open-air market is only a replica of the 1745 original, the site has recently been reborn as a fantastic local farmers' market that's open weekends spring through fall. Flanked by cobblestone streets, the "headhouse" at the top of Pine Street is an 1804 firehouse. *15 min. 2nd St., btw. Pine & Lombard sts.*

10 ★ kids Independence Seaport Museum. Just across Columbus Boulevard, this modern, user-friendly attraction celebrates Society Hill's proximity to the Delaware River (which was, after all, the reason the neighborhood was established). The maritime collection here is first class, but so are the interactive, all-ages exhibits. Especially of note: Workshop on the Water, where visitors can observe classes in traditional wooden boat building and restoration. *1 hr. 211 S. Columbus Blvd. (at Walnut St.) ☎ 215/925-5439. www.phillyseaport.org. Admission Mon–Sat $12 adults, $10 seniors, $7 children 3–12, students & military; Sun 10am–noon pay what you wish. Daily 10am–5pm. Closed major holidays.*

Headhouse Square hosts a local farmers' market that is open weekends from spring through fall.

The Independence Seaport Museum has interactive, all-ages exhibits.

City Hall/Midtown

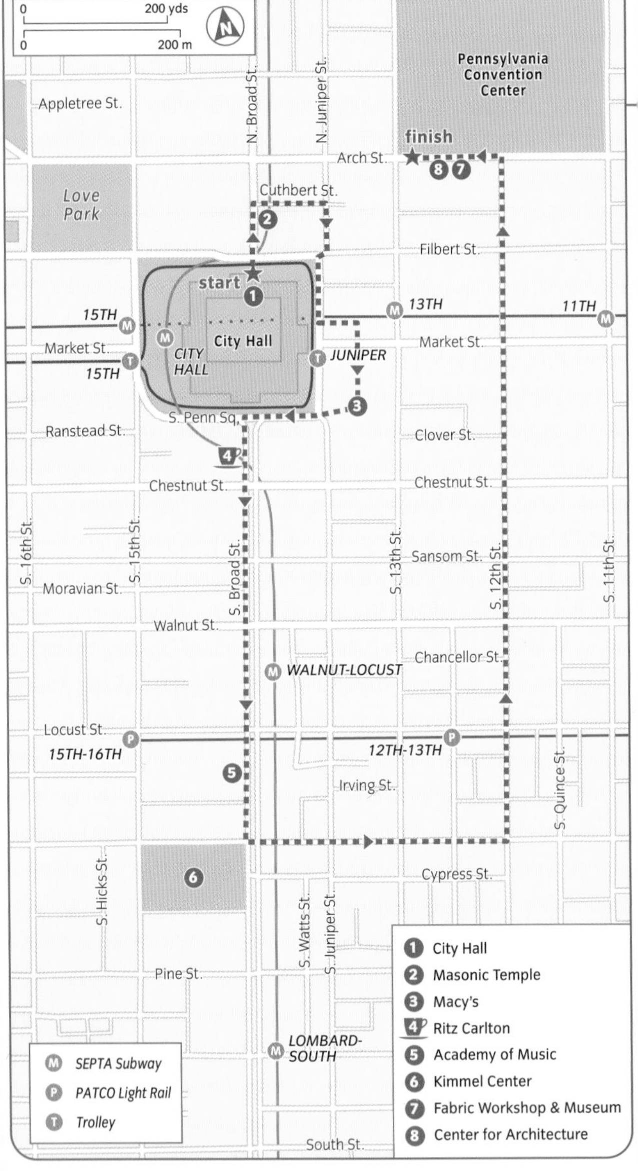

In the past decade, the heart of Philadelphia has experienced a major renaissance. Broad Street's theaters have grown to become the glittery "Avenue of the Arts": trendy bistros, shops, and condos transformed a once-dingy corridor of South 13th Street into hip "Midtown Village," and even City Hall has had a facade-brightening facelift. START: **City Hall, Broad & Market sts.**

1 ★★ City Hall. At the very center of Center City stands this wedding-cake of an all-masonry building, topped off with a 37-foot, 27-ton bronze statue of city "founder" William Penn. Treaty in hand, Penn faces east toward the Delaware River and Penn Treaty Park, where he signed a peace pact with the Native American Leni Lenape (or "Delaware") tribe. City Hall's best parts are its exterior sculpture (including Penn) by Alexander Milne Calder (1846–1923) and its glassed-in observation deck, located just below Penn's statue, 500 feet above ground, accessed by a sporadically available six-person elevator, with views clear to verdant New Jersey. *1 hr.* *(See p 20, 8.)*

The views are excellent from City Hall's 500-foot-high observation deck.

2 ★ Masonic Temple. Across from City Hall is a grand lodge of American Freemasonry, a fraternity of obscure, antique origins. A tour of the seven halls offers a crash course in classical architecture—and a glimpse of this fairly secret society (of which Washington and Franklin were members). *1 hr. 1 N. Broad St. ☎ 215/988-1917. Admission $8 adults, $6 students with ID, $5 seniors & children 12 & under. Tours Mon–Fri 10 & 11am, 1, 2, & 3pm; Sat 10 & 11am & noon.*

The Masonic Temple has ornate classical architecture in seven different halls.

The bronze eagle statue at this grand Macy's outlet.

3 **Macy's.** No worries: You're not here to shop. You're just here to admire the site of the old John Wanamaker Store, one of the nation's oldest department stores (now, obviously, a Macy's). Although a shadow of its former self, this stunning retail arena still alludes to grander shopping days, when proper ladies met at the bronze eagle sculpture before lunching at the store's Crystal Tearoom, and children marveled at the wonders of a toy department with its own monorail. Between Thanksgiving and New Year's, the store attracts crowds for its half-hour holiday light show, held right next to women's shoes. ½ *hr. 1300 Market St. (at Juniper St.). ☎ 215/241-9000. www.macys.com.*

4 ★ **Ritz Carlton.** So, it's a little on the fancy side. But it's worth the couple of extra dollars you'll spend to have coffee and warm soft pretzels amid the marble and beneath the grand dome of this Pantheon-like structure, opened as Girard Bank in 1908—and transformed into a, well, ritzy hotel in 2000. ***(See p 142.)***

5 ★★★ **Academy of Music.** Flickering gas-lit lanterns announce this 19th century opera hall, modeled

The Kimmel Center is home to several performing arts venues.

The Center for Architecture's bookstore carries fantastic gift items.

after Milan's La Scala. Gilded and gorgeous, the Academy is known as the "Grand Old Lady of Locust Street." (Her massive crystal chandelier is *to die for*.) If possible, catch a performance of the Pennsylvania Ballet, the Opera Company, or even a pop icon like Prince. ***(See p 129.)*** *15 min.*

6 ★★ Kimmel Center. A few blocks south stands Rafael Viñoly's (1944–) dramatic glass-and-steel, accordion-shaped performing arts center. Opened in 2001, the Kimmel encompasses a 2,500-seat, cello-shaped orchestra hall; a 650-seat theater for smaller performances; an interactive education center; and soaring, community-minded Commonwealth Plaza, which often plays host to free performances. Take the elevator to the rooftop garden for a view of Broad Street, also known as the "Avenue of the Arts." (This is the place to get those tickets to the Academy.) *½ hr. 300 S. Broad St. (at Spruce St.). 215/790-5800. www.kimmelcenter.org. Free admission. Daily 10am–6pm, or 30 min. past last performance.*

7 ★★ Fabric Workshop & Museum. A renovated warehouse—a structure familiar to many Philly artists—houses this unique center for the creation, display, and sale of new work in new materials. Three exhibition galleries and a video lounge show off cutting-edge (and often irresistibly tactile) works of local and international artists. In the permanent collection: Robert Morris' nuclear bed linens, a richly embroidered screen by Carrie Mae Weems, and a rubbery rug by Mona Hatoum. Artists' studios tours are available by appointment, and the gift shop is fantastic. *1 hr. 1214 Arch St. (btw. 12th & 13th sts). 215/561-8888. www.fabricworkshop.org. Admission $3 adults, free for children under 12. Mon–Fri 10am–6pm; Sat–Sun noon–5pm.*

8 Center for Architecture. The Philly chapter of the American Institute of Architects offers pristine design exhibits, such as vintage neon and a 3-D model of Center City. The gift-stocked bookstore is worth the trip alone, especially at Christmastime. *½ hr. 1218 Arch St. 215/569-3186. www.philadelphiacfa.org. Free admission. Mon–Sat 10am–6pm; Sun noon–5pm.*

Rittenhouse

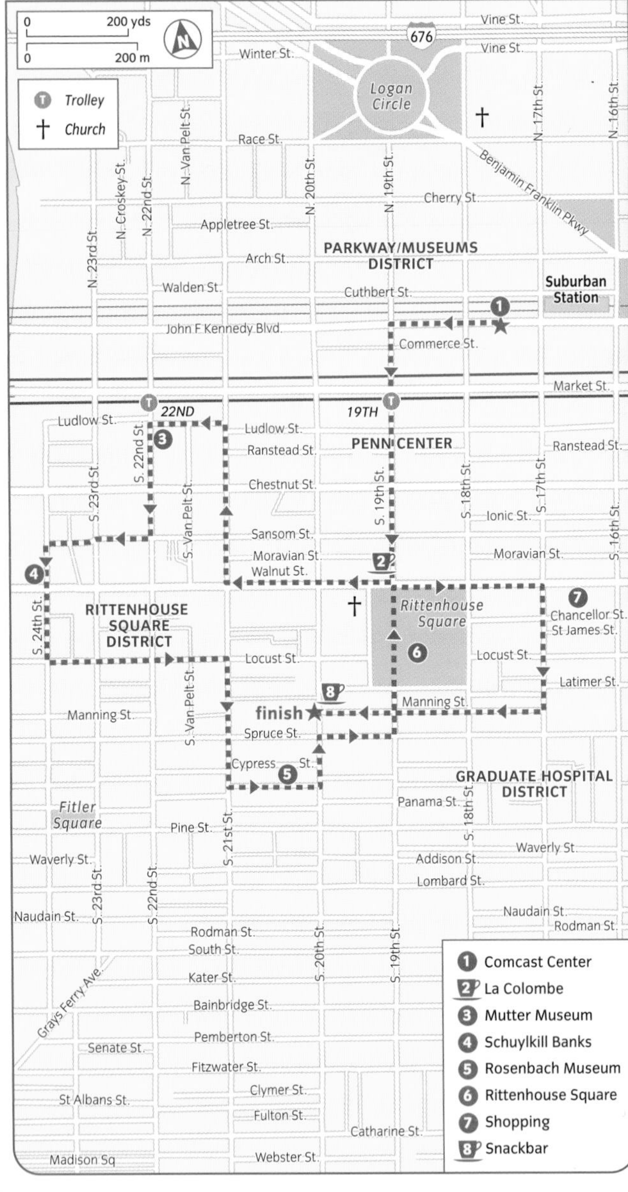

Per capita, more people walk to work in Philadelphia than in any other U.S. city. Many of these pedestrians wind up in this exclusive, residential-meets-commercial neighborhood. If it's a sunny spring day, the Square is the perfect spot to have lunch on a park bench. Fashion tip: If you packed something nice, wear it here. (And if not, take shopping breaks!) START: **19th & Walnut sts.**

❶ **Comcast Center.** Philadelphia's tallest building (975ft) comes courtesy of the 25 million people who pay Comcast's cable bills. When the Center debuted in 2009, the *Philadelphia Inquirer* called it "a giant USB memory stick." Stop in the atrium to ogle the people "walking" along the overhead beams, and watch a stunning, 83-foot, 10-million-pixel video display. A fun aside: In order to break the "curse of William Penn" (that no Philly professional sports team had won a championship since skyscrapers grew taller than Penn's statue on City Hall), workers attached a figurine of Penn to the Center's final beam. A few months later, the Phillies won the World Series. Coincidence? Certainly not! *20 min. 1701 JFK Blvd. www.comcast.com. Free admission.*

❷ **La Colombe.** A Rittenhouse resident wouldn't dream of starting the day without a cappuccino and an almond croissant from this chic cafe. Eat in, and your breakfast will be handed to you on pretty Fima Deruta pottery. *130 S. 9th St. ☎ 215/563-0860. $.*

❸ ★★ kids **Mutter Museum.** Visitors—especially kids—will be fascinated, possibly frightened, and definitely grossed out by the huge collection of medical oddities at this dimly lit, 19th-century building that feels straight out of *Harry Potter*—or, at least, *Young Frankenstein.* A whopping 20,000 strange-to-creepy objects fill the exhibit spaces at the College of Physicians (no longer a college)—including Grover Cleveland's

The 10-million-pixel video display at the Comcast Center.

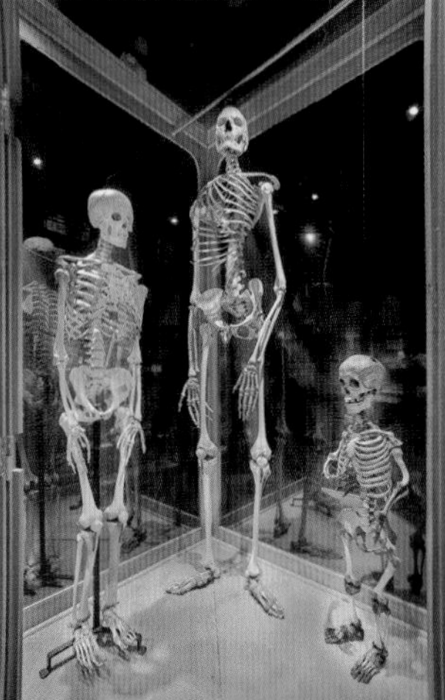

The Mutter Museum is filled with medical oddities.

(1837–1908) "secret tumor," a plaster cast of conjoined twins Chang and Eng (1811–1874), John Wilkes Booth's (1838–1865) thorax—and horrifying antique surgical instruments. ⌚ *1½ hr. 19 S. 22nd St. (btw. Market & Chestnut sts.). ☎ 215/563-3737, ext 293. www.collphyphil.org. Admission $14 adults, $10 students & military with ID, seniors & children 6–17, free for children 5 & under. Sat–Thurs 10am–5pm, Fri 10am–9pm.*

4 ★ Schuylkill Banks. Another welcome improvement to the cityscape is the extension of the paved riverbank trail from the Art Museum to this neighborhood. Check out what urban progress looks like—and sign yourself up for a kayak lesson while you're here. Entrance at 24th and Locust (cross the tracks) or down the staircase at 24th and Walnut. ⌚ *1 hr. 24th and Locust sts. ☎ 215/222-6030. www.schuylkillbanks.org.*

5 ★ Rosenbach Museum. Although it feels like a library, what with the 30,000 rare books and three times as many precious documents, this grand repository is, in fact, a museum. So, as much as you'd like to leaf through James Joyce's (1882–1941) original *Ulysses,* peruse a first-edition Melville (1819–1891), or borrow one of Maurice Sendak's (1928–) paintings for *Where the Wild Things Are,* you can't. These are artifacts, not meant for touching. What you may do: Wander about the lovely townhouse into art- and antique-filled rooms left over from the Rosenbachs' time living here. ⌚ *1 hr. 2010 Delancey Place. ☎ 215/732-1600. www.rosenbach.org. Admission $10 adults, $8 seniors, $5 students. Tues & Thurs–Sun 10am–5pm; Wed 10am–8pm.*

6 ★★★ kids Rittenhouse Square. Nearly a century ago, Paul Philippe Cret (1876–1945), designer of Ben Franklin Parkway, gave this park its rather polished good bones. Today, it's the city's most perfect people-watching spot, with some charming outdoor sculpture,

A paved riverbank trail winds through Schuylkill Banks.

The Rosenbach Museum is home to more than 30,000 rare books.

such as the central plaza's Antoine-Louis Barye's (1796–1875) *Lion Crushing a Serpent* (ca. 1832), Paul Manship's (1885–1966) *Duck Girl* (ca. 1911) near the reflecting pool, and Albert Laessle's (1877–1954) 2-foot-tall *Billy* goat in the Square's SW corner—since 1919, the preferred climbing toy of the Square's younger set, who've worn poor *Billy*'s head, horns, and spine to a golden shine. ½ ***hr. (See p 93, 6.)***

7 ★★ Shopping. There's an Anthropologie (1801 Walnut St.) inside the Square's Van Rensselaer mansion. Adresse (1706 Locust St.) boutique occupies a charming townhouse on Locust. Calderwood Gallery (1622 Spruce St.) bears traces of its genteel former residents. The display window at Joan Shepp (1616 Walnut St.) is downright museum-quality. Around here, "just looking" is quite a pleasant pastime. ***1 hr. (See p 73.)***

8 ★ Snackbar. This elegant, small bistro serves elegant, small snacks and cocktails. Sip a dainty grapefruit daiquiri. Nibble a tiny plate of tuna confit, poached shrimp with honeydew, or caviar-touched pierogies. Feel the glamour. ***253 S. 20th St. (btw. Locust & Spruce sts). 215/545-5655. $$.***

Rittenhouse Square contains several pieces of outdoor sculpture.

Fairmount

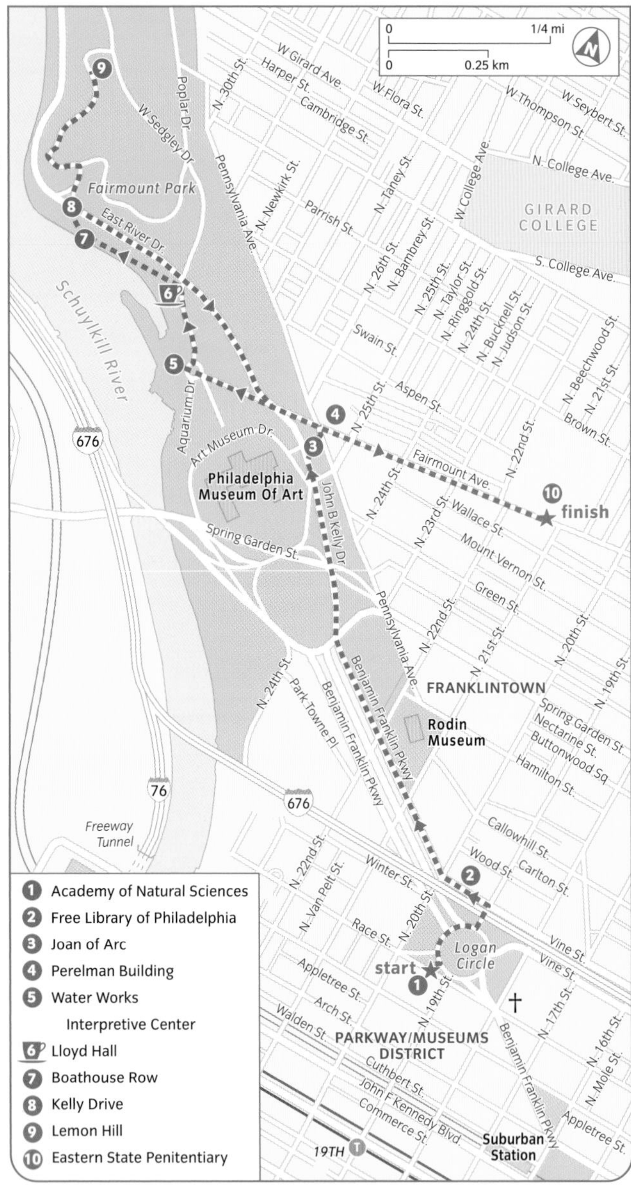
0
1/4 mi
0
0.25 km
N
Fairmount Park
Schuylkill River
Philadelphia Museum Of Art
GIRARD COLLEGE
FRANKLINTOWN
Rodin Museum
Logan Circle
PARKWAY/MUSEUMS DISTRICT
Suburban Station
19TH
start
finish
Freeway Tunnel
676
76
W Girard Ave.
Harper St.
Cambridge St.
W Flora St.
W Thompson St.
W Seybert St.
N. College Ave.
S. College Ave.
Parrish St.
Swain St.
Aspen St.
Brown St.
Fairmount Ave.
Wallace St.
Mount Vernon St.
Green St.
Spring Garden St.
Nectarine St.
Buttonwood Sq
Hamilton St.
Callowhill St.
Wood St.
Carlton St.
Winter St.
Race St.
Vine St.
Appletree St.
Arch St.
Walden St.
Cuthbert St.
John F Kennedy Blvd.
Commerce St.
Poplar Dr.
W Sedgley Dr.
East River Dr.
Aquarium Dr.
Art Museum Dr.
John B Kelly Dr.
Pennsylvania Ave.
Benjamin Franklin Pkwy
Park Towne Pl
N. 30th St.
N. Newkirk St.
N. Taney St.
W College Ave.
N. 26th St.
N. Bambrey St.
N. 25th St.
N. Taylor St.
N. Ringgold St.
N. 24th St.
N. Bucknell St.
N. Judson St.
N. Beechwood St.
N. 21st St.
N. 22nd St.
N. 23rd St.
N. 20th St.
N. 19th St.
N. Van Pelt St.
N. 17th St.
N. 16th St.
N. Mole St.
1 Academy of Natural Sciences
2 Free Library of Philadelphia
3 Joan of Arc
4 Perelman Building
5 Water Works Interpretive Center
6 Lloyd Hall
7 Boathouse Row
8 Kelly Drive
9 Lemon Hill
10 Eastern State Penitentiary

Bound by Vine and Girard, Broad and the Schuylkill, Fairmount is often called the "Museum District." And, while it's true that the Philadelphia Museum of Art, Franklin Institute, and Academy of Natural Sciences all exist here, so do some marvelous examples of elegant urban living: Stroll along Green Street to admire beautiful townhouses. START: **19th St. & Ben Franklin Pkwy.**

1 ★ kids Academy of Natural Sciences. If it's dinosaurs you seek, look no further. More than a dozen impressive specimens, including a massive T-Rex with jaws agape, are on display in the main hall. On weekends, kids can even "dig" for fossils. This natural history museum is also home to enormous moose, bison, and bears; a second floor filled with Asian and African flora and fauna; a tropical butterfly exhibit ($2 extra); and a children's museum where kids can touch a meteorite—and whatever animals happen to stop by that day. ⏲ *1 hr. 19th St. & Ben Franklin Pkwy. ☎ 215/299-1000. www.ansp.org. Admission $12 adults, $10 seniors, students with ID & children 3–12. Mon–Fri 10am–4:30pm, Sat–Sun 10am–5pm.*

2 Free Library of Philadelphia. Stoic and splendid from its perch at the top of Logan Circle, the central branch of the public library is (after this book) the best place to delve into writing about local travel and history (second floor). ⏲ *½ hr. 1901 Vine Street. ☎ 215/686-5322. www.library.phila.gov. Free admission. Mon–Wed 9am–9pm, Thurs–Sat 9am–5pm, Sun 1–5pm.*

3 ★ Joan of Arc. The shiniest monument in town marks the entrance to Kelly Drive and Fairmount Park. Built originally in 1874, Napoleon III (1808–1873) commissioned this equestrian statue of the French heroine for Paris. In 1890 the city of Philadelphia asked for a copy, but sculptor Emmanuel Frémiet (1824–1910) gave the original to them

The Academy of Natural Sciences boasts a tropical butterfly exhibit among its many attractions.

The Joan of Arc monument was originally commissioned by Napoleon III for Paris.

instead, sculpting a new version for Paris. The work's most recent gilding happened in late 2009. *10 min.*

4 ★★ Perelman Building. Across the street from the Philadelphia Museum of Art—which is worth a visit, when you have a couple of hours *(see p 13, 2)*—the Perelman offers a glimpse of the PMA's rich permanent collections. The restored Art Deco office building has textile and design treasures, smaller exhibits, and a lovely cafe. *1 hr. (See p 34, 11).*

5 ★★ kids Water Works Interpretive Center. Behind the Art Museum and atop Fairmount Dam is a charming line of miniature classical facades that appear as if they might be inhabited by mini Romans. They mark the restored location of the country's first municipal water delivery systems, which although not quite as fantastical, does hold, er, water today. This center aims to teach the importance of clean water via high-tech exhibits—a simulated helicopter ride takes visitors from the Delaware Bay to the headwaters of the Schuylkill River—and offers an engaging message of environmental awareness. *1 hr. 640 Waterworks Dr. ☎ 215/685-0719. www.fairmountwaterworks.com. Free admission. Tues–Sat 10am–5pm, Sun 1–5pm.*

6 Lloyd Hall. This newest of boathouses is owned and operated by the City of Philadelphia; despite that, it serves some tasty salads, sandwiches, and pastries—and, if you arrive early enough on a weekend, they'll even rent you a bike. *1 Boathouse Row (Kelly Dr.). ☎ 215/685-3936. www.fairmountpark.org. Daily 7am–9pm. $.*

7 ★★ Boathouse Row. Although these 10 Victorian-era crew-team

The Water Works Interpretive Center includes several miniature classical facades.

Kelly Drive is popular with cyclists and joggers.

clubhouses are most famously viewed lit up and from the other side of the river, they're great to peek into as you pass by. Together, the houses form the "Schuylkill Navy" and are most often used by college and high school teams. Frank Furness (1839–1912) designed #13, Undine Barge Club. ½ ***hr. #2–#14 Boathouse Row, Kelly Dr.***

8 ★★ Kelly Drive. Named for champion Olympian oarsman Jack Kelly (father of Grace Kelly [1929–1982]), this winding road has an adjacent path popular with cyclists and joggers. Even a short walk here leads to some marvelous sculpture, including one of Kelly himself. But look carefully: Frederic Remington's (1861–1909) *Cowboy* (ca. 1905), for example, hides atop a rock. ½ ***hr. Kelly Dr., btw. Fairmount Ave. and Strawberry Mansion Bridge.***

9 ★ Lemon Hill. High above Kelly Drive is the summer home of merchant Henry Pratt. Built in the 1800, this Federal-style "country" estate boasts an impressive trio of stacked oval rooms and serene gardens. ½ ***hr. Sedgeley & Lemon Hill drs.*** ☎ ***215/232-4337. www.lemonhill.org. Admission $5 adults, $3 seniors & students. Apr to mid-Dec Wed–Sun 10am–4pm; Jan–Mar by appt.***

10 ★ Eastern State Penitentiary. Smack-dab in the center of residential Fairmount is this frightening former prison, placed atop the nearest hill to Center City to serve as a warning to criminals. It didn't work: Eastern State stayed in business from 1829 to 1971, and is busiest now around Halloween and Bastille Day (July 14). ***1 hr.*** ***(See p 48, 8).***

Lemon Hill is a country estate built in 1800.

University City

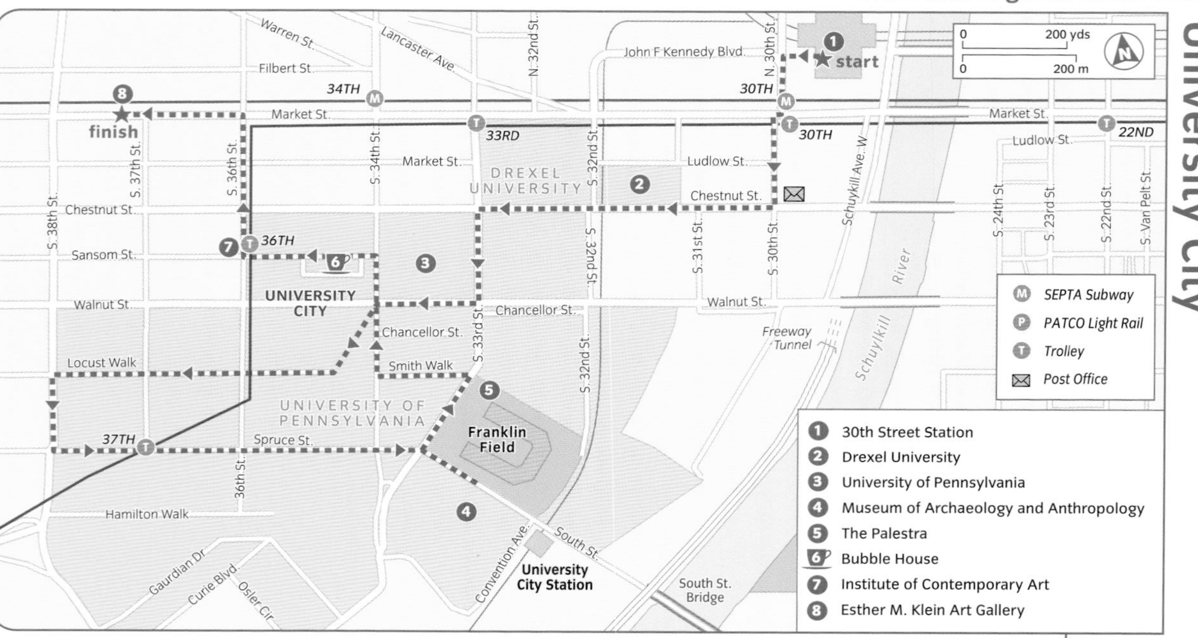

West of the Schuylkill River lies Philly's first suburb, known today as University City. Its centerpiece is the University of Pennsylvania, founded in 1740 by (who else but) Franklin and friends, which boasts the country's first medical, law, and business schools. START: **30th St. Station, btw. 29th & 30th sts. on Market St.**

1 ★★ 30th Street Station. 20,000 Amtrak, SEPTA, and NJ Transit commuters pass through this circa-1933 train station daily. Notice the ornate Art Deco decor, roof built to accommodate small aircraft, and PA Railroad World War II Memorial of archangel Michael. *15 min. 2955 Market St. 215/349-3196. www.30thstreetstation.com. Daily 24 hr.*

2 ★★ Drexel University. This high-tech university is the first to greet entrants to West Philly. Founded in 1891, Drexel has gone through several name changes, developed a world-class engineering program, and added contemporary architecture, including a dorm by Michael Graves at 33rd and Race sts. *1 hr. Btw. 31st & 35th sts, Chestnut & Powelton sts. www.drexel.edu.*

3 ★★★ University of Pennsylvania. One of the country's oldest universities, "Penn" belongs both to the Ivy League and to the long list of Philadelphia establishments founded by Ben Franklin. The city campus is a mix of modern and antique, with a well-heeled and international student body. Penn's heart is "Locust Walk," a vibrant pedestrian thoroughfare bisecting campus, passing between ivy-covered 19th-century Gothic buildings, student-populated College Green, giant contemporary sculpture (Claes Oldenburg's [1929–] *Split Button*), and modern, Louis Kahn-designed (1901–1974) Fine Arts Library. Look carefully, and find Franklin (in bronze) seated on a park bench, too. *½ hr. Locust Walk btw. 34th & 38th sts. 215/898-5000. www.upenn.edu.*

4 ★★★ kids University of Pennsylvania Museum of Archaeology and Anthropology. Since 1887—through 400-some archeological and anthropological international expeditions—Penn's major museum has collected more than 1 million ancient objects. A vast portion of them are displayed (and intelligently explained) within this massive Beaux Arts building's 25 galleries, distributed among three floors. The basement-level Egyptian collection, considered one of the finest in the world, includes a colossal Sphinx, enormous columns, and *Mummies, Secrets, and Science,* a favorite among families. The third floor's world-renowned excavation display of Sumerian jewelry and household objects from the royal tombs of Ur is not to be missed. Nearby, ogle giant cloisonné lions from Beijing's Imperial Palace, Chinese court treasures, and tomb figures. Basically, if it's ancient, it's here: Mesopotamia; the Bible

Locust Walk is the heart of the University of Pennsylvania.

The Museum of Archaeology and Anthropology has collected more than 1 million ancient objects.

Lands; Mesoamerica; the ancient Mediterranean; and native peoples of the Americas, Africa, and Polynesia are also all represented. Most Wednesday mornings, the University Museum holds multicultural kid-friendly performances such as dance, storytelling, drumming, or puppetry. ◷ *2 hrs. 3260 South St. (near Spruce St.). ☎ 215/898-4000. www.museum.upenn.edu. Admission $10 adults, $7 seniors, $6 students with ID & children over 5, free for children 5 & under. Tues–Sat 10am–4:30pm, Sun 1–5pm (except holidays).*

5 ★ The Palestra. If you know college hoops, you know Penn's circa-1927 gymnasium, a.k.a. "The Cathedral of College Basketball." More NCAA men's b-ball games, more tournaments, and more visiting teams have played here than anywhere else. The tradition continues today, so when you visit, you might catch a St. Joe's, Villanova, Temple, or (of course) Penn game. ◷ *½ hr. 215 S. 33rd St. (btw. Walnut & Spruce sts.).*

6 Bubble House. On a petite stretch of restaurants and retail, this cozy cafe-bar offers yummy tapioca "bubble" teas, lemongrass shrimp dumplings, burgers and wraps, fruity cocktails (yum: lychee margarita), plus more of a sit-down menu. *3404 Sansom St. ☎ 215/243-0804. $.*

7 ★★ Institute of Contemporary Art. Edgy modern art is always on display at this spare, Penn-run gallery. The first museum to show Andy Warhol (1928–1987), Laurie Anderson (1947–), and Robert Indiana (1928–), the ICA's installations have ranged from rocketry to music, couture to comics. ◷ *1 hr. 118 S. 36th St. (at Sansom St.). ☎ 215/898-5911. www.icaphila.org. Free admission. Wed–Fri noon–8pm, Sat–Sun 11am–5pm.*

8 ★ Esther M. Klein Art Gallery. If you have one more stop in you, visit this unique and up-and-coming gallery. EKG puts on contemporary exhibits with a science and technology bent—so that photo you're admiring might have a bio lesson behind it. ◷ *½ hr. 3711 Market St. ☎ 215/966-6188. www.kleinartgallery.com. Free admission. Mon–Sat 9am–5pm.* ●

4 The Best **Shopping**

Center City **Shopping**

AIA Bookstore **31**
Antiquarian's Delight **35**
Art Star **60**
Benjamin Lovell Shoes **56, 9**
Blendo **38**
Born Yesterday **11**
Boyd's **1**
Bus Stop Boutique **54**
Calderwood Gallery **20**
Children's Boutique **17**
DiBruno Brothers **6**
Eyes Gallery **53**
Fleisher/Ollman Gallery **21**
Foster's Homeware **50**
Freeman's/Fine Arts of Philadelphia **2**
Gene's Boutique **59**
Halloween **24**
Head House Books **57**
Joan Shepp **26**
Locks Gallery **36**
Lolli Lolli **34**
Loop and Spool **15**
Lost & Found **43**
M. Finkel & Daughter **39**
Macy's **27**
Matthew Izzo **44**
Minima **46**
Mitchell & Ness Sporting Goods **29**
Mode Moderne **45**
Moderne Gallery **47**
Newman Galleries **19**
Open House **28**
The Original I. Goldberg **30**
Petulia's Folly **7**
Philadelphia Art Alliance **16**
Philadelphia Runner **5**
Piccolini **13**
Reading Terminal Market **32**
Rittenhouse Sports Specialties **3**
Rosie's Yarn Cellar **12**
Scarlett Alley **41**
Shops at Liberty Place **4**
Shops at the Bellevue **23**
Smak Parlor **51**
Sophie's Yarns **55**
Sugarcube **40**
Third Street Habit **42**
Town Home **22**
Vagabond **48**
Vintage Modern **58**
W. Graham Arader III Gallery **25**

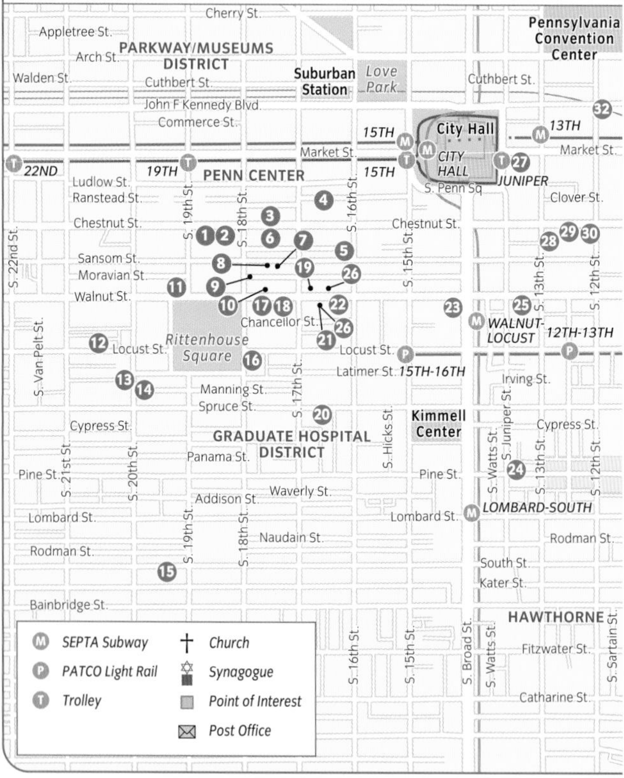

Previous page: Sugarcube features many up-and-coming fashion labels.

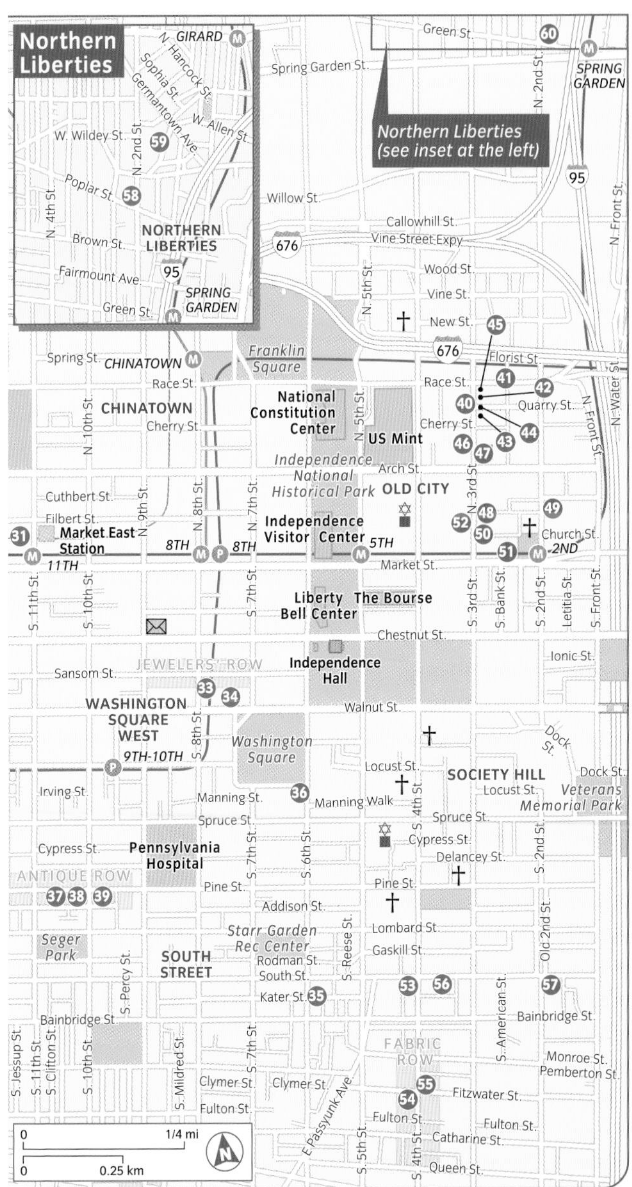
Northern Liberties
GIRARD
N. Hancock St.
Sophia St.
Germantown Ave.
W. Allen St.
W. Wildey St.
N. 2nd St.
Poplar St.
N. 4th St.
NORTHERN LIBERTIES
Brown St.
Fairmount Ave.
SPRING GARDEN
Green St.
Northern Liberties (see inset at the left)
Spring Garden St.
SPRING GARDEN
N. 2nd St.
Willow St.
Callowhill St.
Vine Street Expy
Wood St.
Vine St.
New St.
N. 5th St.
Florist St.
Franklin Square
Spring St.
CHINATOWN
Race St.
CHINATOWN
Cherry St.
N. 10th St.
National Constitution Center
US Mint
Quarry St.
N. Front St.
N. Water St.
N. Front St.
Independence National Historical Park
Arch St.
OLD CITY
N. 3rd St.
Cuthbert St.
Filbert St.
N. 9th St.
N. 8th St.
N. 7th St.
Market East Station
Independence Visitor Center
Church St.
11TH
8TH
8TH
5TH
2ND
Market St.
S. 11th St.
S. 10th St.
S. 7th St.
Liberty Bell Center
The Bourse
S. 3rd St.
S. Bank St.
S. 2nd St.
Letitia St.
S. Front St.
Chestnut St.
Ionic St.
Sansom St.
JEWELERS' ROW
Independence Hall
WASHINGTON SQUARE WEST
Walnut St.
S. 8th St.
Washington Square
9TH-10TH
Dock St.
Locust St.
SOCIETY HILL
Dock St.
Locust St.
Veterans Memorial Park
Irving St.
Manning St.
Manning Walk
S. 4th St.
Spruce St.
Spruce St.
Cypress St.
Pennsylvania Hospital
Cypress St.
Delancey St.
S. 7th St.
S. 6th St.
S. 2nd St.
ANTIQUE ROW
Pine St.
Pine St.
Addison St.
Seger Park
Starr Garden Rec Center
Lombard St.
Gaskill St.
S. Reese St.
Old 2nd St.
SOUTH STREET
S. Percy St.
Rodman St.
South St.
Kater St.
S. American St.
Bainbridge St.
Bainbridge St.
S. Jessup St.
S. 11th St.
S. Clifton St.
S. 10th St.
S. Mildred St.
S. 7th St.
FABRIC ROW
Monroe St.
Pemberton St.
Clymer St.
Clymer St.
E Passyunk Ave.
Fitzwater St.
Fulton St.
Fulton St.
Fulton St.
Catharine St.
S. 5th St.
S. 4th St.
Queen St.
0
1/4 mi
0
0.25 km

Shopping Best Bests

Best for **Gifts**
★★ Open House, *107 S. 13th St. (p 83)*

Best **Bookshop**
★★ Joseph Fox, *1724 Sansom St. (p 79)*

Best for **Precious Baubles**
★★★ Halloween, *1329 Pine St. (p 83)*

Best for **Antiques with Provenance**
★★ M. Finkel & Daughter, *936 Pine St. (p 77)*

Best for **Emerging Art**
★★ Larry Becker Contemporary Art, *43 N. 2nd St. (p 78)*

Best **Children's Shop**
★★ Gene's Boutique, *1050 N. Hancock St. (p 79)*

Best **Edible Souvenirs**
★★★ Reading Terminal Market, *12th and Arch sts. (p 83)*

Best for **Crafters**
★★★ Loop and Spool, *1912–1914 South St. (p 80)*

Best **Women's Designer Clothing**
★★★ Joan Shepp, *1616 Walnut St. (p 81)*

Best **Edgy Women's Wear**
★★★ Vagabond, *37 N. 3rd St. (p 82)*

Best for **Shoes**
★★ Bus Stop Boutique, *750 S. 4th St. (p 84)*

Best for **Browsing**
★ Macy's, *1300 Chestnut/Market St. (p 81)*

Best for **Foodies**
★★ DiBruno Brothers, *1730 Chestnut St. (p 83)*

Best for **Sports Fanatics**
★★★ Mitchell & Ness, *1318 Chestnut St. (p 84)*

Best **Cheap and Chic Clothing**
★★ Lost & Found, *133 N. 3rd St. (p 81)*

Gene's Boutique is a popular choice for children's gifts.

Shopping A to Z

M. Finkel & Daughter carries antique furnishings and paintings.

Antiques/Vintage

Antiquarian's Delight SOUTH STREET A former synagogue, now full of independently-run kiosks hawking slightly quirky to wholly quirky old things. *615 S. 6th St. (btw. South & Bainbridge sts.). ☎ 215/592-0256. Some kiosks accept some credit cards. Bus: 40, 57. Map p 74.*

★★ **Blendo** ANTIQUE ROW Feels like grandma's attic, with all of the clutter and more of the treasures (including brand-new finds, too). *1002 Pine St. (btw. 10th & 11th sts.) ☎ 215/351-9260. AE, DISC, MC, V. Bus: 23, Alternate 40. Map p 74.*

★★ **Calderwood Gallery** RITTENHOUSE Rare, French Art Deco, plus an elite handful of more current shelter collectibles, fill Janet and Gary Calderwood's elegant, multi-floor, ring-to-get-in townhouse. *1622 Spruce St. ☎ 215/546-5357. www.calderwoodgallery.com. AE, MC, V. Bus: 2, 40. Map p 74.*

★★ **Freeman's/Fine Arts of Philadelphia** RITTENHOUSE The local version of Sotheby's or Christy's, with catalogued auctions of art, jewelry, antiques, decorative arts, and fashion. *1808 Chestnut St. (btw. 18th & 19th sts.). ☎ 215/563-9275. www.freemansauction.com. No credit cards. Bus: 9, 17, 21, 42. Map p 74.*

★★ **M. Finkel & Daughter** ANTIQUE ROW Known for restored schoolgirl samplers from the 17th through mid-19th century, this well-appointed shop also stocks American folk art, furnishings, and paintings. *936 Pine St. (at 10th St.) ☎ 215/627-7797. www.samplings.com. AE, MC, V. Bus: 23, Alternate 40. Map p 74.*

★★ **Mode Moderne** OLD CITY More vintage than antique, the mint-condition furniture at this two-level shop hails from the dawn of the "atomic" modern era; think Charles and Ray Eames, not Chippendale. *159 N. 3rd St. (btw. Arch and Race sts.) ☎ 215/627-0299. www.modemoderne.com. AE, DISC, MC, V. Bus: 5, 17, 48, 57. Map p 74.*

★★ **Moderne Gallery** OLD CITY Robert Aibel's artful collection includes early Nakashima (1905–1990); French ironwork; and sculpture, furnishings, and woodcuts from the American craft movement. *111 N. 3rd St. (btw. Arch & Race sts.). ☎ 215/923-8536. www.modernegallery.com. MC, V. Bus: 5, 17, 48, 57. Map p 74.*

★★ **Vintage Modern** NORTHERN LIBERTIES Well-priced mid-century-and-beyond wares move fast out of this laid-back spot. Owner James Miller is fanatical about properly reupholstering vintage finds. *906 N. 2nd St. (at Poplar St.). ☎ 215/238-1997. www.vintagemodern.net. AE, MC, V. Bus: 5, 25. Subway: Spring Garden St. Map p 74.*

★★ **W. Graham Arader III Gallery** MIDTOWN Rare 16th-through 19th-century maps, water-colors, and prints—including some by renowned naturalist John James Audubon (1785–1851)—are the specialty inside Arader's landmark building. *1308 Walnut St. ☎ 215/735-8811. www.aradergalleries.com. AE, MC, V. Bus: 9, 12, 21, 42. Subway: Walnut-Locust. Map p 74.*

Art

★ **Eyes Gallery** SOUTH STREET Sometimes religious, often offbeat, and always colorful Latin American folk art bursts from the seams of this multi-floor, 30-something-year-old shop, which is covered in mosaics by local artist Isaiah Zagar (1940–). *402 South St. (at 4th St.) ☎ 215/925-0193. www.eyesgallery.com. AE, DISC, MC, V. Bus: 40, 57. Map p 74.*

★ **Fleisher/Ollman Gallery** RITTENHOUSE This second-floor gallery carries fine, variable works by emerging contemporary and self-taught American artists. *1616 Walnut St. (btw. 16th & 17th sts). ☎ 215/545-7562. www.fleisher-ollmangallery.com. AE, DISC, MC, V. Bus: 9, 12, 21, 42. Map p 74.*

Larry Becker Contemporary Art offers an intimate space for showcasing modern artists.

★★ **Larry Becker Contemporary Art** OLD CITY An intimate space for new, often spare paintings and sculpture from modern artists such as Steve Riedell (1954–) and Stuart Arends (1953–). *43 N. 2nd St. (btw. Market & Arch sts.) ☎ 215/925-5389. No credit cards. Bus: 5, 17, 33, 44. Subway: 2nd St. Map p 50.*

★★★ **Locks Gallery** WASHINGTON SQUARE A Beaux Arts building houses a powerhouse gallery exhibiting big-deal works by de Kooning (1904–1997), Hockney (1937–), and Rauschenberg (1925–2008). *600 Washington Sq. (at 6th St., btw. Walnut & Spruce sts.). ☎ 215/629-1000. www.locksgallery.com. No credit cards. Bus: 9, 12, 21, 42, 47. Map p 74.*

★★ **Minima** OLD CITY More "design" than "art," the wares in this glossy-white space consist of pristinely modern furnishings by Piero Lissoni (1956–), Phillippe Starck (1949–), Jasper Morrison (1959–), and Marcel Wanders (1963–).

118 N. 3rd St. (btw. Arch & Race sts.). ☎ 215/922-2002. www.minima.us. AE, DISC, MC, V. Bus: 5, 17, 33, 44, 48, 57. Subway: 2nd St. Map p 74.

★ **Newman Galleries** RITTENHOUSE Philadelphia's oldest gallery (ca. 1865) represents Bucks County artists, American sculptors, and traditional painters. *1625 Walnut St. (btw. 16th & 17th sts.). ☎ 215/563-1779. www.newmangalleries.com. AE, DISC, MC, V. Bus: 2, 9, 12, 21, 42. Map p 74.*

★ **Philadelphia Art Alliance** RITTENHOUSE A striking mansion on the Square houses three floors of exhibition space for a variety of shows that have included photography, fine craft, and more. *251 S. 18th St. (at Rittenhouse Sq.). ☎ 215/545-4302. www.philartalliance.org. No credit cards. Bus: 9, 12, 17, 21, 42. Map p 74.*

Bookstores

★★ **AIA Bookstore** MIDTOWN Moleskine journals, modern cards, great office supplies, and holiday decorations stand out among hundreds of books about design and architecture. *1218 Arch St. (btw. 12th & 13th sts.). ☎ 215/569-3188. www.aiabookstore.com. AE, DISC, MC, V. Bus: 17, 23, 33, 44, 48. Subway: 13th St. Map p 74.*

★ kids **Head House Books** SOUTH STREET This neat-as-a-pin neighborhood shop stocks classics, bestsellers, and fantastic children's books—and invites local authors for readings. *619 S. 2nd St. (btw. South & Bainbridge sts.). ☎ 215/923-9525. www.headhousebooks.com. AE, DISC, MC, V. Bus: 40, 57. Map p 74.*

★★ **Joseph Fox Bookshop** RITTENHOUSE This tiny walkup is cozy and well organized, and has a bookish staff who know their stock inside and out. (David Sedaris [1956–] gives readings here.) *1724 Sansom St. (btw. 17th & 18th sts.). ☎ 215/563-4184. www.foxbookshop.com. AE, MC, V. Bus: 2, 9, 12, 21, 42.*

Children's

★ **Born Yesterday** RITTENHOUSE For the Bugaboo stroller set, a haute boutique for hand-knit sweaters, French onesies, and trendy ensembles for newborns on up. *1901 Walnut St. (across from Rittenhouse Sq.). ☎ 215/568-6556. www.bornyesterdayphila.com. AE, DISC, MC, V. Bus: 9, 12, 17, 21, 42. Map p 74.*

★ **Children's Boutique** RITTENHOUSE Design-your-own cotton sweaters and kiddie "it" brands, plus shoes, toys, and *très* impressive baby shower baskets. *1702 Walnut St. (btw. 17th & 18th sts.). ☎ 215/732-2661. www.echildrensboutique.com. AE, DISC, MC, V. Bus: 2, 9, 12, 21, 42. Map p 74.*

★★ **Gene's Boutique** NORTHERN LIBERTIES Shrunken versions of trendy labels—Ella Moss, Splendid, C&C California—plus everything

Joseph Fox Bookshop has hosted readings from the likes of David Sedaris.

Loop and Spool has a wide range of colorful patterns for crafts.

you'd need to furnish the modern nursery are for sale and custom order at this Piazza shop. *1050 N. Hancock St. (btw. Girard Ave. & Poplar St., in the Piazza). ☎ 215/735-4300. www.shopgenes.com. AE, DISC, MC, V. Bus: 5, 57. Subway: Girard Ave. Map p 74.*

Lolli Lolli WASHINGTON SQUARE This cheerful walk-up stocks classic toys, cute placemats, and plenty of oh-so adorable clothes for children through age 12. *713 Walnut St. (across from Washington Sq.). ☎ 215/625-2655. www.lollilolli.net. AE, DISC, MC, V. Bus: 9, 21, 42, 47. Map p 74.*

★ **Piccolini** RITTENHOUSE Rocker t-shirts, chic changing tables, organic burp cloths for the baby who has—or, at least, deserves—everything. *264 S. 20th St. (btw. Locust & Spruce sts.). ☎ 215/545-0395. www.piccolinionline.com. AE, DISC, MC, V. Bus: 7, 12, 17, 40. Map p 74.*

Crafts

★★ **Art Star** NORTHERN LIBERTIES If you like Etsy, you'll love this youthful gallery's stock of handmade clothing, accessible art, and sculptural jewelry. *623 N. 2nd St. (btw. Spring Garden St. & Fairmount Ave.). ☎ 215/238-1557. www.artstarphilly.com. MC, V. Bus: 5, 57. Subway: Spring Garden St. Map p 74.*

★★★ **Loop and Spool** SOUTH STREET/RITTENHOUSE These colorful, gallery-like, always friendly, side-by-side shops offer beautiful yarns, pretty fabrics, and tons of patterns (and advice). *1912–1914 South St. (btw. 19th & 20th sts.). ☎ 215/893-9939 & 215/545-0755. www.loopyarn.com & www.spoolsewing.com. DISC, MC, V. Bus: 17, 40. Map p 74.*

Rosie's Yarn Cellar RITTENHOUSE This below-ground shop has fueled the knitting pastimes of hundreds of Philadelphians. *2017 Locust St. (btw. 20th & 21st sts.). ☎ 215/977-9276. www.rosiesyarncellar.com. AE, DISC, MC, V. Bus: 7, 12, 17, 40. Map p 74.*

★ **Sophie's Yarns** QUEEN VILLAGE On the short stretch of "Fabric Row," this sunny shop sells natural yarns, tons of books, and tools for beginning to advanced knitters. *739 S. 4th St. (btw. Monroe & Fitzwater sts.). ☎ 215/925-5648. www.sophiesyarns.com. AE, DISC, MC, V. Bus: 40, 57. Map p 74.*

Department Store/Shopping Centers

★ **Macy's** MIDTOWN This standby stands out for its antique, 30,000-pipe organ and holiday light show, carryovers from its days as one of the country's first department stores. *Btw. 13th & Juniper sts., Chestnut & Market sts. ☎ 215/241-9000. www.macys.com. AE, DISC, MC, V. Bus: C, 17, 27, 32, 33, 44, 48, 62, 121, 124, 125. Subway: City Hall or 13th St. Map p 74.*

Shops at the Bellevue RITTENHOUSE On the ground floor of the Park Hyatt is a kick-off to the upscale retail chains along Walnut Street: Ralph Lauren, Nicole Miller, Origins, and Williams-Sonoma. *200 S. Broad St. (at Walnut St.). ☎ 215/875-8350. www.bellevuephiladelphia.com. Bus: C, 9, 12, 21, 27, 32, 42. Subway: Walnut-Locust. Map p 74.*

★ **Shops at Liberty Place** RITTENHOUSE This mini mall, on the first levels of one of the city's tallest buildings, has J. Crew, Express, Nine West, Aveda, Jos. A. Bank, and about a dozen more stores. *Btw. 16th & 17th sts., Chestnut & Market sts. ☎ 215/851-9055. www.shopsatliberty.com. Bus: 2, 9, 21, 42. Map p 74.*

Fashion

★ **Boyd's** RITTENHOUSE Selling bespoke suits, $25,000 watches, Dolce & Gabbana frocks, Manolo Blahniks—and sushi—this family-run business occupies a beautiful old building and has a staff of obsessively attentive salespeople and 65 tailors. *1818 Chestnut St. (btw. 18th & 19th sts.). ☎ 215/564-9000. www.boydsphila.com. AE, DISC, MC, V. Bus: 9, 12, 17, 21. Map p 74.*

★★★ **Joan Shepp** RITTENHOUSE The mother-daughter doyennes of the local fashion scene run this industrial-chic boutique, where big-deal designers (such as Yohji Yamamoto, Dries Van Noten, Marni, and Yves Saint Laurent) come to roost. *1616 Walnut St. (btw. 16th & 17th sts.). ☎ 215/735-2666. www.joanshepp.com. AE, DISC, MC, V. Bus: 2, 9, 12, 21, 42. Map p 74.*

★ **Knit Wit** RITTENHOUSE The go-to boutique for generations of neighborhood fashionistas offers essentials from Miu Miu, Habitual, and Bluemarine, plus estate jewelry. *1718 Walnut St. (btw. 17th & 18th sts.). ☎ 215/564-4760. www.knitwitonline.com. AE, DISC, MC, V. Bus: 2, 9, 12, 21, 42.*

★★ **Lost & Found** OLD CITY A mother-daughter team runs this new-plus-vintage shop, known for its reasonable prices on cute, youthful clothing for men and women, Orla Kiely bags, and fun jewelry. *133 N. 3rd St. (btw. Arch & Race sts.). ☎ 215/928-1311. AE, DISC, MC, V. Bus: 5, 17, 48, 57. Map p 74.*

★ **Petulia's Folly** RITTENHOUSE Phillip Lim, Jovovich-Hawk, and

This Macy's location was one of the first department stores in the country.

Foster's Homeware is outstanding for loft-style furniture.

Rachel Comey are the bread-and-butter of this luxe women's boutique, which also stocks some beautiful gifts for the home. *1710 Sansom St. (btw. 17th & 18th sts.). ☎ 215/569-1344. www.petuliasfolly.com. AE, DISC, MC, V. Bus: 2, 9, 12, 21, 42. Map p 74.*

★ **Smak Parlour** OLD CITY Adorable designers Abby Kessler and Katie Lofuts create each trendy skirt, flirty dress, and cool top in this girly shop, which also sells a smattering of shoes, jewelry, and gifts. *219 Market St. (btw. 2nd & 3rd sts.). ☎ 215/625-4551. www.smakparlour.com. AE, DISC, MC, V. Bus: 5, 17, 33, 48. Subway: 2nd St. Map p 74.*

★★ **Sugarcube** OLD CITY Up-and-coming labels are the not-inexpensive specialty of this mostly women's and men's shop, a must for the fashion set. *124 N. 3rd St. (btw. Arch and Race sts.). ☎ 215/238-0825. www.sugarcube.us. AE, MC, V. Bus: 5, 17, 48, 57. Map p 74.*

★★ **Third Street Habit** OLD CITY Philly's version of Barney's women's department, with great little designers like Dagmar, Hudson, Isabel Marant, and Rag & Bone. *153 N. 3rd St. ☎ 215/925-5455. www.thirdstreethabit.com. AE, MC, V. Bus: 5, 17, 48, 57. Map p 74.*

★★★ **Vagabond** OLD CITY This pioneering women's shop offers Twinkle by Wenlan, Built by Wendy, and knits and dresses by the shop's stylish owners. *37 N. 3rd St. (btw. Market & Arch sts.). ☎ 267/671-0737. www.vagabondboutique.com. AE, DISC, MC, V. Bus: 5, 17, 33, 48, 57. Subway: Market-Frankford Line. Map p 74.*

Gifts

★★ **Foster's Homeware** OLD CITY The ultimate stop for outfitting any city loft sells kitchen goods, Bludot furniture, and Chilewich placemats, plus cards, books . . . and cooking lessons. *33 N. 3rd St. (btw. Market & Arch sts.). ☎ 215/925-0950. www.shopfosters.com. AE, DISC, MC, V. Bus: 5, 17, 33, 48, 57. Subway: 2nd St. Map p 74.*

★ **Hello Home/Hello World** ANTIQUE ROW/RITTENHOUSE Restored vintage furnishings, great new shelter pieces, pretty jewelry, and kids' clothes combine in these two neighborhood shops. ***Hello Home*** *1004 Pine St. (btw. 10th & 11th sts.). ☎ 215/545-7060.Bus: 23, Alternate 40.* ***Hello World*** *257 S. 20th St. (btw. Locust & Spruce sts.). ☎ 215/ 545-5207. www.shophelloworld.com. AE, DISC, MC, V. Bus: 12,17.*

★★ Matthew Izzo OLD CITY Modern furniture. Modern clothing. Modern art. Modern jewelry. Matthew Izzo's eponymous boutique is a must-stop for style in this century. Great sales, too. *151 N. 3rd St. (btw. Arch & Race sts.) ☎ 215/829-0606. www.matthewizzo.com. AE, DISC, MC, V. Bus: 5, 17, 48, 57. Map p 74.*

★★ Open House MIDTOWN Bright vases, clever pillows, pretty coffee cups, great kiddie goodies, and wonderful bath products make this one of the best spots for gift shopping—for yourself. *107 S. 13th St. (btw. Sansom & Chestnut sts.). ☎ 215/922-1415. www.openhouseliving.com. Bus: 9, 21, 42. Subway: Walnut St. or 2nd St. AE, MC, V. Map p 74.*

★★ Scarlett Alley OLD CITY For fantastic, unexpected, stylish souvenirs like Italian cordial glasses, hand-painted bowls, and great table linens. *241 Race St. (btw. 2nd & 3rd sts.). ☎ 215/592-7898. www.scarlettalley.com. AE, MC, V. Bus: 5, 17, 48, 57. Map p 74.*

★★ Town Home RITTENHOUSE Pretty, extra-petite shop known for its amazing jewelry by the likes of ME&Ro, Kasey K., and Heather Moore, plus inimitable Alora diffusers and chic baby onesies.*1616 Walnut St. ☎ 215/972-5100. www.townhomephila.com. AE, MC, V. Bus: 2, 9, 12, 21, 42. Map p 74.*

Gourmet Food

★★ DiBruno Brothers RITTENHOUSE Locals think this two-floor shop with its cheese cave and cafeteria is better than Dean & DeLuca. They're right. *1730 Chestnut St. (btw. 17th & 18th sts.). ☎ 215/665-9220. www.dibruno.com. AE, DISC, MC, V. Bus: 2, 9, 21, 42. Map p 74.*

★★★ Reading Terminal Market MIDTOWN This charming, 80-stall indoor market has oysters, organic produce, ice cream, cookbooks, chocolates, sushi, tacos, gourmet cheeses, Pennsylvania Dutch pretzels, roast pork sandwiches . . . *12th St. (btw. Arch & Filbert sts.). ☎ 215/922-2317. www.readingterminalmarket.org. Some kiosks accept some credit cards. Bus: 23, 48, 61. Subway: 13th St. Map p 74.*

Jewelry

★★★ Halloween ANTIQUE ROW With only an orange business card in the window as signage, this boutique feels like a treasure trove with pearls upon pearls, opals upon opals, silver upon silver—including vintage and custom pieces. *1329 Pine St. (at Juniper St.). ☎ 215/732-7711. No credit cards. Bus: C, 27, 32, Alternate 40. Subway: Lombard South. Map p 74.*

Jeweler's Row WASHINGTON SQUARE A couple blocks' worth of wholesale and retail merchants whose vibe ranges from pawn shop to antiques shop, Jeweler's Row is tailored to sellers of gold and buyers of engagement rings. *Btw. 7th & 8th sts., Walnut & Chestnut sts. Bus: 9, 21, 42, 47. Subway: 8th St.*

★ Lagos RITTENHOUSE Locally-designed jewelry, known for its fashion-forward settings and colored gems. Oprah is a fan. *1735 Walnut St. (btw. 17th & 18th sts.). ☎ 215/567-0770.*

Halloween features vintage and custom jewelry pieces.

www.lagos.com. AE, MC, V. Bus: 2, 9, 12, 21, 42.

Shoes

★ Benjamin Lovell Shoes SOUTH STREET/RITTENHOUSE Locally-based chain best known for its comfort footwear from Merrell, Ugg, Ecco, Dansko, and Naot, plus fresh kicks from Camper and Cole Haan. *South St. 318 South St. (btw. 3rd & 4th sts.). ☎ 215/238-1969. Bus: 40, 57. Rittenhouse 119 S. 18th St. (btw. Sansom & Chestnut sts.). ☎ 215/564-4655.Bus: 9, 12, 21, 42. www.benjaminlovellshoes.com. AE, DISC, MC, V. Map p 74.*

★★ Bus Stop Boutique QUEEN VILLAGE Super-friendly British shopkeep Elena Brennan maintains a stylishly offbeat selection of women's and men's shoes, bags, and jewelry from cutting-edge European and local designers. *750 S. 4th St. (btw. Fitzwater & Catharine sts.). ☎ 215/627-2357. www.busstopboutique.com. AE, DISC, MC, V. Bus: 40, 57. Map p 74.*

★ J. Karma Boutique OLD CITY There are many bags and much silver jewelry at this shop, but well-priced, on-trend shoes for women are definitely the draw. *62 N. 3rd St. (btw. Market & Arch sts.) ☎ 215/627-9625. www.jkarmaboutique.com. AE, MC, V. Bus: 5, 17, 33, 48, 57. Subway: 2nd St.*

Sporting Goods

★★★ Mitchell & Ness Sporting Goods MIDTOWN Find authentic, licensed replicas of the jerseys, caps, and jackets of some of America's best-known athletes. *1318 Chestnut St. (btw. 13th & Broad sts.). ☎ 215/592-6512. www.mitchellandness.com. AE, DISC, MC, V. Bus: C, 9, 21, 23, 27, 32, 38, 42. Subway: Walnut-Locust or 13th St. Map p 74.*

★ The Original I. Goldberg MIDTOWN This classic army-navy sells everything you need to spend the night outdoors, at very fair prices. *1300 Chestnut St. (at 13th St.). ☎ 215/925-9393. AE, DISC, MC, V. Bus: C, 9, 21, 23, 27, 32, 38, 42. Subway: Walnut-Locust or 13th St. Map p 74.*

★ Philadelphia Runner RITTENHOUSE More than 250 styles of running and walking shoes are for sale at the retail home of the Philadelphia Running Club. *1601 Sansom St. (at 16th St.). ☎ 215/972-8333. www.philadelphiarunner.com. AE, DISC, MC, V. Bus: 2, 9, 12, 21, 42. Map p 74.*

★★ Rittenhouse Sports Specialties RITTENHOUSE Forgot your sneaks? Come here, and foot expert Karen McGovern won't just find you a replacement; she'll find you an improvement. *1729 Chestnut St. (btw. 17th & 18th sts.). ☎ 215/569-9957. AE, DISC, MC, V. Bus: 2, 9, 21, 42. Map p 74.*

The fashion choices at Bus Stop Boutique are stylishly offbeat.

5 The Best of the **Outdoors**

Fairmount Park by Bike

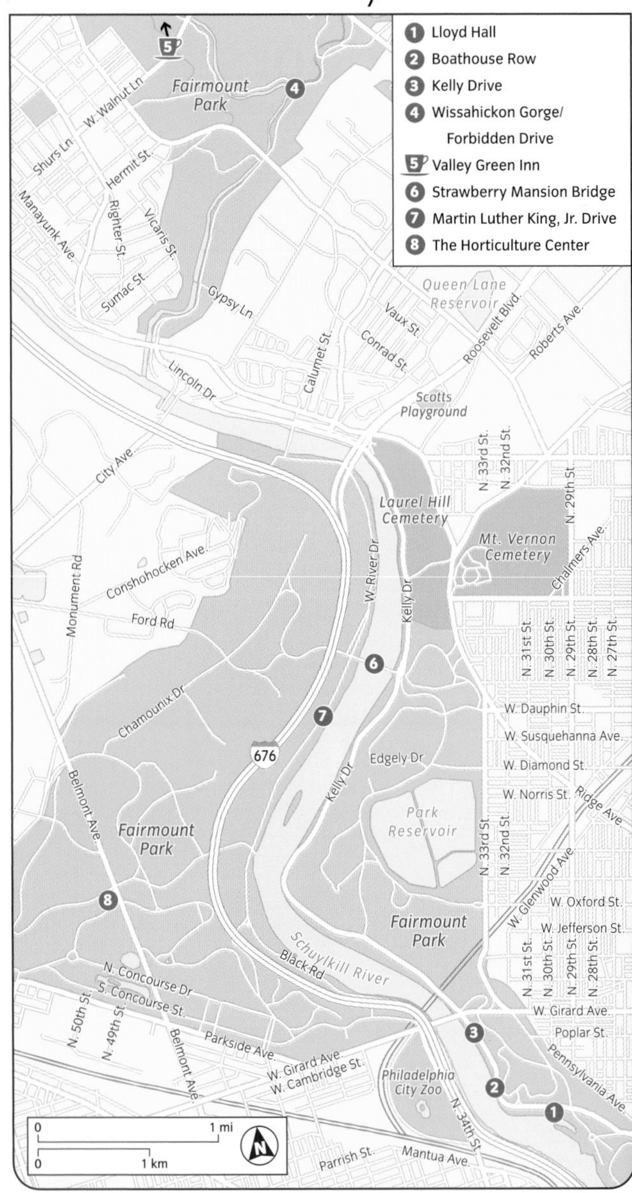

Previous page: A cyclist enjoys Philadelphia's abundant green space.

More than 215 miles of trails exist within the 9,200-plus acres that make Fairmount Park the world's largest landscaped city park (for comparison: NYC's Central Park is a mere 843 acres). This 18- to 22-mile route explores areas easiest accessed from Center City, via trails that are paved or gravel-covered, beginner-friendly, and bucolic. START: **Lloyd Hall, 1 Boathouse Row, behind the Philadelphia Museum of Art.**

1 **Lloyd Hall.** This community boathouse has a bike rental shack operated by Breakaway Bikes, open weekends only. Weekdays, rent from Breakaway's headquarters (1923 Chestnut St., ☎ 215/568-6002, www.breakawaybikes.com. Mon–Sat 10am–7pm, Sun noon–5pm). Helmets included with rental. 🕘 *½ hr. 1 Boathouse Row. ☎ 215/685-3936. www.fairmountpark.org. 7am–9pm (bike rentals 10am–7pm). Rentals $10/hr; $30/day.*

2 ★★ **Boathouse Row.** You'll quickly whiz by these ten Victorian-era crew-team clubhouses, so take some time to peep inside; to note #13, Undine Barge Club, designed by Frank Furness (1839–1912); and to avoid running into an unsuspecting college or high school athlete. 🕘 *10 min.*

3 ★★ **Kelly Drive.** For about 4 miles, you'll ride between the Schuylkill (pronounced "Schoo-kill") River and this winding artery, named after champion Olympian oarsman Jack Kelly (father of Grace [1929–1982]), and peppered with classic to modern sculpture. The Drive ends in a sharp left at Ridge Avenue. Cross Ridge at the light and pick up the trail. 🕘 *1 hr.*

4 ★★ **Wissahickon Gorge/ Forbidden Drive.** As you descend 5 miles along this wooded trail, rocks rising on one side, creek on the other, you're entering the jewel of the park, 1,800 acres of urban nature. Stop to spot owls, titmice, woodpeckers (five species nest here), bluebirds, cardinals, nuthatches, goldfinches—and plenty of mallards. Note the old stone bridges and monuments to Philadelphia's first locals, the Leni Lenape. There's no wading in the creek, and a permit is required to explore dirt trails

The 1,800-acre Wissahickon Gorge is one of the city's jewels.

The Valley Green Inn is a perfect place to stop and refuel.

by bike. Note: Cellphone service here is spotty. *2 hrs. Fairmount Park: 215/683-0200; www.fairmountpark.org. The Friends of the Wissahickon (a good resource for park news and information): 215/247-0417; www.fow.org.*

5 ★ **Valley Green Inn.** This charming, circa-1850 former roadhouse tavern (the last one left in the park) serves sit-down meals—chicken salad sandwiches, salmon clubs, and spinach salads—and has a walk-up stand for drinks and snacks. ***Valley Green Rd. at Wissahickon. 215/247-1730. $$.***

6 ★ **Strawberry Mansion Bridge.** Turn around to come back the way you came—except once back on Kelly Drive, cross the river at this circa-1896-to-1897 former trolley bridge of four intricate, wrought-iron arches atop stone masonry piers, to head to Martin Luther King, Jr. Dr. (From Valley Green, about 7 miles.) *1 hr.*

7 **Martin Luther King, Jr. Drive** Weekend days in April through October, this tree-lined thoroughfare (which you'll also hear referred to as its former name, "West River Drive") is closed to vehicular traffic. Spread out, enjoy the smooth ride. If you're worn out, continue back about 4 miles, passing the Philadelphia Zoo on your right *(see p 45, bullet 8)*, crossing in front of the Philadelphia Museum of

The beautiful century-old Strawberry Mansion Bridge.

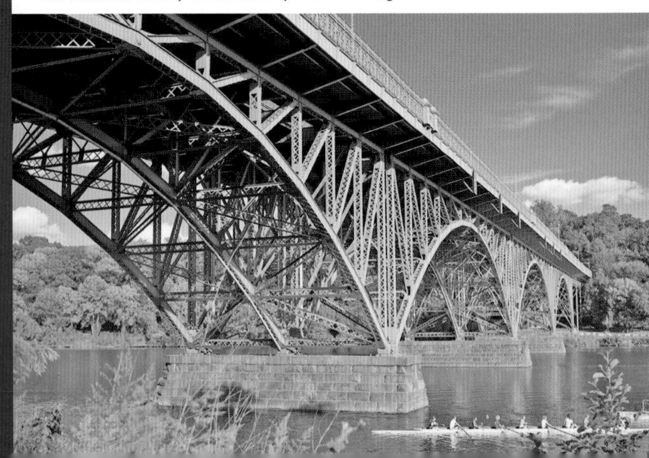

Art *(see p 33, bullet* ⑩*)* and behind the Water Works *(see p 68, bullet* ⑤*)*, and back to Lloyd Hall. If you're up for more scenery, take a right at the trail next to Montgomery Drive (just past the Columbia Railroad Bridge) for an uphill 2 miles and turn left at Belmont Ave. to the entrance of . . . ◷ *½ hr.*

⑧ ★★★ **The Horticulture Center.** In order to enjoy this park-within-a-park, you really must dismount. By foot, you can explore all 27 acres of elegant statuary, ponds, pools, tropical plants, fountains, gazebos, and butterflies. A must-visit while you're here: **Shofuso,** a Japanese garden and teahouse (☎ 215/878-5097; www.shofuso.com; May–Sept Wed–Fri 10am–4pm, Sat–Sun 11am–5pm; admission $6 adults, $3 seniors and students). Renowned architect Yoshimura Junzo (1908–1997) designed the Japanese House in 1953 in Nagoya. Five years later, it landed here, surrounded by lush moss, weeping cherry trees, and koi ponds. Inside are contemporary murals by Hiroshi Senju (1958–) and, occasionally, formal tea ceremonies. ◷ *2 hrs. Belmont Ave. & Montgomery Dr. www.fairmountpark.org/hortcenter.asp. Free admission. Daily Nov–Mar 8am–5pm, Apr–Oct 8am–6pm.*

The Shofusu Japanese garden is full of elegant ponds and fountains.

When you're through here, retrace your tracks back to MLK, Jr. Drive, where you'll take a right toward Center City and head back to Lloyd Hall, about 3½ miles.

Fairmount Park by Other Means

By sneaker or skate: If the sun's out, so are the runners, walkers, and bladers along Kelly and MLK Jr. Drives. From the Philadelphia Museum of Art, over Strawberry Mansion Bridge (at Ford Rd.) and back is 6.5 miles (10.4 km); go as far as the Falls Bridge (at Calumet St.), and you'll cover 8.5 miles (13.7km). Beware bikers—and resident Canadian geese.

By kayak: Get a half-hour kayaking lesson from the outfitters at **Schuylkill Banks** and a one-hour trip to the Schuylkill Falls—or, for more advanced paddlers, a day trip to Bartram's Garden. *25th and Walnut sts. (entrance at 25th and Locust sts.).* ☎ *215/222-6030, ext 103. www.schuylkillbanks.org. Tours $40–$75. Various hours, Sat–Sun, Jun–Oct.*

Park It: Five Squares

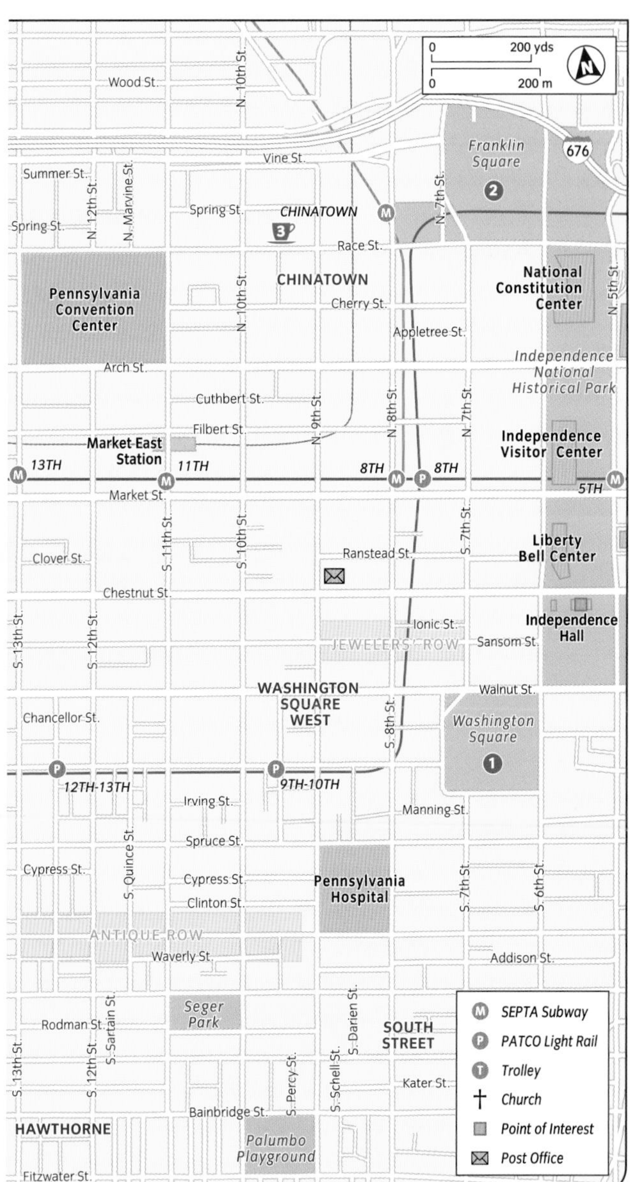
0 200 yds
0 200 m
N
Franklin Square
2
676
Wood St.
N. 10th St.
Vine St.
Summer St.
N. 12th St.
N. Marvine St.
Spring St.
CHINATOWN
Race St.
N. 7th St.
Pennsylvania Convention Center
CHINATOWN
Cherry St.
National Constitution Center
N. 5th St.
Appletree St.
Arch St.
Independence National Historical Park
Cuthbert St.
N. 9th St.
N. 8th St.
Filbert St.
Independence Visitor Center
Market East Station
13TH
11TH
8TH
8TH
5TH
Market St.
S. 11th St.
S. 10th St.
S. 7th St.
Liberty Bell Center
Ranstead St.
Clover St.
Chestnut St.
S. 13th St.
S. 12th St.
Ionic St.
Independence Hall
JEWELERS' ROW
Sansom St.
WASHINGTON SQUARE WEST
Walnut St.
Chancellor St.
S. 8th St.
Washington Square
1
12TH-13TH
9TH-10TH
Irving St.
Manning St.
Spruce St.
Cypress St.
S. Quince St.
Cypress St.
Pennsylvania Hospital
S. 7th St.
S. 6th St.
Clinton St.
ANTIQUE ROW
Waverly St.
Addison St.
Seger Park
S. Darien St.
Rodman St.
S. Sartain St.
SOUTH STREET
S. 13th St.
S. 12th St.
S. Percy St.
S. Schell St.
Kater St.
Bainbridge St.
HAWTHORNE
Palumbo Playground
Fitzwater St.
SEPTA Subway
PATCO Light Rail
Trolley
Church
Point of Interest
Post Office

In 1682, William Penn planned five green squares for his "Green Countrie Towne." Because of his modest Quaker values, he named the spaces after their locations (Northwest Square, Centre Square), not proper names. Today, Penn's parks are named and, somewhat ironically, are also the city's proudest al fresco showpieces. You can easily see them all in one day. START: **6th & Locust sts.**

1 ★★ Washington Square. The most historically significant park on the list, the 6½-acre "Southeast Square" was once pasture with a pair of fish-able creeks. Starting in 1704, a portion of these grounds became a modest burial ground for the city's unknown and poor, a potter's field. In 1776, troops who died fighting in the burgeoning Revolutionary War were interred here, as were victims of yellow fever in 1793. At the park's center, an eternal flame and bronze statue of Washington serve as the Tomb of the Unknown Revolutionary Soldier. In later years, Washington Square became the centerpiece of the city's active publishing business, with the still-extant Farm Journal (in the southwest corner), and Curtis Publishing Company (occupying all of Walnut St. between 6th and 7th sts.), at onetime the home of *Ladies' Home Journal.* Stop in the Curtis Building (through the 7th St. entrance) and walk toward 6th Street to see Maxfield Parrish (1870–1966) and Louis Comfort Tiffany's (1848–1933) gorgeous, 100,000 mosaic *Dream Garden* mural, a hidden gem. Also available for your perusal (on weekdays) is the Athenaeum, an elegant collections library of rare books (219 S. 6th St.; ☎ 215/925-2688). ⏱ *1 hr. Btw. 6th & 7th, Spruce & Walnut sts.*

2 ★★★ kids Franklin Square. The most recently refreshed of the squares is the most kid-friendly, too. In 2006, after years of neglect , the city cleaned up the space and added 18 holes of Philadelphia-themed mini-golf, toddler-to-tween-friendly jungle gyms, a giant sand sculpture, a carousel, benches for "Once Upon A Nation" performers, and more recently, a really fantastic Square Shack for better-than-average burgers, shakes, and fries. Although you can walk through the square anytime, the best time to visit is in spring through fall, when the amusements are up and running. ⏱ *1 hr.* *(See p 38, bullet 3.)*

Franklin Square is one of the most kid-friendly spaces in the city.

3 ★★ St. Honoré Pastries. On your way between the squares, you'll hit Chinatown, where you'll find this bakery and its just-baked Hong Kong buns stamped with lucky red characters and stuffed with sweet sesame, red bean, or azuki fillings. Other specialties of this walk-up shop include mango shakes, tiny cakes, and pastry-wrapped hot dogs. *935 Race St.* ☎ *215/925-5298. $.*

4 Centre Square. This least green (more granite-hued) of squares was once on the outskirts of the city. Today, it's the gray home of ornate City Hall *(see p 20, bullet 8)*, offering only a few trees on its western side, a plot formally known as Dilworth Plaza (named after beloved 1950s mayor Richardson Dilworth [1916–1997]). 🕘 *15 min. Broad & Market sts.*

5 ★★ Logan Circle. The only square that became a circle, "Northwest" is the nearly bucolic jewel of Ben Franklin Parkway, a boulevard that 20th-century architect Paul Philippe Cret (1876–1945) modeled after the Champs-Elysées. Logan's centerpiece is Alexander Stirling Calder's (1870–1945) Swann Fountain *(see p 15, bullet 6)*, with its sky-high arcs of water and three giant bronze horses surrounded by turtles, nymphs, and angels. (No one would blame you for wading in; in fact, a splash in Swann has become a popular local tradition.) From here, you'll have lovely views of the central branch of the Free Library of Philadelphia *(see p 67, bullet 2)*, the Philadelphia Museum of Art *(see p 13, bullet 2)*, and City Hall *(see p 20, bullet 8)*. 🕘 *½ hr. 19th & Race sts.*

6 ★★ kids Rittenhouse Square. "Southwest Square" is the best known and highest (foot) trafficked in the group. This sublime urban landscape, with its tall sycamores, diagonal paths, reflecting pool, and scattered sculpture is also the work of Cret (see above). If you plan to sit on a bench and people-watch at anyplace on this list, do it here, paying special attention to the comings and goings around the Rittenhouse Hotel *(see p 141)*, which seems to be the preferred overnight spot for movie stars in town for filming. Rittenhouse is even pretty on winter evenings, when its trees glitter with giant ornament lights. 🕘 *1 hr. Btw. 18th & 19th sts., Walnut & Rittenhouse sts.*

7 ★ Le Bus Bakery. Grab a cold drink, a just-grilled panini (try the tuna or roast beef), a chocolate-chip cookie to go, and a bench in the Square, and you're all set. *129 S. 18th St. (btw. Walnut & Sansom sts.).* ☎ *215/569-8299. $.*

Rittenhouse Square is a prime spot to relax and indulge in some people-watching.

Penn's Landing

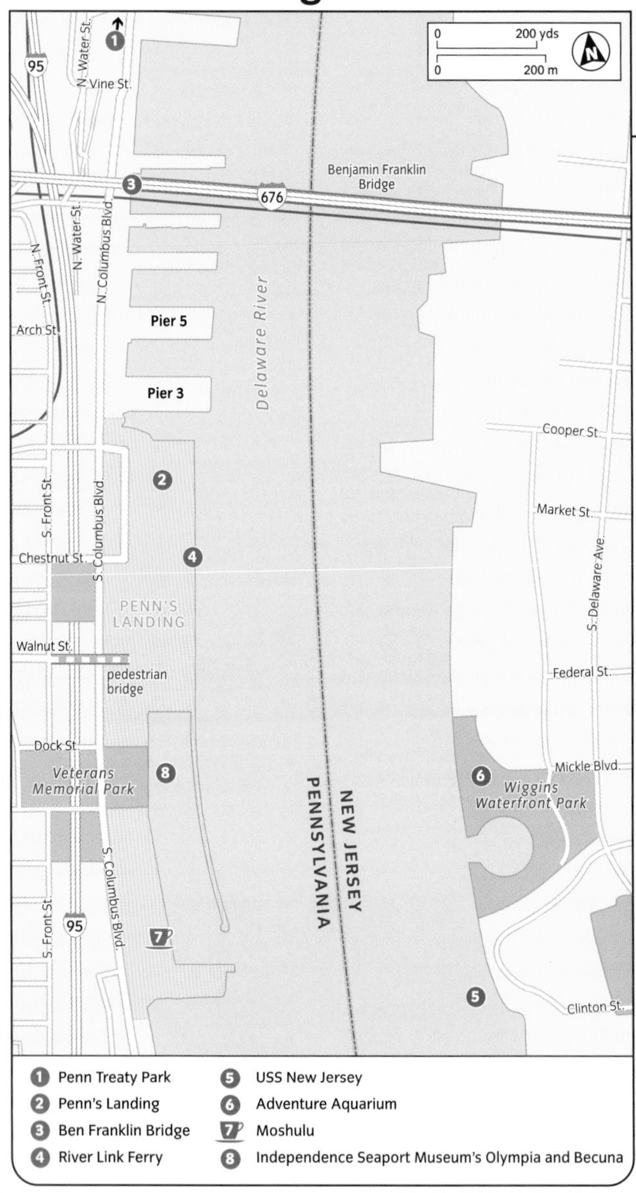

Spanned by Ben Franklin Bridge, bordered by tree- and ship-lined shores, Center City's wide section of Delaware River has been the subject of much recent controversy—to dredge or not to dredge? to gamble or not to gamble? For now, however, it's a nice enough place to explore, to hop a ferry to Camden, and to consider potential over reality. START: **Penn Treaty Park.**

1 Penn Treaty Park. Formerly Shackamaxon, a village of the Native American Leni Lenape tribe, this riverside park hosted the 1683 meeting of William Penn and chief Tamanend, who stood under an elm to sign a peace treaty that endured 99 years. Today, the tranquil, loosely landscaped plot is bordered by industry and features a small obelisk where the elm once stood. *½ hr. Columbus Blvd & Beach St. (off of Delaware Ave.).*

2 ★ Penn's Landing. Philadelphia started out as a major freshwater port, and as recently as 1945, 155 "finger" piers jutted out into the river. Today, 14 remain. Replacing some of them are the more visitor-centric circa-1976 Great Plaza, stretching from Spring Garden Street southward, and consisting of a multi-tiered, tree-lined amphitheater, space for summer festivals and concerts, and in winter, a fantastic outdoor ice skating "River Rink." South of Market Street, there's an esplanade with blue guardrails and charts that identify the New Jersey shoreline opposite. *½ hr. Columbus Blvd btw. Spring Garden & South sts., Visitor's Center at 301 S. Columbus Blvd. ☎ 215/928-8801. www.delawareriverwaterfrontcorp.com.*

3 ★ Ben Franklin Bridge. Great cities have great bridges, and this circa-1926 suspension model is Philadelphia's. Paul Cret, architect of the Ben Franklin Parkway and Rittenhouse Square, designed it. At night, each of its cables is lit and its span changes color. Pedestrians and cyclists can make the long climb across (it takes about an hour round-trip), but there's not much to do on the immediate other side (Camden, NJ), other than turn around and come back. *15 min. Entrance at 5th & Vine sts. Daily 6am–dusk.*

4 ★★ kids River Link Ferry. Next to the Seaport Museum, catch a ride across the Delaware to Camden, NJ's, riverfront. The scenic trip takes about 10 minutes and deposits you at a pair of attractions (below). *15 min. ☎ 215/925-5464. www.riverlinkferry.org. May–Oct Mon–Thurs 9:30am–5:50pm, Fri–Sun 9:30am–6:30pm. Round-trip $6 adults, $5 seniors & children 3–12, free for children under 3.*

5 ★ kids USS *New Jersey*. This giant, circa-1942 battleship, usually referred to as BB-62, is the most decorated of its *Iowa*-class of "fast battleships." A tour involves climbing ladders, peering into 16-inch

"River Rink," at the Great Plaza in Penn's Landing, is fantastic for outdoor ice skating during the winter.

gun turrets, cramming into living quarters, and learning a history that stretches from tours in World War II to the Persian Gulf. A guided tour costs a dollar or so more, but is a must for military, especially Navy, buffs. *2 hr. 100 Clinton St., Camden, NJ. ☎ 866/877-6262. www.battleshipnewjersey.org. Admission $19 adults; $14 seniors, veterans & children 6–11; free for children under 6, active military & BB-62 vets. Guided tour additional $1. Feb to mid-Mar Fri–Mon 10am–3pm; mid-Mar to Apr daily 9:30am–3pm; May–Aug daily 9:30am–5pm, Sept–Dec daily 9:30am–3pm. Closed Jan.*

6 ★ kids **Adventure Aquarium.** Two million gallons of water fill this expansive museum of the life aquatic, where hippos bob for heads of lettuce; penguins perform and seals cavort at outdoor arenas; stringrays skim through open tanks; jellyfish morph before your eyes; and, for the right price, you can feed sea turtles, train seals, or (for grown-ups only) swim with the sharks. Among the must-see animals: alligators in the wild West Africa River Experience, rarely exhibited bluefin tuna in the 760,000-gallon Ocean Realm tank, and small sharks swimming in a petting tank for kids. *2 hr. 1 Aquarium Dr., Camden, NJ. ☎ 866/451-2782. www.adventureaquarium.com. Admission $20 adults, $16 children 2–12. Daily 9:30am–5pm.*

Adventure Aquarium lets you get up close to a wide array of aquatic creatures.

7 **Moshulu.** You'll notice there are few places to grab much more than a hotdog along the waterfront, so head to the top deck of this four-masted ship for a burger and a piña colada. *401 S. Columbus Blvd. (btw. Pine & South sts.). ☎ 215/923-2500. $$.*

8 ★ kids **Independence Seaport Museum's Olympia and Becuna.** Just south of the Independence Seaport Museum's main building *(see p 57, bullet 10)*, this pair of historic ships offer a self-guided glimpse of the U.S. Navy of yore. The larger of the two is the *Olympia,* Admiral Dewey's circa-1892 steel flagship during the Spanish-American War, featuring a restored bridge and handsome, originally-furnished examples of an officers' saloon and wardroom, flag officer's cabin, and junior officers' mess. *Becuna* is the 1944-launched submarine that served from World War II into the Cold War, and will impart a newfound appreciation for tight quarters. *1 hr.* ●

6 The Best Dining

Dining Best Bets

Best for **Tapas**
★★★ Amada, *217-219 Chestnut St. (p 102)*

Best **BYOB**
★★ Bistro 7, *7 N. 3rd St. (p 103)*

Best **Steakhouse**
★★ Butcher & Singer, *1500 Walnut St. (p 103)*

Best for **Breakfast**
★ Sam's Morning Glory Diner, *735 S. 10th St. (p 110)*

Best for **Sunday Brunch**
★★★ Fountain Restaurant, *1 Logan Sq. (p 106)*

Best **Deli**
★ Famous Fourth Street Delicatessen, *700 S. 4th St. (p 105)*

Best for **Burgers**
★★★ Village Whiskey, *114 S. 20th St. (p 112)*

Best **Date Spot**
★★★ Fork, *306 Market St. (p 106)*

Best for **Vegetarians**
★★ Horizons Café, *611 S. 7th St. (p 106)*

Best for **Seafood**
★★ Sansom Street Oyster House, *1516 Sansom St. (p 111)*

Best for **Sushi**
★★ Zento, *138 Chestnut St. (p 112)*

Best for **Haute Japanese**
★★ Morimoto, *723 Chestnut St. (p 108)*

Best for **Chinese**
★ Lee How Fook, *219 N. 11th St. (p 107)*

Best for **Gourmet Italian**
★★★ Osteria, *640 N. Broad St. (p 109)*

Best for **Italian-American**
★ Villa di Roma, *936 S. 9th St. (p 112)*

Best for **Israeli Fare**
★★★ Zahav, *237 St. James Pl. (p 112)*

Best for **Pizza**
★ Marra's, *1734 E. Passyunk Ave. (p 108)*

Best **Cheesesteak**
★ Cosmi's Deli, *1501 S. 8th St. (p 105)*

Fork is a great place to take a date.

Previous page: The Famous Fourth Street Delicatessen makes some of the city's best sandwiches.

South Philly Dining

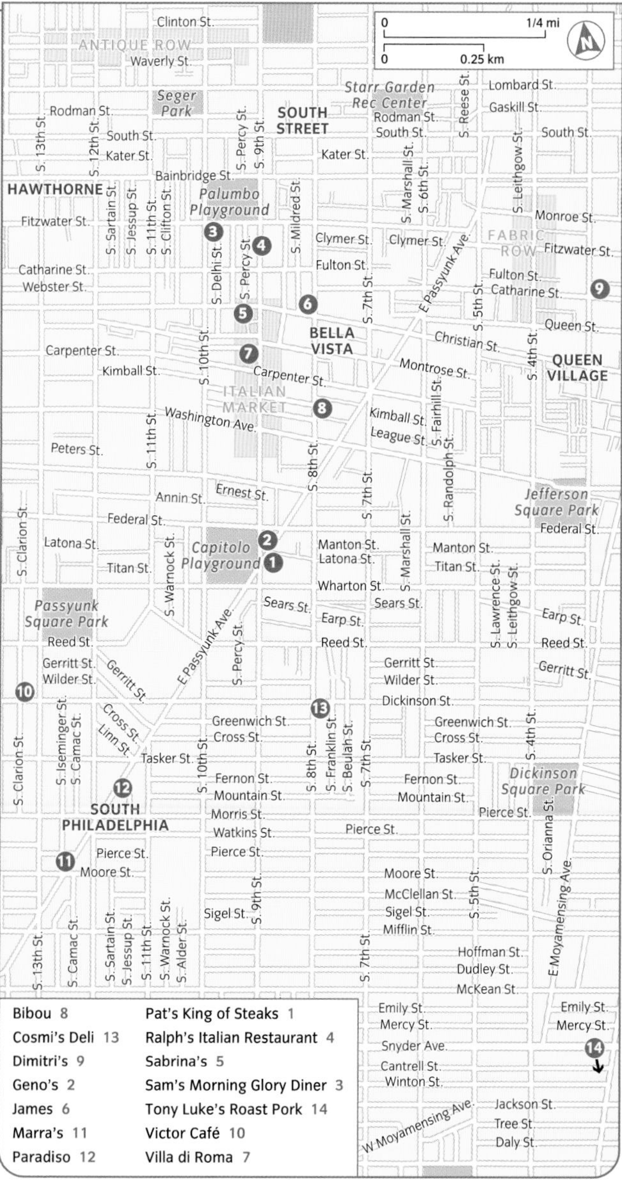

Center City Dining

Alma de Cuba 23
Amada 49
Audrey Claire 21
Barclay Prime 20
Beau Monde 54
Bindi 8
Bistro 7 45
Brauhaus Schmitz 52
Buddakan 48
Butcher & Singer 26
Caribou Café 30
Chifa 39
City Tavern 50
Continental 47
Continental Mid-Town 9
Devil's Alley 11
Distrito 15
El Vez 28
Famous Fourth Street Delicatessen 10, 56
Farmacia 46
Fork 44
Fountain Restaurant 2
Good Dog 27
Horizons Café 53
Jim's Steaks 55
Jones 40
Kanella 41
Kong 43
Lacroix 17
Le Bec-Fin 4
Lee How Fook 36
Lolita 7
Los Catrines & Tequila's 24
Melograno 16
Mercato 33
Meritage 22
Morimoto 37
Nineteen 29

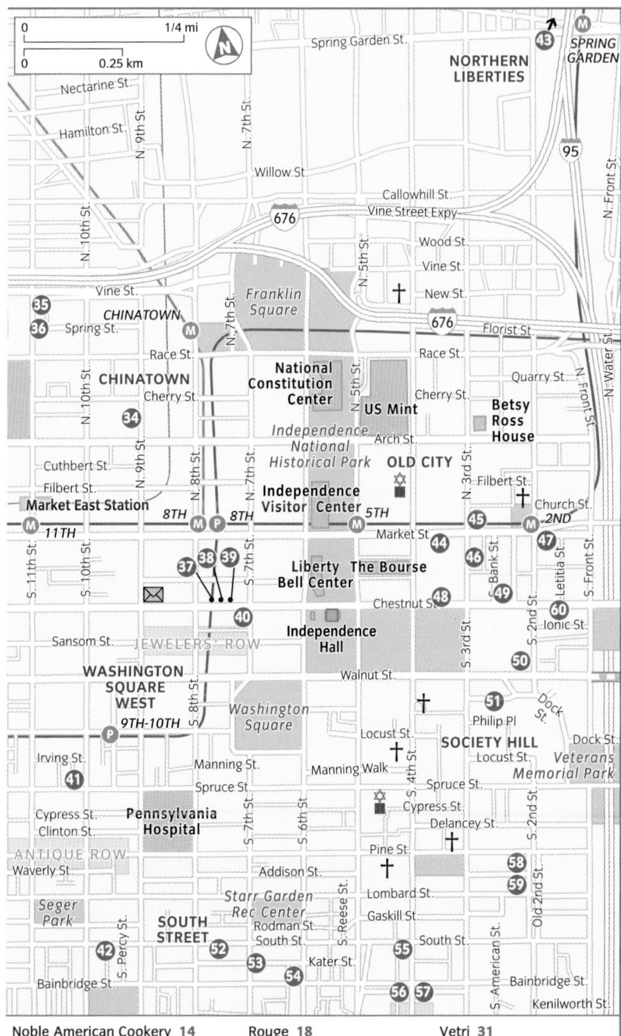
0 1/4 mi
0 0.25 km
N
Spring Garden St.
NORTHERN LIBERTIES
SPRING GARDEN
Nectarine St.
Hamilton St.
N. 9th St.
N. 7th St.
95
Willow St.
N. Front St.
Callowhill St.
Vine Street Expy
676
N. 10th St.
N. 5th St.
Wood St.
Vine St.
New St.
Vine St.
Franklin Square
CHINATOWN
Spring St.
Florist St.
Race St.
Race St.
N. Water St.
Quarry St.
National Constitution Center
CHINATOWN
Cherry St.
US Mint
Cherry St.
Betsy Ross House
N. Front St.
Independence National Historical Park
Arch St.
OLD CITY
N. 3rd St.
Cuthbert St.
Filbert St.
Filbert St.
N. 8th St.
Independence Visitor Center
Church St.
Market East Station
8TH
8TH
5TH
2ND
11TH
Market St.
S. 11th St.
S. 10th St.
S. 7th St.
Liberty Bell Center
The Bourse
S. Bank St.
Letitia St.
S. Front St.
Chestnut St.
S. 2nd St.
Ionic St.
Independence Hall
Sansom St.
JEWELERS' ROW
S. 3rd St.
WASHINGTON SQUARE WEST
Walnut St.
S. 8th St.
Washington Square
Dock St.
Philip Pl
9TH-10TH
Locust St.
SOCIETY HILL
Dock St.
Locust St.
Veterans Memorial Park
Irving St.
Manning St.
Manning Walk
S. 4th St.
Spruce St.
Spruce St.
Cypress St.
Pennsylvania Hospital
S. 7th St.
S. 6th St.
Cypress St.
Clinton St.
Delancey St.
S. 2nd St.
ANTIQUE ROW
Pine St.
Waverly St.
Addison St.
Seger Park
Starr Garden Rec Center
Lombard St.
Gaskill St.
S. Reese St.
Old 2nd St.
SOUTH STREET
Rodman St.
South St.
South St.
S. Percy St.
S. American St.
Kater St.
Bainbridge St.
Bainbridge St.
Kenilworth St.
43 35 36 34 37 38 39 40 41 42 44 45 46 47 48 49 50 51 52 53 54 55 56 57 58 59 60

Dining A to Z

★ **Alma de Cuba** RITTENHOUSE *MODERN CUBAN* Nuevo Latino cuisine—lobster ceviche, Kobe beef tacos, sugarcane tuna—plus Rockwell-designed decor makes for a glamorous night-on-the-town. *1623 Walnut St. ☎ 215/988-1799. www.almadecubarestaurant.com. Entrees $20–$34. AE, DC, DISC, MC, V. Dinner daily. Bus: 5, 21, 42, 48, 57. Map p 100.*

★★★ **Amada** OLD CITY *CONTEMPORARY TAPAS* Chic and rustic; don't miss the Spanish cheeses and meats, plantain empanadas, sangria, and flamenco dancing. *217–219 Chestnut St. ☎ 215/625-2450. www.amadarestaurant.com. Plates $5–$32. AE, DC, DISC, MC, V. Lunch & dinner Mon–Sat; dinner Sun. Bus: 21, 38, 42. Map p 100.*

★ **Audrey Claire** RITTENHOUSE *MEDITERRANEAN BYOB* Grilled Romaine salad, Gorgonzola-and-pear-topped flatbread, and pomegranate roast chicken are on the menu of this stylish little village bistro. *276 S. 20th St. (at Spruce St.). ☎ 215/731-1222. www.audreyclaire.com. Entrees $16–$24. No credit cards. Dinner daily. Bus: 17. Map p 100.*

★★ **Barclay Prime** RITTENHOUSE *STEAKS* Red meat with a boutique vibe, this low-lit emporium offers Gauchot & Gauchot beef, Kobe sliders, and a splurge-worthy $100 "cheesesteak." *237 S. 18th St. (btw. Locust & Spruce sts.). ☎ 215/732-7560. www.barclayprime.com. Entrees $29–$56. AE, DC, MC, V. Dinner daily. Bus: 2, 12. Map p 100.*

★ **Beau Monde** SOUTH STREET *FRENCH* Known for its crepes, this pretty, bustling Bretagne-inspired brasserie also serves up lovely salads and romantic ambiance. *624 S. 6th St. (at Bainbridge St.). ☎ 215/592-0656. www.creperie-beaumonde.com. Entrees $6.50–$19. AE, DC, DISC, MC, V. Lunch & dinner Tues–Sun. Bus: 40, 47. Map p 100.*

★★ **Bibou** BELLA VISTA *FRENCH BYOB* Chanterelles, foie gras, escargots, and very little elbow room: a gem of a bring-your-own-Bordeaux bistro, just off the Italian Market. *1009 S. 8th St. (before Washington Ave.). ☎ 215/965-8290. www.biboubyob.com. Entrees $21–$26. No credit cards. Dinner Wed–Sun. Bus: 47. Map p 99.*

Rustic Amada has excellent Spanish cuisine.

Butcher & Singer is located in a former bank.

★★★ **Bindi** MIDTOWN *MODERN INDIAN BYOB* Clever twists on Indian flavors make this cozy, contemporary spot a true foodie find. (Bring rum for the mango-cardamom mixer.) *105 S. 13th St. (btw. Chestnut & Sansom sts.). ☎ 215/922-6061. www.bindibyob.com. Entrees $18–$24. No credit cards. Dinner Tues–Sun. Bus: 4, 21, 23, 38, 42. Subway: Walnut-Locust or 13th St. Map p 100.*

★★ **Bistro 7** OLD CITY *MODERN FRENCH BYOB* A local favorite for Provençal seafood stew, homemade gnocchi, roast chicken, and crème brûlée. *7 N. 3rd St. (btw. Market & Arch sts.). ☎ 215/931-1560. www.bistro7restaurant.com. Entrees $22–$31. AE, DC, MC, V. Dinner Tues–Sun. Bus: 17, 33, 48, 57. Subway: 2nd St. Map p 100.*

★ **Brauhaus Schmitz** SOUTH STREET *GERMAN* Schnitzel, wieners, brats, *spätzle,* strudel, and 100 kinds of hearty Belgian and German brews make this convivial beer garden the best wurst place in town. *718 South St. (btw. 7th & 8th sts.). ☎ 267/909-8814. www.brauhausschmitz.com. $15–$28. Lunch & dinner daily. AE, DC, DISC, MC, V. Bus 40, 47. Map p 100.*

★ **Buddakan** OLD CITY *ASIAN FUSION* A trendy spot for lobster mashed potatoes, *edamame* ravioli, wok-seared lobster, and chocolate pagodas meant for sharing at a communal table beneath a giant gold Buddha. *325 Chestnut St. ☎ 215/574-9440. www.buddakan.com. Entrees $18–$32. AE, DC, MC, V. Lunch & dinner Mon–Fri; Dinner Sat–Sun. Bus: 5, 17, 21, 42, 57. Subway: 2nd St. Map p 100.*

★★ **Butcher & Singer** RITTENHOUSE *STEAKS* Beneath the soaring ceiling of an old bank are enormous versions of haute meat-and-potatoes for enormous expense accounts. *1500 Walnut St. ☎ 215/732-4444. www.butcherandsinger.com. Entrees $26–$65. AE, DC, MC, V. Lunch & dinner Mon–Fri; Dinner Sat–Sun. Bus: 9, 12, 21, 42. Subway: Walnut-Locust. Map p 100.*

Bistro 7 is a local French favorite.

Chinatown

The country's fourth largest Chinatown (just north of the Convention Center) represents many more populations and cultures than just Chinese; a few bustling blocks boast residents and businesses from Vietnam, Burma, Thailand, Korea, Japan, Malaysia, and beyond. To notice here: Four suspended 1,500lb bronze dragons at 9th and Arch streets, the Friendship Arch at 10th and Arch streets, and (of course) a vibrant, morning-to-late-night dining scene. Among more than 100 restaurants are daytime dim sum palaces **Ocean Harbor** (1023 Race St.; ☎ **215/574-1398**) and **Dim Sum Garden** (59 N. 11th St.; ☎ **215/627-0218**), and for non-carnivores, **Singapore Chinese Vegetarian Restaurant** (1029 Race St.; ☎ **215/922-3288**). For quick, inexpensive snacks in the form of bubble tea, red bean buns, and mango shakes, seek out **St. Honore** (935 Race St.; ☎ **215/925-5298**) and **KC's Pastries** (109 N. 10th St.; ☎ **215/238-8808**).This is definitely an area to explore by foot, as car traffic is almost always clogged in this centrally located neighborhood. ◷ *1 hr. Btw. 9th & 11th sts, Arch & Vine sts.*

★ **Caribou Café** MIDTOWN *FRENCH* This friendly, well-located brasserie is known for its steak frites, cassoulet, goat cheese salad, and wine list. *1126 Walnut St.* ☎ *215/625-9535. www.cariboucafe.com. Entrees $16–$25. AE, MC, V. Lunch & dinner daily. Bus: 9, 21, 23, 42. Map p. 100.*

★★★ **Chifa** WASHINGTON SQUARE *PERUVIAN-CANTONESE* Artful tapas-style versions of ceviche, dim sum, empanadas, and hot pots meld diverse cuisines in a sexy, modern setting. *707 Chestnut St.* ☎ *215/ 925-5555. www.chifarestaurant.com. Plates $8–$23. AE, DC, DISC, MC, V. Lunch & dinner Mon–Sat; dinner Sun. Bus: 9, 21, 38, 42, 47. Subway: 8th St. Map p 100.*

Continental has an exceptionally diverse menu.

City Tavern OLD CITY *AMERICAN* The replica of the pub where Washington and Adams knocked back mead and pepper-pot soup features Colonial-garbed servers, Martha Washington's turkey potpie, and Jefferson's home brew. *138 S. 2nd St. (at Walnut St.).* ☎ *215/413-1443. www.citytavern.com. Entrees $18–$33. AE, DISC, MC, V. Lunch & dinner daily. Map p 100.*

★ **Continental** OLD CITY *MODERN INTERNATIONAL* Something for everyone—from grilled cheese to Thai curry lobster to sugary martinis. (Elder sibling to below.) *138 Market St. (at 2nd St.).* ☎ *215/923-6069.*

The burgers at Good Dog are legendary.

www.continentalmartinibar.com. Entrees $14–$24. AE, DC, MC, V. Lunch & dinner daily. Bus: 5, 17, 33, 48. Subway: 2nd St. Map p 100.

★ kids **Continental Mid-Town** RITTENHOUSE *MODERN INTERNATIONAL* Seats that swing and cocktails that buzz are the hallmarks of this three-floor lounge. Order a big salad and Szechuan shoestring fries. *1801 Chestnut St. (at 18th St.). ☎ 215/567-1800. www.continental midtown.com. Entrees $7.50–$28. AE, DC, MC, V. Lunch & dinner daily. Bus: 9, 17, 21, 42. Map p 100.*

★ **Cosmi's Deli** SOUTH PHILLY *CHEESESTEAKS* Looks like a bodega, delivers like a champion: This neighbor to Pat's and Geno's has bested the big guys in taste tests time after time. *1501 S. 8th St. (at Dickinson St.). ☎ 215/468-6093. Steaks $6–$11. AE, DISC, MC, V. Lunch & dinner daily. Bus: 23, 47. Map p 99.*

★ kids **Devil's Alley** RITTENHOUSE *AMERICAN* A casual, popular spot for BBQ sliders, ribs, Cobb salad, creative burgers, and cold beers. *1907 Chestnut St. (btw. 19th & 20th sts.). ☎ 267/751-0707. www.devilsalley barandgrill.com. $7–$22. AE, DISC, DC, MC, V. Lunch & dinner Mon–Fri; brunch & dinner Sat–Sun. Bus: 9, 17, 21, 33, 42. Map p 100.*

★★ **Dimitri's** QUEEN VILLAGE *GREEK BYOB* Seated elbow-to-elbow, locals dig into grilled octopus, fresh bluefish, amazing hummus, and rice pudding: worth the first-come first-served wait. *795 S. 3rd St. (at Catharine St.). ☎ 215/625-0556. Entrees $10–$20. No credit cards. Dinner daily. Bus: 57. Map p 99.*

★★★ kids **Distrito** UNIVERSITY CITY *MODERN MEXICAN* Mexico City yum and fun: neon booths, private karaoke, wrestling masks, and fancied-up *tacqueria* fare. *3945 Chestnut St. (at 40th St.). ☎ 215/ 2222-1657. www.distritorestaurant. com. Entrees $24–$58. AE, DISC, MC, V. Lunch & dinner Mon–Fri; dinner Sat–Sun. Subway: 40th St. Map p 100.*

★ **El Vez** MIDTOWN *MODERN MEXICAN* Made-to-order guac and margaritas that rock keep this colorful spot busy night after night. Don't miss the arcade photo booth. *121 S. 13th St. (at Sansom St.). ☎ 215/928-9800. www.elvezrestaurant.com. Entrees $15–$26. AE, DISC, MC, V. Lunch & dinner daily. Bus: 4, 21, 23, 38, 42. Subway: Walnut-Locust or 13th St. Map p 100.*

★ kids **Famous Fourth Street Delicatessen** SOUTH STREET *JEWISH DELI* This place has pastrami sandwiches thicker than

James serves up modern, high-end Italian food.

Midtown's Mercato has an inviting atmosphere alongside great food.

phone books, matzo balls as big as grapefruit, marble cake that could double as a checkerboard. ***700 S. 4th St. (at Bainbridge St.). ☎ 215/ 922-3274. Entrees $6–$20. AE, MC, V. Breakfast, lunch & dinner daily. Bus: 40, 57. Map p 100.***

★ **Farmacia** OLD CITY *MODERN AMERICAN* This bakery-owned restaurant has super-fresh, sustainably grown fare. Great for brunch. ***15 S. 3rd St. (btw. Market & Chestnut sts.) ☎ 215/627-6274. www.farmicia restaurant.com. Entrees $13–$26. AE, MC, V. Lunch & dinner Mon–Fri; brunch & dinner Sat–Sun. Bus: 5, 17, 33, 48, 57. Subway: 2nd St. Map p 100.***

★★★ **Fork** OLD CITY *CONTINENTAL* Fresh ingredients—Cape May fluke, house-made sausage, spring rhubarb—shine at this softly lit neighborhood brasserie, a date-night favorite. ***306 Market St. ☎ 215/625-9425. www.forkrestaurant.com. Entrees $24–$32. AE, DC, DISC, MC, V. Lunch & dinner Mon–Fri; dinner Sat; brunch & dinner Sun. Bus: 17, 33, 48, 57. Subway: 2nd St. Map p 100.***

★★★ **Fountain Restaurant** LOGAN CIRCLE *INTERNATIONAL* The elegant Four Seasons hosts this tailored special-occasion affair, where service is king and the Sunday brunch is to die for. ***1 Logan Sq. (at 18th St.). ☎ 215/963-1500. www.fourseasons.com/philadelphia. Entrees $42–$60. AE, DC, MC, V. Breakfast, lunch & dinner daily. Bus: 32, 33, 48. Map p 100.***

Geno's SOUTH PHILLY *CHEESESTEAKS* Pat's across-the-street rival is bigger, brighter, and more controversial, thanks to its "This is America. Order in English" policy. Zoinks. ***1219 S. 9th St. (at E. Passyunk Ave.) ☎ 215/389-0659. www.genosteaks.com. Cheesesteaks $7–$9. No credit cards. Open 24 hr. Bus: 23, 47. Map p 99.***

★ **Good Dog** RITTENHOUSE *PUB FARE* Wooden booths, great microbrews, and a big-time jukebox are just background noise to a blue-cheese-stuffed burger that's the bomb. ***224 S. 15th St. (btw. Walnut & Locust sts.). ☎ 215/985-9600. www.gooddogbar.com. Entrees $9–$15. AE, DC, DISC, MC, V. Lunch & dinner daily. Bus: C, 12, 27, 32. Subway: Walnut-Locust. Map p 100.***

★★ **Horizons Café** SOUTH STREET *VEGETARIAN/VEGAN* Lookout, carnivores: One dip into the *edamame* hummus, one bite of mock chicken wing, and you might convert. ***611 S. 7th St. (btw. South and Bainbridge sts.). ☎ 215/923-6117. www.horizons philadelphia.com. AE, MC, V. Dinner Tues–Thurs. Bus: 40, 47, Map p 100.***

★★★ **James** BELLA VISTA *MODERN ITALIAN* Rabbit *agnolotti* in walnut sauce, langostinos and warm ricotta, duck *ragu* with shaved chocolate: Haute Italian in a chic jewel box. ***834 S. 8th St. (btw. Catharine & Christian sts.). ☎ 215/629-4980. www.jameson8th.com. Entrees $28–$34. AE, DC, MC, V. Dinner Mon–Sat. Bus: 47. Map p 99.***

★ **Jim's Steaks** SOUTH STREET *CHEESESTEAKS* The friendlier uptown cousin to Pat's and Geno's won't balk if you ask for lettuce and tomato. Plus, they have indoor seating—and beer. ***400 South St. (at 4th St.) ☎ 215/928-1911. www.jimssteaks.com. Cheesesteaks $7–$9. No credit cards. Lunch & dinner daily. Bus: 40, 57. Map p 100.***

kids **Jones** OLD CITY *AMERICAN COMFORT* Just what the family ordered: mac and cheese, glazed carrots, meatloaf, and chicken nachos in a Brady-Bunch retro sunken dining room. ***700 Chestnut St. (at 7th St.). ☎ 215/223-5663. www.jones-restaurant.com. AE, DC, MC, V. Entrees $10–$26. Lunch & dinner daily. Bus: 9, 21, 38, 42, 47. Subway: 8th St. Map p 100.***

★ **Kanella** WASHINGTON SQUARE *GREEK BYOB* From the island of Cypriot, this place offers rustic (goat stew) and Mediterranean (pasta with capers and mint) fare. ***1001 Spruce St. (at 10th St.). ☎ 215/922-1773. www.kanellarestaurant.com. Entrees $18–$25. DISC, MC, V. Lunch & dinner Thurs–Sat; dinner Tues–Wed; brunch Sun. Bus: 23, Alternate 40, 47. Map p 100.***

★ **Kong** NORTHERN LIBERTIES *MODERN CHINESE* Find Cantonese graffiti, birdcage pendant lights, and Hong-Kong street fare–inspired dim sum, pork belly buns, and rice bowls. ***702–704 N. 2nd St. (at Fairmount Ave.). ☎ 215/922-5665. www.eatatkong.com. Plates $5–$16. AE, MC, V. Lunch Tue–Fri; dinner daily. Bus, 5, 25, 57. Subway: Spring Garden St. Map p 100.***

★★★ **Lacroix** RITTENHOUSE *MODERN INTERNATIONAL* Overlooking the Square, each gracious meal seems more elegant than the last. ***The Rittenhouse Hotel, 210 W. Rittenhouse (at 19th St.). 215/790-2533. www.lacroixrestaurant.com. AE, DC, DISC, MC, V. Entrees $34–$55. Breakfast, lunch & dinner daily. Bus: 9, 12, 17, 21, 42. Map p 100.***

★ **Le Bec-Fin** RITTENHOUSE *FRENCH* The city's oldest, most formal restaurant *français* has a dessert cart to die for and a downstairs bar that's superbly clubby (and less expensive). ***1523 Walnut St. ☎ 215/567-1000. www.lebecfin.com. Entrees $29–$42. AE, DC, MC, V. Lunch & dinner Mon–Fri; dinner Sat. Bus: 9, 12, 21, 42. Subway: Walnut-Locust. Map p 100.***

★ **Lee How Fook** CHINATOWN *CHINESE BYOB* Garlicky good-for-you greens, hearty duck noodle soup, and salt-baked squid pack this family place night after night. ***219 N. 11th St. (btw. Race & Vine sts.). ☎ 215/925-7266. www.leehowfook.com. Entrees $6–$25. MC, V. Lunch & dinner Tues–Sun. Bus: 23, 61. Map p 100.***

★★ **Lolita** MIDTOWN *MODERN MEXICAN BYOB* Classic dishes get dressed up for a night on the town at

Rangoon is a casual place to sample Burmese cuisine.

this funky little spot. Bring your own tequila for fresh-fruit margaritas. *106 S. 13th St. (btw. Sansom & Chestnut sts.). ☎ 215/456-7100. www.lolitabyob.com. Entrees $18–$24. No credit cards. Dinner daily. Bus: 4, 21, 23, 38, 42. Subway: Walnut-Locust or 13th St. Map p 100.*

★ **Los Catrines & Tequila's** RITTENHOUSE *UPSCALE MEXICAN* Classic fare, snappy delivery, smooth tequilas served up in a mural-covered mansion. *1602 Locust St. (btw. 16th & 17th sts.). ☎ 215/546-0181. www.tequilasphilly.com. Entrees $16–$22. AE, DC, MC, V. Lunch & dinner Mon–Fri; dinner Sat–Sun. Bus: 2, 12. Map p 100.*

★ **Marra's** EAST PASSYUNK *ITALIAN/PIZZA* One meal at this no-nonsense eatery, with its sublimely simple pies and homemade escarole soup, and you'll never eat Pizza Hut again. *1734 E. Passyunk Ave. (between Morris & Moore sts.). ☎ 215/463-9249. Entrees $7–$16. DISC, MC, V. Lunch & dinner Tues–Sat; dinner Sun. Bus: 23. Subway: Tasker-Morris. Map p 99.*

★★ **Melograno** RITTENHOUSE *MODERN ITALIAN BYOB* House-cured pancetta, fig and walnut stuffing, home-made *pappardelle:* This ever-bustling bistro offers Roman fare for modern times. *2021 Sansom St. (btw. 20th & 21st sts.). ☎ 215/875-8116. Entrees $15–$32. MC, V. Dinner Tues–Sun. Bus: 9, 17, 21, 42. Map p 100.*

★★ **Mercato** MIDTOWN *MODERN ITALIAN BYOB* This glittering, no-reservations bistro makes every meal feel like a dinner party—only with better short ribs and risotto than you could ever pull off at home. *1216 Spruce St. (at Juniper St.). ☎ 215/985-2962. www.mercatobyob.com. Entrees $19–$25. No credit cards. Dinner daily. Bus: C, 23, 37. Subway: Walnut-Locust. Map p 100.*

★★ **Meritage** RITTENHOUSE *MODERN FUSION* A corner spot with the three essential elements of a romantic bistro: cozy environs, ample wine list, and foie gras dumplings. *500 S. 20th St. (at Lombard St.) ☎ 215/985-1922. www.meritagephiladelphia.com. Entrees $15–$21. AE, DISC, MC, V. Dinner Tues–Sat. Bus: 17, 40. Map p 100.*

★★ **Morimoto** OLD CITY *JAPANESE* The Iron Chef's signature flash in an aptly futuristic showplace. Splurge on tableside-made tofu, luscious *toro,* and a sake martini. *723 Chestnut St. (btw. 7th & 8th sts.). ☎ 215/413-9070. www.morimotorestaurant.com. Entrees $23–$49. AE, DC, MC, V. Lunch & dinner Mon–Fri;*

Morimoto is owned by the famed Iron Chef.

Osteria's menu features gourmet Italian comfort food.

dinner Sun. Bus: 9, 21, 38, 42, 47. Subway: 8th St. Map p 100.

★ **Nineteen** BROAD STREET *CONTINENTAL* On the Bellevue's 19th floor, giant pearls drip from ceilings where formal tea, fresh oysters, and dress-up dinners are served. *Park Hyatt, 200 S. Broad St. (at Walnut St.). ☎ 215/790-1919. www.nineteenrestaurant.com. Entrees $16–$38. AE, DC, DISC, MC, V. Breakfast, lunch & dinner daily. Bus: C, 9, 12, 21, 23, 37, 42. Subway: Walnut-Locust. Map p 100.*

★ **Noble American Cookery** RITTENHOUSE *GOURMET AMERICAN* Simple dishes, made chic—roast chicken with morels, short ribs with fava relish—are served in a setting that matches. *2025 Sansom St. (btw. 20th & 21st sts.). ☎ 215/568–7000. www.noblecookery.com. Entrees $23–$35. AE, MC, V. Dinner daily. Bus: 9, 17, 21, 42. Map p 100.*

★★★ **Osteria** NORTH BROAD *ITALIAN* Casual Boot fare, made gourmet. Sample egg-topped pizza, wild boar Bolognese, and anything from the 100% Italian wine list. Reserve ahead. *640 N. Broad St. (at Wallace St.). ☎ 215/763-0920. www.osteriaphilly.com. Entrees $15–$35. AE, DC, MC, V. Lunch & dinner Thurs–Fri; dinner Sat–Wed. Bus: C, 27. Subway: Spring Garden St. Map p 100.*

★★ **Parc** RITTENHOUSE *FRENCH* Classic Parisian bistro fare in a see-and-be-seen setting. Homemade bread, *coq au vin,* steak *au poivre,* and quiet breakfasts are standouts. *227 S. 18th St. (at Locust St.). ☎ 215/545-2262. www.parc-restaurant.com. Entrees $13–$36. AE, DC, MC, V. Breakfast, lunch & dinner daily. Bus: 9, 12, 17, 21, 42. Map p 100.*

★★ **Paradiso** EAST PASSYUNK *ITALIAN* Swanked-out South Philly neighbors nibble smoked trout salads and airy fried calamari before tucking into rabbit cacciatore and olive-dressed ahi tuna. *1627 E. Passyunk Ave. (between Tasker & Morris sts.). ☎ 215/271-2066. www.paradisophilly.com. Entrees $21–$25. AE, MC, V. Lunch & dinner daily. Bus: 23. Subway: Tasker-Morris. Map p 99.*

Pat's King of Steaks SOUTH PHILLY. *CHEESESTEAKS* The originator, in all its roadside glory. Order one "wid" onions, and/or (Cheez) Whiz. *1237 E. Passyunk Ave. (at Wharton St.). ☎ 215/468-1546. www.patskingofsteaks.com. Cheesesteaks $7–$9. No credit cards. Open 24 hr. Bus: 23, 47. Map p 99.*

★★ **Pizzeria Stella** SOCIETY HILL *PIZZA* This place offers thin-crust, cleverly topped (*guanciale,* pistachios) pies, plus juice glasses of Prosecco, egg-topped asparagus, and olive oil gelato. *420 S. 2nd St. (at Lombard St.). ☎ 215/320-8000. www.pizzeriastella.net. Pizzas $11–$17. AE, DISC, MC, V. Lunch & dinner daily. Bus: 40, Alternate 40, 57. Map p 100.*

★★ **Pumpkin** RITTENHOUSE *AMERICAN BYOB* Little and locavore, this minimalist, homey neighborhood gem excels at seasonal cuisine, seafood, and steak. (Reservations very recommended.) *1713 South St. (btw. 17th & 18th sts.). ☎ 215/545/4448. Entrees $23–$25. No credit cards. Dinner Tues–Sun. Bus: 2, 40. Map p 100.*

Ralph's Italian Restaurant BELLA VISTA *ITALIAN* Meatballs and "red gravy" (marinara), chicken Sorrento, and unpretentious service are staples at this century-old family trattoria. *760 S. 9th St. (between Fitzwater & Catharine sts.). ☎ 215/627-6011. www.ralphsrestaurant.com. Entrees $11–$23. No credit cards. Lunch & dinner daily. Bus: 47. Map p 99.*

★ **Rangoon** CHINATOWN *BURMESE* If you've never had the pleasure of digging into a tealeaf salad, coconut rice, or 1,000-layer bread, do it at this casual, women-run spot. *112 N. 9th St. (btw. Arch & Cherry sts.). ☎ 215/829-8939. Entrees $8.50–$20. MC, V. Lunch & dinner daily. Bus: 47, 48, 61. Map p 100.*

★★ **Rouge** RITTENHOUSE *AMERICAN-FRENCH* In the mood for a lavish burger or a teensy salad or a bottle of Dom for lunch? This luxe little bistro understands, as long as you're wearing the good jewelry. *205 S. 18th St. (btw. Walnut & Locust sts.). ☎ 215/732-6622. Entrees $15–$34. AE, DISC, MC, V. Lunch & dinner daily. Bus: 9, 12, 17, 21, 42. Map p 100.*

Sabrina's BELLA VISTA *AMERICAN BYOB* The reason folks wait hours for a seat in this pink-and-blue-hued eatery? Must be something in the humongous French toast. *910 Christian St. (btw. 9th & 10th sts.). ☎ 215/574-1599. www.sabrinascafe.com. Entrees $6–$11. AE, MC, V. Breakfast, lunch & dinner Tues–Sat; breakfast & lunch Sun–Mon. Bus: 23, 47. Map p 99.*

★ kids **Sam's Morning Glory Diner** BELLA VISTA *AMERICAN* "Be nice or leave" is the motto of this corner luncheonette, where ketchup is homemade, coffee comes in steel mugs, and frittatas and pancakes are worth the wait. *735 S. 10th St. (at Fitzwater St.). ☎ 215/413-3999. $5–$12. No credit cards. Breakfast & lunch daily. Bus: 23, 47. Map p 99.*

★★ **Southwark** SOUTH STREET *CONTINENTAL* The ultimate spot to eat is at the bar, from your first Manhattan to your last bite of Bosc pear stuffed with fontina and duck confit. *701 S. 4th St (at Bainbridge St.). ☎ 215/238-1888. www.southwarkrestaurant.com. Entrees $18–$28. AE, MC, V. Dinner Tues–Sat; brunch Sun. Bus: 40, 57. Map p 100.*

★★ **Supper** SOUTH STREET *MODERN AMERICAN* Unexpected send-ups of comfort fare (latkes, cioppino,

The menu at Southwark is as high-class as the surroundings.

The Oyster House boasts some of the best shuckers around.

deviled eggs, pork BBQ) star at this chic brasserie, where the "Sunday supper" and happy hour deals are not to be missed. *928 South St. ☎ 215/592-8180. www.supperphilly.com. AE, MC, V. $16–$29. Dinner daily. Bus: 40, 47. Map p 100.*

★★ **Table 31** RITTENHOUSE *AMERICAN* A snazzy, suit-and-tie steakhouse in the Comcast Center. Bring the titanium card. *1701 JFK Blvd. (at 17th St.). ☎ 215/567-7111. www.table-31.com. Entrees $24–$58. AE, DC, MC, V. Lunch & dinner Mon–Fri; dinner Sat. Bus: 2, 32, 48. Subway: 15th St. Map p 100.*

★★ **The Oyster House** RITTENHOUSE *AMERICAN SEAFOOD* Everything that swims (and is classic), including oysters opened by shuckers who've been at it for decades. *1516 Sansom St. (btw. 15th & 16th sts.). ☎ 215/567-7683. www.oysterhousephilly.com. Entrees $14–$28. AE, DISC, MC, V. Lunch & dinner Mon–Sat; dinner Sun. Bus: C, 9, 12, 21, 23, 38, 42. Subway: Walnut-Locust or 15th St. Map p 100.*

★★ **Tinto** RITTENHOUSE *BASQUE TAPAS* Chef Garces' cozy lounge offers delicious snacks like Serrano-wrapped figs and cockle-studded sea bass. *116 S. 20th St. (btw. Sansom & Chestnut sts.). ☎ 215/665-9150. www.tintorestaurant.com. Plates $4–$18. AE, DC, MC, V. Lunch & dinner Mon–Fri; dinner Sat–Sun. Bus: 9, 17, 21, 42. Map p 100.*

★★ **Tony Luke's Roast Pork** SOUTH PHILLY *ITALIAN SANDWICHES* Neon-lit, two-handed dining: Have the roast pork with garlicky broccoli rabe and sharp provolone. *39 E. Oregon Ave. (btw. Columbus Blvd. & 2nd St.). ☎ 215/551-5725. www.tonylukes.com. Entrees $7–$9. No credit cards. Breakfast, lunch & dinner daily. Bus: G, 7. Map p 99.*

★★ **Union Trust** OLD CITY *STEAKHOUSE* Opulence, thy name is a $50-per-person seafood "cascade," followed by a $100 "vertical rib-eye tasting," served in a grand old bank. *717 Chestnut St. (btw. 7th & 8th sts.). ☎ 215/925–6000. www.uniontruststeakhouse.com. Entrees $26–$49. AE, MC, V. Lunch & dinner Mon–Fri; dinner Sat–Sun. Bus: 9, 21, 38, 42, 47. Subway: 8th St. Map p 100.*

★ **Valanni** MIDTOWN *MEDITERRANEAN-LATIN TAPAS* Enjoy the modern lounge vibe, spicy-sweet snacks (mmm: stuffed figs, chickpea frites), and paella meant for sharing. *1229 Spruce St. (btw. 12th & 13th sts.). ☎ 215/790-9494. www.valanni.com. Entrees $14–$26. AE, DISC, MC, V. Dinner daily; brunch Sun. Bus: C, 27, 32. Subway: Walnut-Locust. Map p 100.*

★★★ **Vetri** MIDTOWN *ITALIAN* When Esquire critic John Mariani called chef Marc Vetri's brownstone the best Italian restaurant in the U.S. Order the tasting menu. *1312 Spruce St. (btw. 13th & Broad sts.). ☎ 215/732-3478. www.vetriristorante.com. Entrees $30–$40. AE, MC, V. Dinner Mon–Sat. Bus: C, 27, 32. Subway: Walnut-Locust. Map p 100.*

★ **Victor Café** SOUTH PHILLY *ITALIAN* The giant veal chops and homemade pastas try, but they can't compete with this trattoria's opera-singing servers. *1303 Dickinson St. (btw. 13th & Broad sts.). ☎ 215/468-3040. www.victorcafe.com. AE, MC, V. Main courses $17–$28. AE, MC, V. Dinner daily. Bus: C, 27, 32. Subway: Tasker-Morris. Map p 99.*

★ **Vietnam** CHINATOWN *VIETNAMESE* Peanut-dusted rice vermicelli, charbroiled pork, lime-glazed chicken, and handsome surroundings make this gently exotic spot popular with the neighbors. *221 N. 11th St. (btw. Race & Vine sts.). ☎ 215/592-1163. Entrees $7–$15. AE, DISC, MC, V. Lunch & dinner daily. Bus: 23, 61. Map p 100.*

★ **Villa di Roma** ITALIAN MARKET *ITALIAN* Behind red-brick tile, extra casual Italian-American fare includes classic meatballs, fried asparagus, and homemade gnocchi. *936 S. 9th St. (btw. Montrose & Carpenter sts.). ☎ 215/592-1295. www.delucasvilladiroma.com. Entrees $10–$30. No credit cards. Lunch & dinner Fri–Sat; dinner Sun–Thurs. Bus: 47. Map p 99.*

★★★ **Village Whiskey** RITTENHOUSE *GOURMET PUB* Find Philly's longest whiskey list (and longer barstool wait) and a burger that'll knock you off that hard-won seat. *114 S. 20th St. (at Sansom St.). ☎ 215/665-1088. www.villagewhiskey.com. Entrees $8–$28. AE, DISC, MC, V. Lunch Mon–Sat; dinner daily. Bus: 9, 17, 21, 42. Map p 100.*

★ **Water Works Restaurant** FAIRMOUNT *AMERICAN, GREEK* This restaurant is so pretty, with history, a view, grilled specialties—and a gourmet H2O menu. *640 Waterworks Dr. (btw. Philadelphia Museum of Art & Boathouse Row). ☎ 215/236-9000. www.thewaterworksrestaurant.com. Entrees $19–$37. AE, DC, DISC, MC, V. Lunch & dinner Sun, Tue–Fri; dinner Sat. Bus: 32, 33, 38. Map p 100.*

The hummus and kebabs at Zahav have a legion of fans.

★★ **Xochitl** SOCIETY HILL *MODERN MEXICAN* Distinctive, refined, understated, and lounge-y, the fare and the vibe at sleek "So-cheet" are refreshingly sophisticated. *408 S. 2nd St. (btw. Pine & Lombard sts.). ☎ 215/238-7280. www.xochitlphilly.com. Entrees $18–$26. AE, DISC, MC, V. Dinner Tues–Sun. Bus: 40, Alternate 40, 57. Map p 100.*

★★★ **Zahav** OLD CITY/SOCIETY HILL *ISRAELI* The best restaurant in town? Fans say yes and swear by the rich hummus and savory kebabs. *237 St. James Place. (btw. 2nd & 3rd sts.). ☎ 215/625-8800. www.zahavrestaurant.com. Plates $6–$18. AE, DISC, MC, V. Lunch & dinner Mon–Fri; dinner Sat–Sun. Bus: 21, 42, 57. Subway: 2nd St. Map p 100.*

★★ **Zento** OLD CITY *JAPANESE BYOB* Tiny but mighty, this friendly spot offers stellar staples and clever square *maki,* plus excellent teriyaki and tempura for the sushi-shy. *138 Chestnut St. (btw. Front & 2nd sts.). ☎ 215/925-9988. www.zentocontemporary.com. Entrees $18–$30. AE, MC, V. Lunch & dinner Mon–Sat; dinner Sun. Bus: 21, 42. Subway: 2nd St. Map p 100.* ●

7 The Best Nightlife

Nightlife Best Bets

Best for **Bowling**
★ North Bowl, *909 N. 2nd St. (p 115)*

Best **Beer List**
★★ Monk's Café, *264 S. 16th St. (p 122)*

Best **Dive Bar**
★ Dirty Frank's, *347 S. 13th St. (p 119)*

Best for **Local Brews**
★★★ Standard Tap, *901 N. 2nd St. (p 122)*

Best for **Canoodling**
★ Friday Saturday Sunday, *261 S. 21st St. (p 122)*

Best for **Eating**
★★ Pub and Kitchen, *1946 Lombard St. (p 118)*

Best for **the DJ Scene**
★★ Fluid, *613. S. 4th St. (p 118)*

Best for **a Long-Term Relationship**
★★★ Swann Lounge at the Four Seasons, *1 Logan Sq. (p 121)*

Best for **Salsa Dancing**
Brasil's, *112 Chestnut St. (p 115)*

Best for **Overall Chic-ness**
★★ Snackbar, *253 S. 20th St. (p 118)*

Best **Classic Gay Bar**
★ Tavern on Camac, *243 S. Camac St. (p 119)*

Best for **Dancing**
Shampoo, *417 N. 8th St. (p 118)*

Best for **Martinis**
★★ Nineteen Bar, *200 S. Broad St. (p 120)*

Monk's Café has the city's best beer list.

Previous page: Nineteen Bar is renowned for its martinis.

Nightlife in Northern Liberties

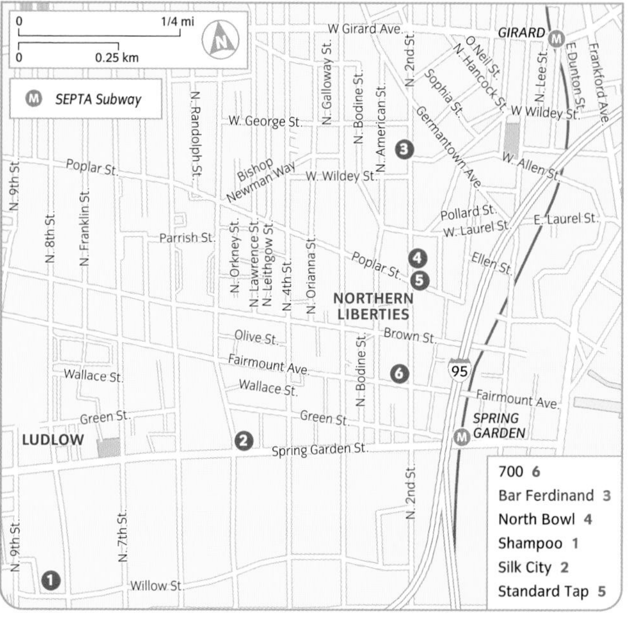

Nightlife A to Z

Bowling

Lucky Strikes Lanes MIDTOWN This swank chain alley has 24 lanes, two floors, a low-slung lounge, cocktails, buckets of beers, and sliders galore. *1336 Chestnut St. (btw. 13th & Broad sts.). ☎ 215/545-2471. www.bowlluckystrike.com. $45–$65 per hr. Shoe rental $4. Bus: C, 9, 21, 27, 32, 38, 42. Subway: Walnut-Locust or 13th St. Map p 116.*

★ **North Bowl** NORTHERN LIBERTIES This retro-chic, locally-owned alley has 17 lanes, two bars, and a major local following. On the menu: corn dogs and local brews. *909 N. 2nd St. (btw. Poplar & N. Hancock sts.). ☎ 215/238-2695. www.northbowlphilly.com. $4–$6 per game. Bus: 5. Subway: Spring Garden St. Map p 115.*

Dance Clubs

Brasil's OLD CITY This compact upstairs club serves up the hottest Latin groove scene (and coolest *caipirinhas*) in town. From 9 to 10:30pm, dance pros offer free salsa lessons. *112 Chestnut St. (btw. Front & 2nd sts.). ☎ 215/413-1700. Cover $5–$10. Bus: 5, 9, 17, 21, 38, 42. Map p 116.*

D'Angelo's Lounge RITTENHOUSE Like a party scene from *The Sopranos*, this trattoria-with-a-dance-floor caters to a mature crowd who groove to Sinatra and Miami Sound Machine. *256 S. 20th*

Nightlife in Center City

12th Air Command 25
Black Sheep 10
Bob & Barbara's 15
Brasil's 31
Bridgid's 1
D'Angelo's Lounge 7
Dark Horse 30
Dirty Frank's 26
Drinker's Tavern and Pub 3, 32
Fergie's 19
Fluid 28
Friday Saturday Sunday's "Tank Bar" 6
Il Bar 33
Latest Dish 29
L'Etage 27
Lucky Strikes Lanes 17
McGillin's Olde Ale House 18
McGlinchey's 14
Monk's Café 11
Nineteen Bar 16
Nodding Head Brewery and Restaurant 13
Oscar's Tavern 12
The Pub and Kitchen 9
Ray's Happy Birthday Bar 34
Sisters 20
Snackbar 8
Swann Lounge at the Four Seasons 2
Tavern on Camac 23
Tria 4, 24
Voyeur 21
Walnut Room 5
Woody's 22

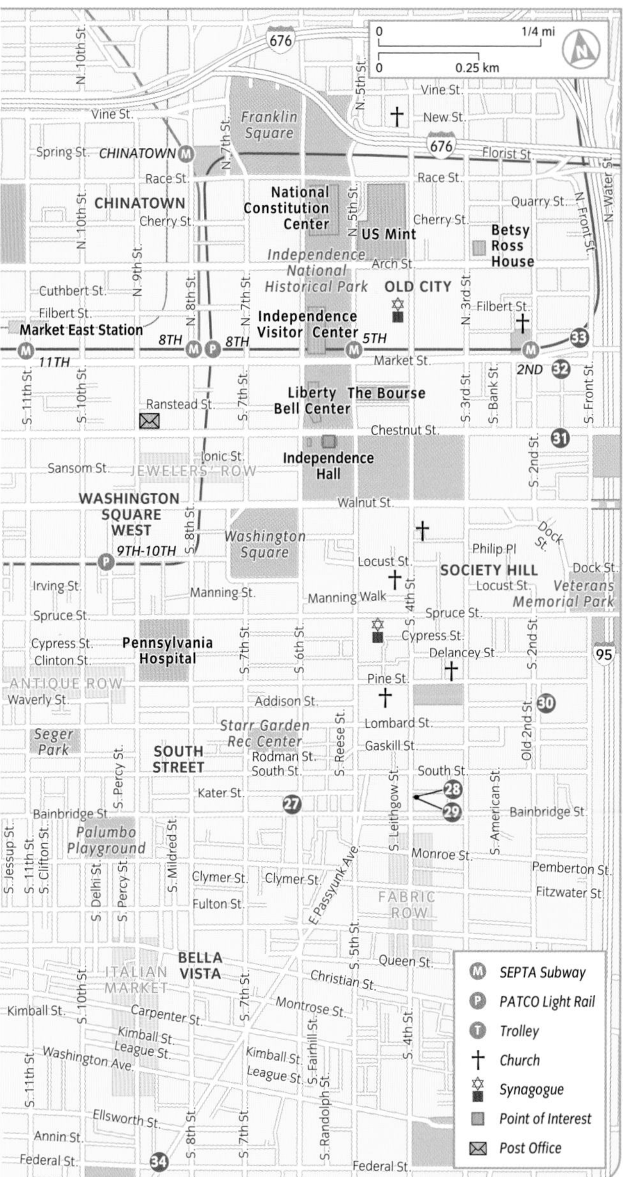

676
0
1/4 mi
0
0.25 km
Vine St.
New St.
Florist St.
Race St.
Quarry St.
Cherry St.
Arch St.
Filbert St.
Market St.
Chestnut St.
Walnut St.
Locust St.
Spruce St.
Cypress St.
Delancey St.
Pine St.
Lombard St.
Gaskill St.
South St.
Bainbridge St.
Monroe St.
Pemberton St.
Fitzwater St.
Queen St.
Christian St.
Montrose St.
Carpenter St.
Kimball St.
League St.
Washington Ave.
Ellsworth St.
Annin St.
Federal St.
Spring St.
CHINATOWN
Franklin Square
National Constitution Center
US Mint
Betsy Ross House
Independence National Historical Park
OLD CITY
Independence Visitor Center
Market East Station
8TH
5TH
11TH
2ND
Liberty Bell Center
The Bourse
Ranstead St.
Ionic St.
Sansom St.
JEWELERS' ROW
Independence Hall
WASHINGTON SQUARE WEST
9TH-10TH
Washington Square
Philip Pl
Dock St.
SOCIETY HILL
Veterans Memorial Park
Irving St.
Manning St.
Manning Walk
Pennsylvania Hospital
Clinton St.
ANTIQUE ROW
Waverly St.
Addison St.
Starr Garden Rec Center
Rodman St.
Seger Park
SOUTH STREET
Kater St.
Palumbo Playground
Clymer St.
Fulton St.
E. Passyunk Ave.
FABRIC ROW
BELLA VISTA
ITALIAN MARKET
Kimball St.
95
N. 10th St.
N. 9th St.
N. 8th St.
N. 7th St.
N. 5th St.
N. 3rd St.
N. Front St.
N. Water St.
S. 11th St.
S. 10th St.
S. 8th St.
S. 7th St.
S. 6th St.
S. 5th St.
S. 4th St.
S. 3rd St.
S. Bank St.
S. 2nd St.
S. Front St.
Old 2nd St.
S. Reese St.
S. Leithgow St.
S. American St.
S. Percy St.
S. Jessup St.
S. Clifton St.
S. Delhi St.
S. Mildred St.
S. Fairhill St.
S. Randolph St.
27
28
29
30
31
32
33
34
SEPTA Subway
PATCO Light Rail
Trolley
Church
Synagogue
Point of Interest
Post Office

Fluid showcases different musical styles via local DJs.

St. (btw. Locust & Spruce sts.). ☎ 215/546-3935. www.dangeloristorante.com. No cover. Bus: 12, 17. Map p 116.

★★ Fluid SOUTH STREET Above a funky bistro, this petite, quintessentially Philly club shows love for diverse musical genres via homegrown DJs. *613 S. 4th St. (btw. South & Bainbridge sts.). ☎ 215/629-0565. www.fluidnightclub.com. Cover $5–$10. Bus: 40, 57. Map p 116.*

Shampoo NORTHERN LIBERTIES A thumping maze that's all things to all clubbers: three floors and eight bars with Goth, 80s, drag, hip-hop—even, on some Sunday afternoons, disco for toddlers. *417 N. 8th St. (btw. Callowhill & Spring Garden sts.). ☎ 215/922-7500. www.shampooonline.com. Cover $7–$12. Bus: 47. Map p 115.*

Dine-In Bars

★★ Bar Ferdinand NORTHERN LIBERTIES Sangria; $2 wine specials; and tapas of smoked fish, curried ham, and spiced almonds star at this artsy spot. Tabs here can add up fast. *1030 N. 2nd St. (btw. W. Wildey & W. George sts.). ☎ 215/923-1313. www.barferdinand.com. No cover. Bus: 5. Subway: Spring Garden St. Map p 115.*

★ Latest Dish SOUTH STREET Downstairs from Fluid (see above), stylish diners sit at a copper-top bar or tables for comfort-minded nibbles and anything from the above-average cocktail list. *613 S. 4th St. (btw. South & Bainbridge sts.). ☎ 215/629-0565. www.latestdish.com. No cover. Bus: 40, 57. Map p 116.*

★★ The Pub and Kitchen RITTENHOUSE Rustic and refined, this corner spot has the menu of a bistro and the vibe of a stylish bar. Expect waits on weekends. *1946 Lombard St. (at 20th St.). ☎ 215/545-0350. www.thepubandkitchen.com. No cover. Bus: 17, 40. Map p 116.*

★★ Snackbar RITTENHOUSE Stylishly tiny, this spot offers precious small bites to go with elegant little drinks. *253 S. 20th St. (btw. Locust & Spruce sts.). ☎ 215/545-5655. www.snackbarltd.com. No cover. Bus: 12, 17. Map p 116.*

Dive Bars

★ Bob & Barbara's SOUTH STREET This retro-style spot comes replete with vintage beer ads and lighting, $3 Jim Beam shots and can of PBR specials, and on Thursday night, drag performances. *1509 South St. (btw. 15th & 16th sts.).*

☎ *215/545-4511. No cover. Bus: 2, 40. Map p 116.*

★ **Dirty Frank's** MIDTOWN No sign, just a mural of famous "Franks" announces this more shabby than chic watering hole, where locals play darts and sink into booths. To be safe, order a bottle, not a pint. *347 S. 13th St. (at Pine St.).* ☎ *215/ 732-5010. No cover. Bus: Alternate 40. Map p 116.*

★ **McGlinchey's** RITTENHOUSE Ms. Pac Man tables. Grumpy bartenders. 25-cent hotdogs. Cheap shots and even cheaper beer. No wonder this place is where the down-and-out chill, the glamorous slum, and the business folk hole up. *259 S. 15th St. (btw. Locust & Spruce sts.).* ☎ *215/ 735-1259. No cover. Subway: Walnut-Locust. Map p 116.*

Oscar's Tavern RITTENHOUSE The textbook spot to hide from the boss, this dirt-cheap place dodged the smoking ban, allowing patrons to light up later into the night. Hungry? Don't fear the roast beef. *1524 Sansom St. (btw. 15th & 16th sts.).* ☎ *215/972-9938. No cover. Bus: 2, 9, 21, 42. Map p 116.*

★ **Ray's Happy Birthday Bar** SOUTH PHILLY Lou runs this corner joint (recently discovered by irony-dealing hipsters) and will be seriously bummed if you don't call ahead to tell him it's your b-day. Also: This is the best place to go for a brew after a stint at Pat's or Geno's. *1200 Passyunk Ave. (at Federal St.).* ☎ *215/365-1169. No cover. Bus: 47, 47m. Map p 116.*

Gay Bars

Sisters MIDTOWN The only lesbian bar in town covers 5,000 square feet to satisfy a diverse group of women that range from buzz-cut to glammed up. Best nights: Thursday's karaoke and Saturday's singles dance party. *1320 Chancellor St. (btw. 13th & Juniper sts., Walnut & Locust sts.).* ☎ *215/ 735-0735. www.sistersnightclub.com. Cover $6–$10. Bus: 9, 12, 21, 42. Subway: Walnut-Locust. Map p 116.*

★ **Tavern on Camac** MIDTOWN Tucked along a tiny side street, this friendly 60-year-old piano bar is one of the oldest gay pubs in the U.S. Go on a Friday or Saturday for a famously fun sing-along. *243 S. Camac St. (btw. 12th & 13th sts., Locust & Spruce sts.).* ☎ *215/545-0900.*

The patio at stylish Snackbar.

The elegant L'Etage offers the occasional cabaret act.

www.tavernoncamac.com. No cover. Bus: 23. Map p 116.

12th Air Command MIDTOWN Like a gay amusement park, this all-in-one scene boasts an arcade, disco dance hall, karaoke, deck-top cookouts, hunky barkeeps, and theme nights, including a college party where it's 17 to enter, 21 to drink. *254 S. 12th St. (btw. Locust & Spruce sts.). ☎ 215/545-8088. www.12thair.com. Cover $3–$5. Bus: 23. Map p 116.*

★ **Voyeur** MIDTOWN There's room for 1,000 among the lavishly decorated floors (red velvet, crystal spangles, faux fur), home to some of the East Coast's best DJs—and Philly's biggest circuit parties. Drag queens serve cocktails. *1221 St. James St. (btw. 12th & 13th sts.). ☎ 215/735-5772. www.voyeurnightclub.com. No cover. Bus: 23. Map p 116.*

Woody's MIDTOWN This mega-bar has anchored the gayborhood since the '70s, sort of a community center with booze. Among the umpteen theme nights: Latin, country two-step, karaoke, and college. *202 S. 13th St. (btw. Walnut & Locust sts.). ☎ 215/545-1893. www.woodysbar.com. Cover $5. Bus: 9, 12, 21, 42. Map p 116.*

Lounges

★ **L'Etage** SOUTH STREET A floor above Beau Monde (*see p 102*), this elegant spot offers banquette seating, a nice little wine list, a tiny dance floor, and occasional cabaret acts. *624 S. 6th St. (at Bainbridge St.). ☎ 215/592-0656. Cover $5–$10. Bus: 40. Map p 116.*

★★ **Nineteen Bar** MIDTOWN Known for its fireside coziness, this 19th-floor lounge is nonetheless see-and-be-seen, with an impeccable crowd—and martinis to match. *Park Hyatt at the Bellevue, 200 S. Broad St. (at Walnut St.). ☎ 215/790-1919. www.nineteenrestaurant.com. No cover. Bus: C, 9, 12, 21, 27, 32, 42. Subway: Walnut-Locust. Map p 116.*

700 NORTHERN LIBERTIES Early on, the crowd at this two-floor spot is hipper-than-thou (in a nice way) artists and the like. Later, it's a mixed bag of the same, plus bachelorettes, frat brothers, and on-the-town yuppies. *700 N. 2nd St. (at Fairmount Ave.). ☎ 215/413-3181. No cover. Bus: 5. Subway: Spring Garden St. Map p 115.*

★ **Silk City** NORTHERN LIBERTIES The more dimly-lit arm to a silver car diner, this lounge is known for its hipster clientele and DJs. *435 Spring*

Garden St. (btw. 4th & 5th sts.). ☎ 215/592-8838. www.silkcityphilly.com. Cover $0–$10. Bus: 43, 57. Map p 115.

★★★ Swann Lounge at the Four Seasons LOGAN CIRCLE There's something about perching in a cozy banquette, nibbling cheese straws and sipping a top-dollar grapefruit martini, that makes the day just seem . . . better. *1 Logan Sq. (at 18th St.). ☎ 215/963-1500. www.fourseasons.com. No cover. Bus: 32, 33, 48. Map p 116.*

Walnut Room RITTENHOUSE Great for an early-evening martini, but better for late-night partying, this narrow space has the tiniest of dance floors, for when you really need to get a little closer. *1709 Walnut St. (btw. 17th & 18th sts.). ☎ 215/751-0201. www.walnutroomredux.com. Cover $5–$10. Bus: 2, 9, 12, 21, 42. Map p 116.*

Taprooms

Black Sheep RITTENHOUSE A cozy Irish pub in an old Colonial townhouse, popular among the suit-and-tie crowd. The menu's worthy of staying past happy hour, too. *247 S. 17th St. (at Latimer St.). ☎ 215/545-9473. www.theblacksheeppub.com. No cover. Bus: 2. Map p 116.*

★ Bridgid's FAIRMOUNT Tiny and friendly, this horseshoe-shaped bar stocks an impressive array of Belgian beers—best accompanied by a small menu of inexpensive dinner specials. *726 N. 24th St. (btw. Fairmount Ave & Aspen St.). ☎ 215/232-3232. www.bridgids.com. No cover. Bus: 48. Map p 116.*

Dark Horse SOCIETY HILL If it's 4am and a World Cup match is taking place, chances are a number of onlookers are holed up drinking Harp at this Brit-inspired pub, which is also popular among neighbors during more regular hours. *421 S. 2nd St. (btw. Pine & Lombard sts.). ☎ 215/928-0232. www.darkhorsepub.com. No cover. Bus: Alternate 40. Map p 116.*

Drinker's Tavern and Pub OLD CITY and RITTENHOUSE Never has a bar in Philly been so aptly named. At either location, shotgun (really) a Pabst Blue Ribbon for a buck. *124 Market St. (btw. Front & 2nd sts.); ☎ 215/351-0141. Bus: 5, 17, 44, 121. Subway: 2nd St. 1903 Chestnut St. (btw. 19th & 20th sts.); ☎ 215/564-0914. www.drinkers215.com. No cover. Bus: 9, 17, 21, 42. Map p 116.*

★★ Fergie's MIDTOWN An Irish pub actually *owned* by an Irishman, this find is cozy and candlelit, and offers a large list of brews complimented by some tasty potpies, burgers, and mussels and fries. *1214 Sansom St. (btw. 12th & 13th sts.). ☎ 215/928-8118. www.fergies.com. No cover. Bus: 23. Map p 116.*

Il Bar offers more than 100 wines by the glass.

Tria has a strong European influence.

★ **McGillin's Olde Ale House** MIDTOWN Hard to find—but worth it—Philadelphia's oldest continuously operating tavern is as popular now as its ever been, only now there's Friday-night karaoke with their pitchers of lager. *1310 Drury St. (btw. Chestnut & Sansom sts., 13th & Juniper sts.). ☎ 215/735-5562. www.mcgillins.com. No cover. Bus: 9, 21, 38, 42, 124, 125. Map p 116.*

★★ **Monk's Cafe** RITTENHOUSE For some reason, the Penn crowd has adopted this beer-connoisseur's spot, but you should go regardless of the elbow-throwing crowd, if only for the house's special Flemish sour ale (or a bucket of mussels and the house fries). *264 S. 16th St. (btw. Locust & Spruce sts.). ☎ 215/545-7005. www.monkscafe.com. No cover. Bus: 2. Map p 116.*

★ **Nodding Head Brewery and Restaurant** RITTENHOUSE For the ultimate locavore drinker: Six truly interesting beers brewed on premises: three light to dark; three seasonal; plus a nice, absorptive menu not unlike Monk's (see above). *1516 Sansom St. (btw. 15th & 16th sts.). ☎ 215/569-9525. www.noddinghead.com. No cover. Bus: 2. Map p 116.*

★★★ **Standard Tap** NORTHERN LIBERTIES Local—and *only* local—beer, plus whatever other kind of drink you require, is served at this hip, handsome, vast, and justly popular gastro-pub. If it's nice out, ask for a table on the deck. *901 N. 2nd St. (at Poplar St.). ☎ 215/238-0630. www.standardtap.com. No cover. Bus: 5. Subway: Spring Garden St. Map p 115.*

Wine Bars

★ **Friday Saturday Sunday's "Tank Bar"** RITTENHOUSE Above a neighborhood restaurant known for its retro cuisine, this romantic spot offers wines with the lowest (around 10%) markups in town. *261 S. 21st St. (btw. Locust & Spruce sts.). ☎ 215/546-4232. www.frisatsun.com. No cover. Bus: 7, 12, 40. Map p 116.*

★ **Il Bar** OLD CITY Tucked into the ground floor of the Penn's View Hotel (*see p 140)* are more than 100 wines by the glass, available by flights of five 1.5-ounce pours—all part of the hotel's Italian restaurant. *14 N. Front St. (at Market St.). ☎ 215/922-7800. www.pennsviewhotel.com. No cover. Bus: 5, 17, 33, 48. Subway: 2nd St. Map p 116.*

★★ **Tria** MIDTOWN, RITTENHOUSE This pair of narrow bars feels very Euro, what with their spare handsomeness, little savory plates, and beginner-friendly selection of *vino*, categorized as bubbly, bold, zippy, and so on. *123 S. 18th St. (at Sansom St.); ☎ 215/972-8742. Bus: 9, 12, 21, 42. 12th & Spruce sts.; ☎ 215/629-9200. www.triacafe.com. No cover. Bus: 23. Map p 116.*

8 The Best of Arts & Entertainment

Arts & Entertainment Best Bets

Best Theater for **Children's Performance**
★ Arden Theatre Company, *40 S. 2nd St. (p 125)*

Best for **Orchestra**
★★★ Kimmel Center for the Performing Arts, *300 S. Broad St. (p 130)*

Best for **Local Productions**
★ kids Walnut Street Theater, *825 Walnut St. (p 128)*

Best **Theater Facility, Period**
★★★ Academy of Music, *240 S. Broad St. (p 129)*

Best **Hidden Gem**
★★ Academy of Vocal Arts, *1920 Spruce St. (p 129)*

Best for **Outdoor Concerts**
★ Mann Music Center, *5201 Parkside Ave. (p 130)*

Best for **Free Performances**
★★★ Curtis Institute of Music, *1726 Locust St. (p 129)*

Best **Jazz Club**
★★ Ortlieb's Jazzhaus, *847 N. 3rd St. (p 130)*

Best **Rock Club**
★ The Khyber, *56 N. 2nd St. (p 131)*

Best for **Broadway Productions**
★ The Forrest, *1114 Walnut St. (p 125)*

Best for **Outdoor Concerts**
★ Susquehanna Bank Center, *1 Harbour Blvd., Camden. (p 130)*

Best for **Drama with an Edge**
★ Wilma Theater, *265 S. Broad St. (p 128)*

Best for **Cabaret**
★★ L'Etage, *624 S. 6th St. (p 132)*

Best for **Laid-Back Original Music**
★ Tin Angel, *20 S. 2nd St. (p 132)*

Best for **Family Concerts**
★★ World Café Live, *3025 Walnut St. (p 132)*

The Curtis Institute of Music features free performances from top students.

Previous page: The Philadelphia Opera Company performs at the Academy of Music in Midtown.

Arts & Entertainment

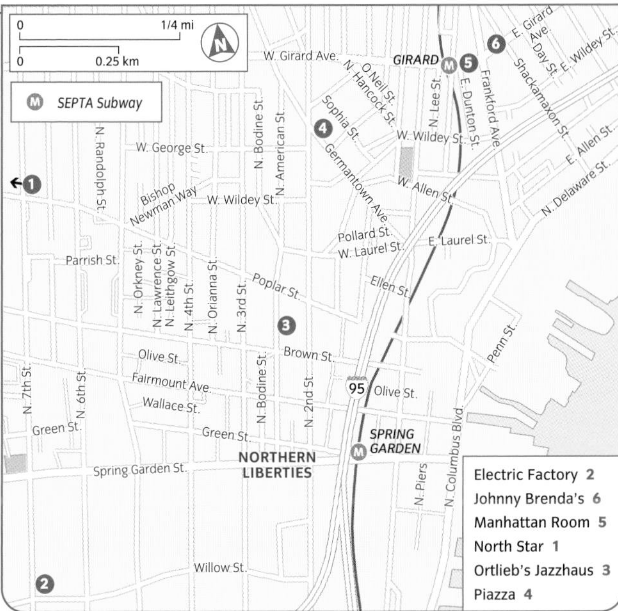

Arts & Entertainment A to Z

Theater

★ kids **Arden Theatre Company** OLD CITY Two contemporary performance spaces (360-seat and 175-seat) offer five popular seasonal productions—adaptations, premieres, and masterpieces—plus two popular children's shows. *40 S. 2nd St. (btw. Market & Arch sts.). ☎ 215/922-1122. www.ardentheatre.org. Tickets $29–$48 Bus: 5, 17, 33, 44, 121. Subway: 2nd St. Map p 126.*

★ **The Forrest** WASHINGTON WEST Best for big musicals (*Phantom of the Opera*, *Pippin*), this spectacular venue was built for $2 million in 1927, around when Gilbert & Sullivan launched productions here. *1114 Walnut St. (btw. 11th & 12th sts.). ☎ 215/923-1515. www.forrest-theatre.com. Tickets $32–$87. Bus: 9, 12, 21, 23, 42. Map p 126.*

Merriam Theater MIDTOWN This turn-of-the-20th-century Avenue of the Arts stunner welcomes top touring Broadway musicals, performers such as Patti LaBelle and Mandy Patinkin, and the Gilbert & Sullivan International Festival. *250 S. Broad St. (btw. Spruce & Pine sts.). ☎ 215/336-1234. Tickets $29–$150. Bus: C, 27, 32. Subway: Walnut-Locust. Map p 126.*

Philadelphia Shakespeare Theatre RITTENHOUSE The Bard's best-loved plays, two or three of them per year, played

Center City Arts & Entertainment

Academy of Music 12
Academy of Vocal Arts 7
Annenberg Center at the University of Pennsylvania 5
Arden Theatre Company 23
Chris' Jazz Café 11
Curtis Institute of Music 8
The Forrest 17
Helium Comedy Club 4
Kimmel Center for the Performing Arts 15
L'Etage 21
Mann Music Center 1
Merriam Theater 13
Painted Bride Art Center 22
Philadelphia Shakespeare Theatre 3
Plays & Players Theater 9
Prince Music Theater 10
Society Hill Playhouse 20
Susquehanna Bank Center 26
Suzanne Roberts Theatre 16
The Khyber 25
Theater of Living Arts 27
Tin Angel 24
Tower Theatre 2
Trocadero 18
Walnut Street Theater 19
Wilma Theater 14
World Café Live 6

0 1/4 mi
0 0.25 km
Willow St.
676
95
Wood St.
Vine St.
New St.
Florist St.
Franklin Square
CHINATOWN
Spring St.
Race St.
CHINATOWN
Cherry St.
National Constitution Center
US Mint
Independence National Historical Park
OLD CITY
Betsy Ross House
Quarry St.
Arch St.
Cuthbert St.
Filbert St.
Church St.
11TH
8TH
8TH
5TH
2ND
Independence Visitor Center
Market St.
Liberty Bell Center
The Bourse
Ranstead St.
Chestnut St.
Ionic St.
Sansom St.
JEWELERS' ROW
Independence Hall
WASHINGTON SQUARE WEST
Walnut St.
Washington Square
Dock St.
Philip Pl
SOCIETY HILL
Dock St.
9TH-10TH
S. Washington Sq
Manning St.
Irving St.
Locust St.
Locust St.
Manning Walk
Veterans Memorial Park
Spruce St.
Spruce St.
Cypress St.
Cypress St.
Pennsylvania Hospital
Clinton St.
Delancey St.
ANTIQUE ROW
Pine St.
Waverly St.
Addison St.
Starr Garden Rec Center
Lombard St.
Seger Park
Gaskill St.
SOUTH STREET
South St.
South St.
Kater St.
Bainbridge St.
Bainbridge St.
Palumbo Playground
Monroe St.
Clymer St.
Clymer St.
FABRIC ROW
Fitzwater St.
Fitzwater St.
Fulton St.
Fulton St.
E Passyunk Ave.
ITALIAN MARKET
BELLA VISTA
Christian St.
Montrose St.
Kimball St.
Carpenter St.
Kimball St.
League St.
Washington Ave.
Kimball St.
League St.
N. 10th St.
N. 7th St.
N. 5th St.
N. 9th St.
N. 8th St.
N. 3rd St.
N. Front St.
N. Water St.
S. 11th St.
S. 10th St.
S. 7th St.
S. 3rd St.
S. Bank St.
Letitia St.
S. Front St.
S. 2nd St.
S. 8th St.
S. 4th St.
S. 6th St.
S. Reese St.
Old 2nd St.
S. Percy St.
S. Leithgow St.
S. American St.
S. Jessup St.
S. Clifton St.
S. Mildred St.
S. Delhi St.
S. 5th St.
S. Randolph St.
SEPTA Subway
PATCO Light Rail
Trolley
Church
Synagogue
Point of Interest
Post Office

The Walnut Street Theater hosts Broadway-style productions.

traditionally, cleverly re-imagined, or with an easy-to-understand, educational bent, in an intimate setting. *2111 Sansom St. (btw. 21st & 22nd sts.). ☎ 215/496-9722. www.phillyshakespeare.org. Tickets $0–$35. Bus: 7, 9, 12, 21, 40, 42. Map p 126.*

★ Plays & Players Theater Charmingly rickety, this side-street landmark is home to the century-old amateur troupe of the same name, known for classic drama, works-in-progress, and interactive shows. *1714 Delancey St. (btw. 17th & 18th sts., Spruce & Pine sts.). ☎ 215/735-0630. www.playsandplayers.org. Tickets $10–$40. Bus: 2, 40. Map p 126.*

★ Prince Music Theater MIDTOWN An old-picture-palace-turned-modern venue hosts new and adventurous productions, reliably enjoyable cabaret, and on very special occasions, old movies and debut films. *1412 Chestnut St. (btw. Broad & 15th sts.). ☎ 215/972-1000. www.princemusictheater.org. Tickets (to live performances) $29–$60. Bus: C, 27, 32. Subway: City Hall. Map p 126.*

Society Hill Playhouse SOCIETY HILL The self-described "theater for people who don't like theater" has an upstairs main stage known for its original and popular comedy, and a downstairs "Red Room" for smaller productions. *507 S. 8th St. (btw. Lombard & South sts.). ☎ 215/923-0210. www.societyhillplayhouse.com. Tickets $10–$55. Bus: 40, 47, 47m. Map p 126.*

Suzanne Roberts Theatre MIDTOWN Universal access is the concept behind this newest and most iridescent of Broad Street's performing spaces, home base to both the "all premieres" of the Philadelphia Theatre and Koresh Dance companies. *480 S. Broad St. (at Lombard St.). ☎ 215/985-1400. www.philadelphiatheatrecompany.com. Tickets to Philadelphia Theatre Co. performances $46–$69. Bus: C, 27, 32. Subway: Lombard-South. Map p 126.*

★ kids Walnut Street Theater WASHINGTON WEST The country's oldest playhouse (ca. 1809) hosts locally-produced Broadway-style productions (*Oliver!, Fiddler on the Roof*) and children's shows in its 1,052-seat theater, plus experimental works in its adjoining studio spaces. *825 Walnut St. (at 9th St.). ☎ 215/574-3550. www.walnutstreettheatre.org. Tickets $10–$70. Bus: 9, 21, 42, 47, 61, 62. Map p 126.*

★ Wilma Theater MIDTOWN For drama buffs: A modern, 300-seat space offering modern works, including premieres of works by playwrights such as Tom Stoppard. *265 S. Broad St. (at Spruce St.). ☎ 215/546-7824. www.wilmatheater.org. Tickets $35–$50. Bus: C, 27, 32. Subway: Walnut-Locust. Map p 126.*

Opera, Ballet, Classical

★★★ Academy of Music MIDTOWN The grandest performance hall in town—from its iconic gaslights to its gilded onstage columns—is home to the Pennsylvania Ballet, Philadelphia Opera Company, visiting performers (Jerry Seinfeld, Feist) and traveling musical theater. *240 S. Broad St. (at Locust St.). ☎ 215/893-1999. Tickets from Kimmel Center. Bus: C, 12, 27, 32. Subway: Walnut-Locust. Map p 126.*

★★ Academy of Vocal Arts RITTENHOUSE One of the world's most exclusive opera schools (only 30 students at a time) makes its home in—and gives marvelously intimate performances from—an ornate old townhouse. *1920 Spruce St. (btw. 19th & 20th sts.). ☎ 215/735-1685. www.avaopera.org. Tickets $48–$83. Bus: 17, 40. Map p 126.*

★★★ Curtis Institute of Music RITTENHOUSE In a rambling limestone mansion, one of the world's finest music schools (Lang-Lang trained here), and free student

The Academy of Vocal Arts is one of the world's most exclusive opera schools.

recitals (Oct–May Mon, Wed & Fri 8pm). Curtis students also perform full-scale opera at the Prince Music Theater (see above) and symphony orchestra at the Kimmel Center (see below). *1726 Locust St. (btw. 17th St. & Rittenhouse Sq.). ☎ 215/893-5252. www.curtis.edu. Tickets $0–$40. Bus: 2, 9, 12, 21, 42. Map p 126.*

Music/Performance Halls

★ Annenberg Center at the University of Pennsylvania UNIVERSITY CITY A mixed bag of productions take place at this

The Kimmel Center for the Performing Arts is home to the Philadelphia Orchestra.

Ortlieb's Jazzhaus hosts some serious jazz musicians, like Mickey Roker (above).

modern, double-stage space, from local jazz to the International Children's Festival to contemporary dance. ***3680 Walnut St. (btw. 36th & 38th sts.). ☎ 215/898-3900. www.pennpresents.org. Tickets $10–$55. Bus: 21. Subway: 34th St. Map p 126.***

★★★ Kimmel Center for the Performing Arts MIDTOWN This dramatic glass and steel vault includes a 2,500-seat cello-shaped concert hall built for the Philadelphia Orchestra (but performed in by all manner of musical acts) and a 650-seat space for chamber music, dance, and drama. ***300 S. Broad St. (at Spruce St.). ☎ 215/790-5800. www.kimmelcenter.org. Tickets for Philadelphia Orchestra $39–$115. Bus: C, 12, 27, 32. Subway: Walnut-Locust. Map p 126.***

★ Mann Music Center FAIRMOUNT PARK This summertime amphitheater has covered seating and picnicking on the grass for concerts by Yo-Yo Ma, the Gipsy Kings, John Legend, and more. No assigned seats. ***5201 Parkside Ave. (at Belmont Ave.). ☎ 215/546-7900. www.manncenter.org. Tickets $25–$79. Bus: 40. Trolley: 10. Map p 126.***

★ Susquehanna Bank Center CAMDEN Just across the Delaware River, this 25,000-capacity summer amphitheater has had Blink 182, Coldplay, and Dave Matthews perform al fresco. ***1 Harbour Blvd., Camden, NJ. ☎ 856/365-1300. www.livenation.com. Tickets $28–$80. Bus (to ferry): 25. Map p 126.***

Jazz & Blues Venues

★ Chris' Jazz Café MIDTOWN Center City's only spot for local jazz, this cozy, casual find has a simple bar menu and a cool vibe. Great for date night. ***1421 Sansom St. (btw. Broad & 15th sts.). ☎ 215/568-3131. www.chrisjazzcafe.com. Cover $3–$20. Bus: C, 27, 32. Subway: Walnut-Locust. Map p 126.***

★★ Ortlieb's Jazzhaus NORTHERN LIBERTIES Dimly lit, hard to find, this joint gets seriously smokin' when Mickey Roker (Dizzy Gillespie's drummer) heads up the "Hausband." ***847 N. 3rd St. (btw. Brown & Poplar sts.). ☎ 215/922-1035. www.ortliebsjazzhaus.com. Cover $3–$10. Bus: 5, 57. Subway: Spring Garden St. Map p 125.***

★ Painted Bride Art Center OLD CITY This effervescent, welcoming art gallery doubles as a performance space for contemporary music, dance, and theater—and

Philadelphia's longest running jazz series. *230 Vine St. (btw. 2nd & 3rd sts.). ☎ 215/925-9914. www.paintedbride.org. Tickets $20–$25. Bus: 5, 25, 57. Map p 126.*

Popular Concert Venues

Electric Factory NORTHERN LIBERTIES A storied industrial setting for medium-large, all-ages shows by The Yeah Yeah Yeahs, Ani DiFranco, Cat Power, Mos Def, and Regina Spektor. *421 N. 7th St. (btw. Callowhill & Spring Garden sts.). ☎ 215/627-1332. www.electricfactory.info. Tickets $17–$50. Bus: 43, 47. Map p 125.*

★ **Johnny Brenda's** NORTHERN LIBERTIES/FISHTOWN This dive-bar turned music venue/hipster gastropub has an upstairs stage for everything from indie folk groups to death metal acts. *1201 Frankford Ave. (at E. Girard Ave.). ☎ 215/739-9684. www.johnnybrendas.com. Tickets $8–$16. Bus: 5, 15. Subway: Girard Ave. Map p 125.*

★ **The Khyber** OLD CITY Philly's oldest taproom—note the carved gargoyles above the bar—puts its small stage to use with nightly visits from up-and-coming local and national rock bands. *56 N. 2nd St. (btw. Market & Chestnut sts.). ☎ 215/238-5888. www.thekhyber.com. Cover $5–$12. Bus: 5, 17, 21, 42, 48, 121. Subway: 2nd St. Map p 126.*

Manhattan Room NORTHERN LIBERTIES/FISHTOWN Original, often experimental music shares the weekly bill with independent films, art openings, and DJs at the out-of-the-way "M" Room. *15 W. Girard Ave. (btw. Front St. & Frankford Ave.). ☎ 215/739-5577. www.themanhattanroom.com. Cover $8. Bus: 5, 15. Subway: Girard Ave. Map p 125.*

North Star FAIRMOUNT On a neighborhood's edge, this mid-size venue specializes in rock, from The Josh Olmstead Band to Jane's Addiction tribute acts. There are pool tables and finger food, too. *2629 Poplar St. (at 27th St.). ☎ 215/787-0488. www.northstarbar.com. Tickets $5–$35. Bus: 32, 48. Map p 125.*

★ **Piazza** NORTHERN LIBERTIES World music festivals, DJ'd dance parties (plus family movies and Phillies games on the big screen) are part of the scene at this al fresco courtyard of shops, bars, and condos. *2nd St. & Germantown Ave. (at Hancock St.). No phone. www.atthepiazza.com. Free admission. Bus: 5, 25. Subway: Girard Ave. Map p 125.*

Theater of Living Arts SOUTH STREET Funk bands, French hip-hop acts, vintage Brit rockers, and all-American comedians fill the marquee of this bare-bones, standing-room-only venue, where big-time local acts like The Roots sell out fast. *334 South St. (btw. 3rd & 4th sts.). ☎ 215/922-1011. www.livenation.com. Tickets $22–$35. Bus: 40, 57. Map p 126.*

Rock bands play nightly at The Khyber.

Scoring Tickets

For week-of discounts, plus an up-to-date list of theatrical and artistic goings-on, visit the Greater Philadelphia Cultural Alliance's website at www.phillyfunguide.com or call ☎ **215/557-7811.** Tickets to the Philadelphia Orchestra, Pennsylvania Ballet, and Philadelphia Chamber Music Society can be had via Ticket Philadelphia ☎ **215/893-1999** or www.ticketphiladelphia.org, or purchased directly from the Kimmel Center's box office open daily until 6pm, later on performance nights *(see p 130)*, where a lucky few can score a single $10 "community rush" ticket at 5:30pm the night of an evening performance or 11:30am for a matinee performance.

★ **Tin Angel** OLD CITY Singer-songwriters are the bread and butter of this subdued upstairs space, starring folks like Melody Gardot, Amos Lee, The Trash Can Sinatras, and Jeffrey Gaines. There's an international restaurant downstairs, too. *20 S. 2nd St. (btw. Market & Chestnut sts.). ☎ 215/928-0978. www.tinangel.com. Tickets $10–$22. Bus: 5, 17, 21, 33, 42, 44, 121. Subway: 2nd St. Map p 126.*

★ **Tower Theatre** WEST PHILLY/UPPER DARBY All post-Depression-era gilt and scrollwork, this shabbily-majestic, 3,500-seat venue is a great spot to catch Tori Amos or Jill Scott. *19 S. 69th St. (btw. Market & Chestnut sts.). ☎ 610/352-2887. www.livenation.com. Tickets $35–$65. Subway: 69th St. Map p 126.*

★ **Trocadero** CHINATOWN Beneath the timeworn vaulted ceilings of this former vaudeville house, Goth acts, punk bands, and Lil' Kim have all performed. (Monday is movie night.) *1003 Arch St. (btw. 10th & 11th sts.). ☎ 215/922-6888. www.thetroc.com. Tickets $12–$24. Bus: 23, 48, 61. Map p 126.*

★★ kids **World Café Live** UNIVERSITY CITY Operated by Penn's indie music radio station, this multi-tasking venue offers a cafe stage and a two-level, 1,000-capacity space for concerts by They Might be Giants, BeauSoleil, Zap Mama, and kids' acts. *3025 Walnut St. (beyond Walnut St. Bridge). ☎ 215/222-1400. www.worldcafelive.com. Tickets $7–$35. Bus:21, 42. Map p 126.*

Cabaret

★★ **L'Etage** SOUTH STREET Upstairs from a *creperie* (*See p 102*), this red-curtained lounge-with-a-dance-floor offers a mixed bag of evening pleasures, from poetry slams to sketch comedy, Thursday night cabaret to DJs. *624 S. 6th St. (at Bainbridge St.). ☎ 215/592-0656. Cover Thurs–Sat $10. Bus: 40, 47. Map p 126.*

Comedy

★ **Helium Comedy Club** RITTENHOUSE Knowns (John Oliver, Rich Vos, and Kevin Pollack) and not-yet-knowns (Tues is open-mic night) take the stage in front of a friendly, small, table-sat crowd. *2031 Sansom St. (btw. 20th & 21st sts.). ☎ 215/496-9001. www.heliumcomedy.com. Tickets $10–$30. Bus: 9, 17, 21, 42. Map p 126.* ●

9 The Best Hotels

Hotel Best Bets

Best at **the Airport**
★ Aloft $$–$$$ *4301 Island Ave. (p 137)*

Best for **Kids**
★ Sheraton Society Hill $$–$$$ *1 Dock St. (p 142)*

Best for **Pets**
★★ Loews Philadelphia Hotel $$ *1200 Market St. (p 139)*

Best for **Beds**
★★ Westin Philadelphia $$$–$$$$ *99 S. 17th St. (p 142)*

Best for **a Splurge**
★★★ Four Seasons $$$$ *1 Logan Sq. (p 138)*

Best for **Views**
★ Hyatt Regency at Penn's Landing $$–$$$ *201 S. Columbus Blvd. (p 139)*

Best **Gym**
★★ Park Hyatt at the Bellevue $$$ *1415 Chancellor Ct. (p 140)*

Best for **a Long-Term Stay**
★★ AKA Rittenhouse Square $$$ *135 S. 18th St. (p 137)*

Best **Near the Convention Center**
★★ Four Points by Sheraton $$ *1201 Race St. (p 138)*

Best for **Celeb Spotting**
★★★ Rittenhouse Hotel $$$ *210 W. Rittenhouse Sq. (p 141)*

Best for **Glamour**
★★★ Ritz-Carlton Philadelphia *$$$–$$$$ 10 S. Broad St. (p 142)*

Best for **Couples**
★★ Penn's View Hotel $$ *Front & Market sts. (p 140)*

Best **Historic Lodging**
★★ Thomas Bond House $$ *129 S. 2nd St. (p 142)*

Best for **Bargain Rooms**
★ Alexander Inn $$ *301 S. 12th St. (p 137)*

Best **Bed & Breakfast**
★ Lippincott House $$ *2023–2025 Locust St. (p 139)*

The posh Ritz-Carlton Philadelphia.

Previous page: The Rittenhouse Hotel is an excellent place to spot celebs.

East of Broad Lodging

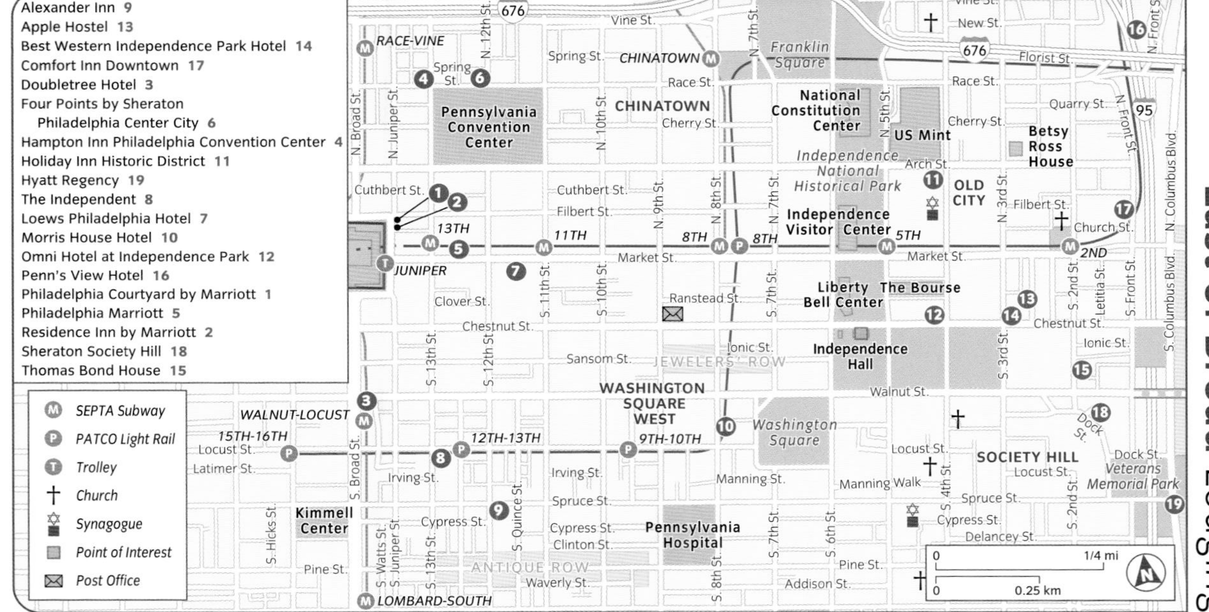

West of Broad Lodging

AKA Rittenhouse Square 8
Aloft Philadelphia 19
Club Quarters Philadelphia 14
Crowne Plaza Philadelphia Center City 5
Embassy Suites Center City 3
Four Seasons Hotel 1
Hotel Palomar 16
Hotel Sofitel 13
The Latham 9
Lippincott House 6
Park Hyatt at the Bellevue 17
Philadelphia Airport Marriott 18
Radisson Plaza—Warwick Hotel 10
Rittenhouse 1715 11
Rittenhouse Hotel 7
Ritz-Carlton Philadelphia 15
Sheraton Philadelphia Center City 2
Westin Philadelphia 12
Windsor Suites Philadelphia 4

Hotels A to Z

★★ AKA Rittenhouse Square RITTENHOUSE SQUARE Chic, just like its address, this all-suites spot is popular among discerning business travelers for week-long stays (although shorter-term stays are often available, too). *135 S. 18th St. (btw. Walnut & Sansom sts.). ☎ 888/252-0180 or 215/825-7000. www.hotelaka.com. 80 units. Suites $195–$265. AE, DISC, MC, V. Bus: 9, 12, 21, 42. Map p 136.*

★ Alexander Inn WASHINGTON WEST Simple little rooms—ask for one of the corners; they're bigger—help make this boutique gayborhood spot affordable and popular. *301 S. 12th St. (at Spruce St.). ☎ 877/253-9466 or 215/923-3535. www.alexanderinn.com. 48 units. Doubles from $129–$169 w/ breakfast. AE, DC, DISC, MC, V. Bus: 23, Alternate 40. Map p 135.*

★ Aloft Philadelphia AIRPORT A modern, lower-priced, fast-paced version of the glitzy W, with platform beds, Wi-Fi, and a 24-hour snack bar. *4301 Island Ave. (near I-95). ☎ 877/462-5638 or 267/298-1700. www.starwoodhotels.com. 136 units. Doubles $129–$279. AE, DC, MC, V. Bus: 68. Train: R1. Map p 136.*

Apple Hostel OLD CITY Dorm-style bunking, a TV lounge with billiards, shared baths, and Thursday night pub crawls with strangers, this place is like college, only cheaper. *32 S. Bank St. (btw. 2nd & 3rd sts., Market & Chestnut sts.). ☎ 800/392-4678 or 215/922-0222. www.applehostels.com. 70 beds. Beds $31–$82. MC, V. Bus: 5, 21, 42, 48. Subway: 2nd St. Map p 135.*

Best Western Independence Park Hotel OLD CITY A circa-1856 dry-goods store offers

The modern Aloft Philadelphia is a stylish alternative near the airport.

high-ceilinged quarters just two blocks from Independence Hall. *235 Chestnut St. (btw. 2nd & 3rd sts.). ☎ 800/624-2988 or 215/922-4443. www.independenceparkhotel.com. 36 units. Doubles $125–$319 w/ breakfast. AE, DC, DISC, MC, V. Bus: 5, 21, 42, 48. Subway: 2nd St. Map p 135.*

★ Club Quarters Philadelphia RITTENHOUSE Officially members-only on weeknights (non-members welcome weekends and holidays), this is a handsome, business-savvy boutique hotel. *1628 Chestnut St. (at 17th St.). ☎ 215/282-5000. www.clubquarters.com. Doubles $94–$169. AE, DC, DISC, MC, V. Bus: 2, 9, 21, 42. Map p 136.*

Comfort Inn Downtown PENN'S LANDING Students and seniors tend to frequent this basic spot, which feels a bit isolated from Old City but has great river views. *100 N. Columbus Blvd. (near Arch St.). ☎ 800/228-5150 or 215/627-7900.*

The Four Seasons Hotel has an outstanding lounge area.

www.comfortinn.com. 185 units. Doubles from $139. AE, DC, DISC, MC, V. Bus: 25, 48. Map p 135.

Crowne Plaza Philadelphia Center City RITTENHOUSE Airline pilots and conventioneers come for the large rooms and easy city access in a nonsense-free setting. *1800 Market St. (btw. 18th & 19th sts.). ☎ 800/980-6429 or 215/561-7500. www.cpphiladelphia.com. 445 units. Doubles $180–$220. AE, DC, MC, V. Bus: 17, 27, 31, 32, 33, 38, 44, 62, 121, 124, 125. Subway: 15th St. Map p 136.*

Doubletree Hotel MIDTOWN Location, location, location (and warm chocolate chip cookies): This business traveler's default has views to the Delaware River from higher floors. *237 S. Broad St. (at Locust St.). ☎ 800/222-8733 or 215/893-1600. www.doubletreehotels.com. 427 units. Doubles $144–$244. AE, DC, DISC, MC, V. Bus: C, 12, 27, 32. Subway: Walnut-Locust. Map p 135.*

★ Embassy Suites Center City LOGAN CIRCLE A cylindrical 1960s apartment building that's been converted to an all-suites hotel with balconies; nice for a longer stay. *1776 Ben Franklin Pkwy. (at 18th St.). ☎ 800/362-2779 or 215/561-5729. 288 units. Suites $195–$249 w/ breakfast. AE, DC, DISC, MC, V. Bus: 2, 32, 33, 48. Map p 136.*

★★ Four Points by Sheraton Philadelphia Center City CONVENTION CENTER The vibe, the bar, and the tiny rooms of a Manhattan boutique hotel; across the street from the Reading Terminal Market. *1201 Race St. (at 12th St.). ☎ 215/496-2700. www.starwoodhotels.com. 92 units. Doubles $155–$185. AE, DC, MC, V. Bus: 23, 48, 61. Subway: 13th St. Map p 135.*

★★★ Four Seasons Hotel LOGAN CIRCLE Top-notch service is the hallmark of this elegant and understated award winner, with a marvelous restaurant, lounge, and spa. *1 Logan Sq. (at 18th St. & Ben Franklin Pkwy.). ☎ 800/332-3442 or 215/963-1500. www.fourseasons.com. 365 units. Doubles $315–$395. AE, DC, MC, V. Bus: 32, 33, 48. Map p 136.*

Hampton Inn Philadelphia Convention Center MIDTOWN This reliable chain offers straightforward lodging, friendly service, and an indoor pool. *1301 Race St. (at 13th St.). ☎ 800/426-7866 or 215/665-9100. www.hamptoninn.com. 250 units. Doubles $129–$159 w/breakfast. AE, DC, DISC, MC, V. Bus: C, 23, 27, 48, 61. Subway: City Hall. Map p 135.*

Holiday Inn Historic District OLD CITY Nothing fancy: Just an easy-to-access, eight-floor hotel, convenient to historical sites, galleries, and shopping. There's a rooftop bar, too. *400 Arch St. (at 4th St.). ☎ 800/972-2796 or 215/923-8660. www.ichotelsgroup.com. 364 units. Doubles $139–$205. AE, DC, DISC, MC, V. Bus: 38, 44, 48, 57 121. Map p 135.*

★★ **Hotel Palomar** RITTENHOUSE Old Art Deco offices, now cozily contemporary and eco-minded, make up this boutique hotel from Kimpton. Most rooms have laptops. Many have great city views. *117 S. 17th St. (at Sansom St.). ☎ 888/725-1778 or 215/563-5006. www.kimptonhotels.com. 230 units. Doubles $159–$349. AE, DISC, MC, V. Bus: 2, 9, 12, 21, 42. Map p 136.*

★★ **Hotel Sofitel** RITTENHOUSE Low-key luxury, a "bonjour" at the door, and fresh croissants at breakfast; this French hotel is close to the city's poshest shopping and dining. *120 S. 17th St. (at Sansom St.). ☎ 800/763-4835 or 215/569-8300. www.sofitel.com. 306 units. Doubles $160–$285. AE, DC, MC, V. Bus: 2, 9, 12, 21, 42. Map p 136.*

Hotel Sofitel has numerous French influences.

★ kids **Hyatt Regency** PENN'S LANDING Your only waterfront option, this Art Deco–style complex boasts an indoor pool overlooking docked old ships and plenty of space for spreading out. *201 S. Columbus Blvd. (at Spruce St.) ☎ 800/233-1234 or 215/928-1234. www.pennslanding.hyatt.com. 350 units. Doubles $154–$299. AE, DC, MC, V. Bus: 25. Map p 135.*

★ **The Independent** MIDTOWN This Georgian Revival building has contemporary appointments, fireplaces in some rooms, and cathedral ceilings in others. It's in the heart of the gayborhood, near a somewhat shady-dealings corner. *1234 Locust St. (btw. 12th & 13th sts.). ☎ 215/772-1440. www.theindependenthotel.com. 24 units. Doubles $169–$184. AE, MC, V. Bus: C, 12, 23, 27, 32. Subway: Walnut-Locust. Map p 135.*

★ **The Latham** RITTENHOUSE A landmark hotel in the first half of the 20th century, this boutique spot brings to mind an efficiently run Swiss hostelry. *135 S. 17th St. (btw. Walnut & Sansom sts.). ☎ 877/528-4261 or 215/563-7474. www.lathamhotel.com. 139 units. Doubles $125–$189. AE, DC, DISC, MC, V. Bus: 2, 9, 12, 21, 42. Map p 136.*

★ **Lippincott House** RITTENHOUSE A pair of circa-1887 townhouses comprise this four-room B&B, which has elegant appointments (a baby grand), high-tech touches (Wi-Fi and satellite TVs), and lovely innkeepers. *2023–2025 Locust St. (btw. 20th & 21st sts.). ☎ 215/523-9251. www.lippincotthouse.com. 4 units. Doubles $199–$249 w/breakfast. AE, DISC, MC, V. Bus: 9, 12, 17, 21, 42. Map p 136.*

★ kids **Loews Philadelphia Hotel** MIDTOWN This hotel is beloved by aesthetes for its international style and Cartier wall clocks,

The boutique Morris House Hotel is located inside a former historic home.

adored by swimmers for its skyline-view pool, and children (and traveling pets) for its toy cache. Rooms tend to be small. *1200 Market St. (at 12th St.). ☎ 800/235-6397 or 215/627-1000. www.loewshotels.com. 581 units. Doubles $149–$199. AE, DC, DISC, MC, V. Bus: 17, 23, 33, 38, 44, 48, 62, 121. Subway: 13th St. Map p 135.*

★★ **Morris House Hotel** WASHINGTON SQUARE Antique portrait paintings, uneven floorboards, and afternoon tea add to the charm of this historic house-turned boutique hotel. Request a courtyard room to avoid street noise. *225 S. 8th St. (btw. Walnut & Locust sts.). ☎ 215/922-2446. www.morrishousehotel.com. 15 units. Doubles $159–$189 w/breakfast. AE, MC, V. Bus: 9, 12, 21, 42, 47. Map p 135.*

★ **Omni Hotel at Independence Park** OLD CITY A primo location for history buffs, this polished, pastel spot is across the street from Independence Park and has a staff known for its knowledge of the district. *401 Chestnut St. (at 4th St.). ☎ 888/444-6664 or 215/925-0000. www.omnihotels.com. 150 units. Doubles $211–$429. AE, DC, DISC, MC, V. Bus: 9, 21, 38, 42, 57. Subway: 5th St. Map p 135.*

★★ **Park Hyatt at the Bellevue** BROAD STREET Once the country's most opulent hotel (in 1904), this Hyatt keeps up-to-date with spacious rooms, goose-down duvets, and a great gym. *1415 Chancellor Ct. (on Broad St. btw. Walnut & Locust sts.). ☎ 800/223-1234 or 215/893-1234. www.parkphiladelphia.hyatt.com. 172 units. Doubles $212–$237. AE, DC, DISC, MC, V. Bus: C, 9, 12, 21, 27, 32, 42. Subway: Walnut-Locust. Map p 136.*

★★ **Penn's View Hotel** OLD CITY This hidden gem has European, family-run appeal—and a fantastic wine bar (*See p 122*). *Front & Market sts. ☎ 800/331-7634 or 215/922-7600. www.pennsviewhotel.com. 51 units. Doubles $149–$199 w/breakfast. AE, MC, V. Bus: 5, 17, 48. Subway: 2nd St. Map p 135.*

★ **Philadelphia Airport Marriott** AIRPORT If you're stuck at the airport and have just a few hours to sleep, this is the quiet, connected place to do it. *1 Arrivals Rd. (via skywalk to PHL Airport). ☎ 800/628-4087 or 215/492-9000. www.marriott.com. 419 units. Doubles $99–$329. AE, DC, DISC, MC, V. Bus: 68. Train: R1. Map p 136.*

★★ **Philadelphia Courtyard by Marriott** MIDTOWN This is my favorite of the trio of Convention Center-ed Marriotts because of its circa-1926 setting and City Hall view. *21 N. Juniper St. (at Broad & Filbert sts.). ☎ 800/321-2211 or 215/496-3200. www.marriott.com. 498 units. Doubles $129–$239. AE, DC, DISC, MC, V. Bus: C, 10, 11, 13, 17, 27, 31, 32, 33, 34, 36, 44, 48, 62, 121, 124, 125. Subway: City Hall or 13th St. Map p 135.*

Philadelphia Marriott MIDTOWN The biggest in town, this high-tech hotel is attached via skyway to the Pennsylvania Convention Center. It often books to capacity with business folk. *1201 Market St. (btw. 12th & 13th sts.). ☎ 800/228-9290 or 215/625-2900. www.marriott.com. 1,409 units. Doubles $149–$289. AE, DC, MC, V. Bus: 17, 23, 33, 38, 44, 48, 61, 62, 121. Subway: 13th St. Map p 135.*

★★ **Radisson Plaza—Warwick Hotel** RITTENHOUSE Windows that open are among the simple yet lovely amenities of this history-touched half-condo, half-hotel. *1701 Locust St. (at 17th St.). ☎ 800/395-7046 or 215/735-6000. www.radisson.com. 301 units. Doubles $139–$239. AE, DC, DISC, MC, V. Bus: 2, 9, 12, 21, 42. Map p 136.*

Residence Inn by Marriott MIDTOWN This suites-only spot is surprisingly quiet, considering its central location. It also has a high-tech fitness center. *1 E. Penn Sq. (at Broad & Market sts.). ☎ 215/557-0005. www.marriott.com. 269 units. Suites $139–$219 w/breakfast. AE, DC, MC, V. Bus: C, 10, 11, 13, 17, 27, 31, 32, 33, 34, 36, 44, 48, 62, 121, 124, 125. Subway: City Hall or 13th St. Map p 135.*

★★ **Rittenhouse 1715** RITTENHOUSE In a city mansion on a leafy little street, this traditional, boutique-y spot has a European vibe. *1715 Rittenhouse Sq. (btw. 17th & 18th sts.). ☎ 877/791-6500 or 215/546-6500. www.rittenhouse1715.com. 23 units. Doubles $249–$699 w/breakfast. AE, DC, MC, V. Bus: 2, 12, 21, 42. Map p 136.*

★★★ kids **Rittenhouse Hotel** RITTENHOUSE This hotel is all suites with a restaurant overlooking the treetops of Rittenhouse Square,

The Park Hyatt at the Bellevue was once the country's most opulent hotel.

an amazing gym, salon, and spa. Jack Nicholson stays here when he's in town. *210 W. Rittenhouse Sq. (btw. Locust & Walnut sts.). ☎ 800/635-1042 or 215/546-9000. www.rittenhousehotel.com. 98 units. Suites $199–$500. AE, DC, MC, V. Bus: 9, 12, 17, 21, 42. Map p 136.*

★★★ **Ritz-Carlton Philadelphia** MIDTOWN This all-marble former bank has butlered bath service and a lounge located inside a former vault. It's *very* posh. *10 S. Broad St. (btw. City Hall & Chestnut St.). ☎ 800/241-3333 or 215/523-8000. www.ritzcarlton.com. 299 units. Doubles $259–$409. AE, DC, DISC, MC, V. Bus: C, 9, 17, 21, 27, 31, 32, 33, 38, 42, 44, 48, 62, 121, 124, 125. Subway: City Hall. Map p 136.*

Sheraton Philadelphia Center City FAIRMOUNT As big as a city block, this one feels like a cross between a convention center and a cruise ship. *17th & Race sts. ☎ 800/325-3535 or 215/448-2000. www.sheraton.com. 759 units. Doubles $95–$249. AE, DC, MC, V. Bus: 2, 32. Map p 136.*

★ kids **Sheraton Society Hill** OLD CITY On a curvy cobblestone street, this short, sprawling spot offers traditional rooms, a lush atrium, and a splashy indoor pool. *1 Dock St. (at 2nd & Walnut sts.). ☎ 800/325-3535 or 215/238-6000. www.sheraton.com/societyhill. 365 units. Doubles $179–$269. AE, DC, MC, V. Bus: 21, 42. Subway: 2nd St. Map p 135.*

★★ **Thomas Bond House** OLD CITY Named for its first occupant (co-founder of Pennsylvania Hospital), Thomas Bond (1712–1784), this cheerful, colonial B&B is as historic as a Philly overnight gets. *129 S. 2nd St. (btw. Chestnut & Walnut sts.). ☎ 800/845-2663 or 215/923-8523. www.thomasbondhousebandb.com. 12 units. Doubles $115–$190 w/ breakfast. AE, DISC, MC, V. Bus: 21, 42. Subway: 2nd St. Map p 135.*

★★ **Westin Philadelphia** RITTENHOUSE Handsomely clubby atmosphere—with the best beds in town—is tucked into one of Philadelphia's iconic skyscrapers. *99 S. 17th St. (btw. Market & Sansom sts.). ☎ 800/228-3000 or 215/563-1600. www.westin.com. 290 units. Doubles $229–$409. AE, DISC, MC, V. Bus: 2, 9, 17, 21, 31, 32, 33, 38, 42, 48, 62, 121, 124, 125. Subway: 15th St. Map p 136.*

kids **Windsor Suites Philadelphia** LOGAN CIRCLE Great for families whose kids don't mind sleeping on a pull-out sofa, this bargain-priced, all-suites offering isn't super fancy, but it's really close to the museums. *1700 Ben Franklin Pkwy. (at 17th St.). ☎ 877/784-8379 or 215/981-5600. www.windsorhotel.com. Suites from $109–$189. AE, DC, DISC, MC, V. Bus: 32, 33, 48. Map p 136.* ●

The historic Thomas Bond House is a cheerful B&B.

10 The Best Day Trips & Excursions

The Best of Brandywine Valley

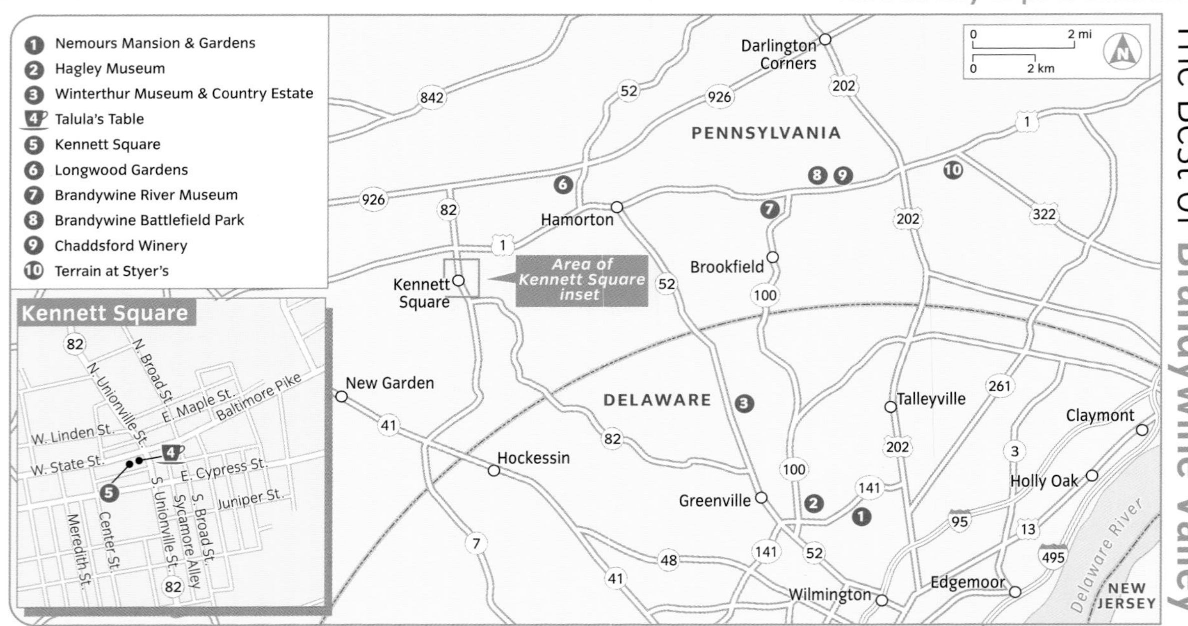

Previous page: An Amish horse-and-buggy travels through Lancaster County.

The bucolic, historic countryside around the Brandywine River in Delaware has largely been defined by its two most famous families: First came the entrepreneurial, elegant, and munificent du Ponts. Next, the earthy, cerebral, prolific, and certainly artistic Wyeths. See this region, and you'll see them, and then some. START: **I-95 S for about 23 miles to Wilmington, then 82 to Kennett Sq., then Baltimore Pike (Rt. 1) to Longwood & Chadds Ford; the drive takes approx. 1 hr.**

1 Nemours Mansion & Gardens. To experience the opulence of Alfred I. du Pont's circa-1910, Louis XVI-style chateau and Petit-Trianon–modeled garden with its 23-karat gold statuary, reserve the required guided tour well in advance. *2 hrs. 1600 Rockland Rd., Wilmington, DE. ☎ 302/651-6912. www.nemoursmansion.org. Free admission. May 1–Dec 31; Closed Jan 1–Apr 30. Tues–Sat tours 9 & 11am, 1 & 3pm; Sun 11am, 1 & 3pm.*

2 ★★ Hagley Museum. More du Pont acreage (235 acres) offers an industrial workmen's community, wisteria-covered Georgian manse, and an ancestral home and gardens. *1 hr. Rte. 141 (200 Hagley Rd.), Wilmington, DE. ☎ 302/658-2400. www.hagley.org. Admission $11 adults, $9 seniors & students, $4 children 6–14. Mid-Mar to Dec daily 9:30am–4:30pm; Jan to mid-Mar Sat–Sun 9:30am–4:30pm.*

3 ★★★ kids Winterthur Museum & Country Estate. Yet another du Pont estate, this one has the country's foremost collection of American decorative arts, including gems from every Eastern seaboard colony: a Montmorenci stair hall, two Shaker rooms, and a grand dining hall. In spring, extensive gardens bloom with azaleas. Year round, kids can explore a 3-acre "enchanted woods." And from March to Christmas, weather permitting, tram tours are offered. Christmastime is busiest, with splendid holiday trimmings. All year, the two gift shops are fabulous. *1 hr. Rte. 52., Winterthur, DE ☎ 800/448-3883 or 302/888-4600. www.winterthur.org. Admission $18 adults, $16 seniors & students, $5 children 2–11. Mar 8–Feb 1 Tues–Sat 10am–5pm, Sun noon–5pm (also Mon 10am–5pm, Fri 10am–8:30pm Thanksgiving–New Year's). Closed Feb 1–Mar 8.*

Winterthur Museum & Country Estate has America's foremost collection of decorative arts.

4 ★★★ **Talula's Table.** This charming country market sells artisan cheeses, homemade soups, petite sandwiches, awesome fruit tarts, and coffee. (Come for lunch; scoring the sole dinner table is next to impossible.) *102 W. State St. ☎ 610/444-8255. www.talulastable.com. $–$$.*

5 ★★ **Kennett Square.** First inhabited by the Lenape Native American tribe, this village became a stopover during the Revolutionary War, then home to free Quakers who established safe havens along the Underground Railroad. A short walk around the historic borough—from State Street to Union, then Mulberry, then back up Broad Street—reveals Queen Anne, Gothic Revival, Italianate, and Tudor architecture. There are plenty of shops. If you dine here, order anything with mushrooms; Kennett Square is the "mushroom capital of the world." Local farmers produce more than a million delicious pounds of fungi each year. *1 hr. Historic Kennett Square Visitors Center, 106 W. State St., Kennett Square, PA. ☎ 610/444-8188. www.historickennettsquare.com.*

6 ★★★ kids **Longwood Gardens.** One of the world's greatest gardens owes its existence to Pierre S.—you guessed it—du Pont, who devoted his life to horticulture and turned a 19th century arboretum into the ultimate 1,050-acre green estate with its own visitor center to get you oriented. Among the must-see attractions: The "main garden fountain," which has special water shows June to September Thursday to Saturday evenings, and a nearby topiary garden surrounding a 37-foot sundial. Four acres of bronze and glass conservatory include the Orangery, practically overflowing with African violets, century-old bonsai trees, tropicals, seasonal plants, and visiting collections—they're just a sampling of Longwood's holdings. Almost everywhere, the "no-touching" rule applies, except in a 3,000-square-foot children's garden, with 17 splash fountains, two mazes, a grotto, and umpteen kid-friendly plants. Du Pont's lovely country residence offers a "heritage" collection that includes 2,000-year-old Native American spear points. Although springtime is a pleasant time to visit, winter holidays are marvelous, too, with strolling carolers, pipe organ and ice-skating performances, and (naturally) decorated trees galore. *1½ hrs. 1001 Longwood Rd. (at Rte. 1), Kennett Square. ☎ 800/737-5500 or 610/388-1000. www.longwoodgardens.org. Admission $16 adults, $14 seniors, $6 students, free for children 4 & under. Sept–Mar daily 9am–5pm; Apr–Aug 9am–6pm.*

The estate at Longwood Gardens is over 1,000 acres.

The Brandywine River Museum displays art from the Wyeth family collection.

7 ★★ Brandywine River Museum. Art by three generations of Wyeths—N.C., Carolyn, Andrew, and Jamie, all locals—are on display at this 19th-century gristmill. (If you're lucky, you can see this work via Victoria Wyeth, Andrew's granddaughter, who leads tours Mon–Sat at 2 and 3pm.) The museum also offers off-site tours (via shuttle bus, and for an additional $5) of N.C.'s house and studio, and the Kuerner Farm, where Andrew found so much inspiration. On-site are other generally soothing illustrations, still life, and landscape painting by American artists. ⌚ *1 hr. Rte. 1 & Rte. 100, Chadds Ford.* ☎ *610/388-2700. www.brandywinemuseum.org. Admission $8 adults, $5 seniors & students, free for children 5 & under. Daily 9:30am–4:30pm.*

8 ★ Brandywine Battlefield Park. Great for a hike, this site hosted a rare full-army clash between Continental and British troops in September 1777 and has a replica of Washington and Lafayette's headquarters. ⌚ *½ hr. 1491 Baltimore Pike (Rte. 1), Chadds Ford.* ☎ *610/459-3342. www.ushistory.org/brandywine. Free admission to grounds; house $5 adults, $3.50 seniors, $2.50 children 6–17. Tues–Sat 9am–4:30pm, Sun noon–4:30pm.*

9 Chaddsford Winery. This 17th-century barn, surrounded by 300 mineral-rich acres, is the closest Pennsylvania gets to Napa. The friendly vintners offer free tastings and cellar tours, allow picnicking, and host al fresco blues bands on Friday evenings in late summer. ⌚ *1 hr. 632 Baltimore Pike (Rte. 1), Chadds Ford.* ☎ *610/388-6221. www.chaddsford.com. Daily noon–6pm.*

10 ★★ Terrain at Styer's. This park-like, Urban Outfitters–owned garden center sells everything from tiny succulents to major trees, with plenty of organic lotions and shelter finds in between. ⌚ *1 hr. 914 Baltimore Pike, Glen Mills.* ☎ *610/459-2400. www.terrainathome.com. Mon–Fri 9am–6pm, Sat 8am–6pm, Sun 9am–5pm.*

Terrain at Styer's is a garden center owned by Urban Outfitters.

The Best of Lancaster County

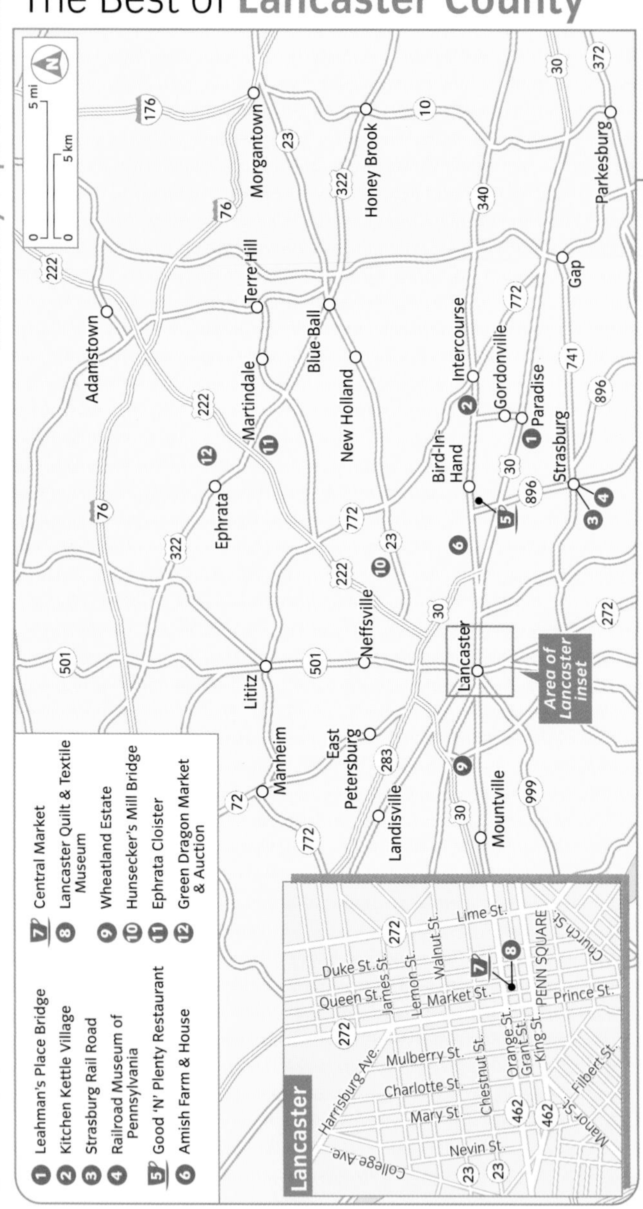

Though it's less than 60 miles from Philadelphia, farm-rich Lancaster County feels ages away. This is mostly because of the region's thousands of Amish residents, who, in the most general terms, live off the land in a devout fashion that shuns many modern ways, choosing horse and buggies over cars, nature over technology, plain over fancy. START: **PA Turnpike (76-W) to Rte. 30; the drive should take approx. 1 hr. during non-rush-hour times.**

1 ★ Leahman's Place Bridge. Also known as Eshleman's Mill or Paradise Bridge, this painted-red covered wooden bridge stands amid cornfields and farms, a pastoral introduction to a pastoral region. Drive slowly: There's only one lane, and, according to lore, a kiss along the span brings good luck. ◷ *¼ hr. Belmont Rd. & Rte. 30.*

2 kids Kitchen Kettle Village. A first pit stop for shoppers: This friendly, countrified (and slightly kitschy) outdoor mall has a few dozen vendors of quilts, crafts, homemade jams, relishes, and ice cream. ◷ *½ hr. Old Philadelphia Pike, Rte. 340, Intercourse.* ☎ *800/732-3538 or 717/768-8261. www.kitchenkettle.com. Nov–Apr Mon–Sat 9am–5pm; May–Oct Mon–Sat 9am–6pm.*

3 ★ kids Strasburg Rail Road. Book an all-day pass for a 45-minute ride in an old-fashioned train from this circa-1832 station through the countryside. Your purchase also earns you entry to train-themed amusements and attractions, such as a circa-1885 switch tower, working vintage pump car, mechanical shop, and a hand-propelled 1930s "cranky car." On occasion, a full-size Thomas-brand tank engine shows up to offer rides to young fans. On other occasions, the trains offer wine and cheese rides to slightly more mature riders. ◷ *1½ hr. Rte. 741-East, Strasburg.* ☎ *717/687-7522. www.strasburgrailroad.com. First class fare $20 adults, $15 children 3–11, free children under 3 years. Mid-Mar to Nov & Dec 26–31 daily; Feb to mid-Mar weekends, Hours vary, usually noon–5pm.*

4 kids Railroad Museum of Pennsylvania. Need more train? Cross the street to this history-rich display, where dozens of stationary engines tell the tale of America's preferred transit of yore. ◷ *½ hr. Rtes. 896 & 741-East, Strasburg.* ☎ *717/687-8628. www.rrmuseumpa.org. Admission $10 adults, $9*

The 45-minute ride on the Strasburg Rail Road departs from a station circa 1832.

Etiquette for the "English"

To the typically friendly, gently private Christian Amish—who are locally divided into Amish, Brethren, and Mennonite sects—any non-member of their societies is "English." The preservation of their "plain" way of life is paramount to their existence. Visitors should drive with great caution, especially along roads frequented by horse-and-buggies. No photos, either: Photography violates religious rules. Trespassing upon private homes, farms, schoolhouses, and religious grounds is as forbidden here as it is anywhere. And, although the Amish are most likely used to being stared at, it might be nice if you didn't.

seniors, $8 children 3–11. Apr–Oct Mon–Sat 9am–5pm, Sun noon–5pm (closed Mon Nov–Mar).

5 Stick-to-yer-ribs country grubbing is the name of the game in these parts. Diners sit at tables for 10 or 12 to dig into family-style fried chicken, chow chow, and shoofly pie at **★★ Good 'N' Plenty Restaurant.** *Rte. 896 (btw. Rtes. 340 and 30), Smoketown; ☎ 717/394-7111; $$.*

6 ★ kids Amish Farm & House. Outsiders (or "English") are, respectfully, unwelcome trespassers upon Amish farms, and inside Amish homes or schoolhouses. The next best thing is to visit this facsimile thereof. This attraction's location—sandwiched between a Target and a strip mall—may seem quite odd, but tune out the suburban surroundings, and the experience feels sublimely authentic. Basic admission includes access to a 204-year-old, 10-room formerly Amish-owned house, a newer one-room schoolhouse, old covered bridge, and 15-acre farm with live animals. *1½ hr. 2395 Lincoln Hwy., Lancaster. ☎ 717/394-6185. www.amishfarmandhouse.com. Admission $7.95 adults, $7.25 seniors, $5.25 children 5–11. Apr–May daily 8:30am–5pm; June–Aug daily 8:30am–6pm; Nov–Mar daily 8:30am–4pm.*

The replica Amish Farm & House feels sublimely authentic.

7 **★★ Central Market.** In the heart of Lancaster, the nation's oldest farmer's market—housed in a stunning Romanesque Revival building—offers 80 stalls of local delicacies, from sweet bologna to shoofly pie to scrapple to schnitzel to whoopie pies. (Don't ask. Just eat.) *23 N. Market St., Lancaster. ☎ 717/735-6890. $–$$.*

The Lancaster Quilt & Textile Museum is located inside a bank built in 1912.

8 ★★ **Lancaster Quilt & Textile Museum.** Nearby, a 1912 Beaux Arts bank—with a very modern addition—houses one of the world's finest collections of hand-wrought, American textile art. For centuries Amish women have communed and collaborated in creating symbolic, geometrically patterned quilts, quietly proving their community is anything but "plain." Established in 2004, the museum is a branch of the nearby Heritage Center, the region's cultural objects museum, displaying Amish toys, printmaking, decorative objects, and folk art (5 W. King St., www.heritagecentermuseum.com). *1 hr. 37 Market St., Lancaster. ☎ 717/299-6440. www.quiltandtextilemuseum.com. Admission $9 adults, $4 students, free children 17 & under. Mon–Sat 9am–5pm (first Fri of month until 9pm).*

Hershey Park Happy

The "sweetest place on Earth" is just a 30 minute drive from downtown Lancaster. At the turn of the 20th century, chocolate-bar-maker Milton Hershey became Pennsylvania's Walt Disney. His eponymous town features chocolate kiss lampposts, a **Chocolate World** for tastings and factory tours (251 Park Blvd.; ☎ **717/534-4900;** www.hersheys.com/chocolateworld), and if the wind is blowing in the right direction, air scented of cocoa. Today, however, the main attraction is 110-acre ★★ kids **Hersheypark** (Rtes. 743 and 422; ☎ **800/HERSHEY [800/437-7439]** or 717/534-3900; www.hersheypark.com), a family-friendly amusement park featuring a dozen roller coasters—including the marvelous wooden Comet—a full-fledged zoo, a water-play area, and al fresco concerts (for performances that are more Rick Springfield than Jonas Brothers). Hersheypark is open daily from May to early September, and the zoo is open year-round. Admission costs $52 for adults, $31 for ages 3 to 8 and 55 to 69, $21 for seniors 70 or over, and it's free for ages 2 and under. For overnights—and more grown-up pleasures (read: "Chocolate Spa")—book a room at the elegant and historic ★★★ **Hotel Hershey** (100 Hotel Rd., Hershey; ☎ **717/533-2171;** www.thehotelhershey.com; 278 units; doubles $353; AE, DC, DISC, MC, V).

Wheatland Estate is a mansion formerly owned by President James Buchanan.

9 ★ Wheatland Estate. About 2 miles west is the gracious Federal mansion and arboretum of James Buchanan, the 15th U.S. president. Costumed guides offer hour-long tours. *1 hr. 1120 Marietta Ave., Rte. 23, Lancaster. ☎ 717/392-8721. www.lancasterhistory.org. Admission $8 adults, $7 seniors, $6 students, $3 children 6–11. Apr–Oct Tues–Sat 10am–4pm; Nov–Dec Fri–Sat 10am–4pm; Jan–Mar by appt.*

10 Hunsecker's Mill Bridge. Photo op! The country's longest single-span covered bridge (180 ft) divides two townships and turns Hunsecker Road into Hunsicker Road. Think of it as Lancaster's version of the equator. (No word on whether smooching along the span brings good luck, but it can't hurt as long as you drive carefully, right?) *¼ hr. Mondale & Hunsecker rds., (1 mile southeast of Rte. 272; ½ mile north of Rte. 23), Upper Leacock & Manheim townships.*

11 ★ Ephrata Cloister. Like the Pyramids, the austere structures of this 18th-century society were built with nary a nail. In the 1720s, Conrad Beissel moved from Germany to Pennsylvania to establish a monastic version of Christianity. Unfortunately, Beissel's rules about celibacy weren't a strong selling feature. He died in 1768, and the cloister's members soon became German Seventh Day Adventists. See how these folks lived, alone and apart. Pay special detail to their beautiful *frakturschriften* (calligraphy used in printmaking), pottery, and book binding. *1½ hr. 633 W. Main St., Ephrata (near junction of rtes. 272 & 322). ☎ 717/733-6600. www.ephratacloister.org. Mar–Dec Mon–Sat 9am–5pm, Sun noon–5pm;*

The austere Ephrata Cloister was built without the use of a single nail.

Fridays are the time to stop at the Green Dragon Market & Auction.

Jan–Feb Wed–Sat 9am–5pm, Sun noon–5pm.

⑫ ★★★ **Green Dragon Market & Auction.** If it's Friday, make sure you stop at this super giant, super authentic spread of 400 stalls manned by growers, merchants, and artisans; an auction house for hay and small animals, and (weather permitting) an outdoor flea market and arcade. It's a true taste of rural America, Pennsylvania Dutch–style. (And you just might find yourself driving home with a gal named "Bessy" in tow.) 🕘 ***1 hr. 955 N. State St. (at Garden Spot Rd.). ☎ 717/738-1117. www.greendragonmarket.com. Fri 9am–9pm.***

Country Sleepovers

With towns named Paradise and Lititz, who wouldn't want to spend the night? Favorite rooms include the modern suites in the 1790 farmhouse at the ★ **Best Western Revere Inn** (3063 Lincoln Hwy./Rte. 30, Paradise; ☎ **800/429-7383** or 717/687-7683; www.revereinn.com; 95 units; doubles $70–$130 w/breakfast; AE, DC, DISC, MC, V). A great outdoor pool, playground, and pet-friendly policies make the ★ **Historic Strasburg Inn** (1 Historic Dr., Strasburg; ☎ **800/872-0201** or 717/687-7691; www.historicinnofstrasburg.com; 102 units; doubles $109; AE, DC, DISC, MC, V), a great B&B for the whole family, including Fido. Slightly more romantic—and in the heart of Lancaster's historic district—is the modernized Victorian manse of the ★ **Alden House** (62 E. Main St.; ☎ **800/584-0753** or 717/627-3363; www.aldenhouse.com; 6 units; doubles $99–$130; AE, DISC, MC, V). Guests choose from modern or traditional suites—from Jacuzzis to stained-glass windows—in the two vintage homes that comprise ★★ **The Inns at Doneckers** (322 N. State St., near rtes. 322 and 222, Ephrata; ☎ **717/738-9502;** www.doneckers.com; 31 units; doubles $75–$125; AE, DC, DISC, MC, V).

The Best of Atlantic City

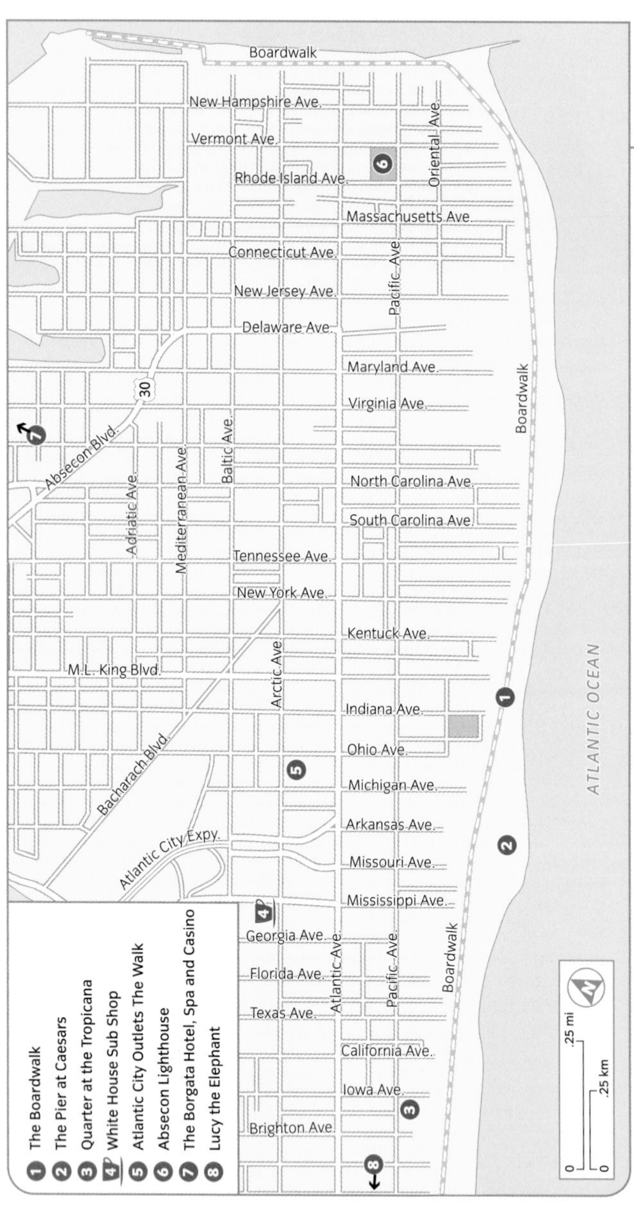

At some point in every Philadelphian's life, he or she believes a midnight road trip to A.C. is an absolutely brilliant idea. And why not? New Jersey's own Vegas-by-the-sea is one big neon-lit, adults-only, all-night party (sort of). And if the casinos don't take your money, the shopping, spas, and steakhouses will. Beach? What beach? START: **Ben Franklin Bridge to 42-South to Atlantic City Expressway; driving time is approx. 1 hr.**

1 The Boardwalk. Once a fashionable seaside pedestrian thoroughfare, A.C.'s wooden 4-mile Boardwalk has taken a decades-long turn for the seedy, with little to recommend but a view of the Atlantic, a ride in a rolling chair, and salt water taffy—for that, go to historic Fralinger's (Park Place and the Boardwalk; ☎ 609/344-0758; www.fralingers.com), preserved in Bally's. 🕘 *½ hr. Along Pacific Ave. & ocean.*

2 ★ The Pier at Caesars. This glamorously rehabbed pier stretches from Caesars Palace out into the Atlantic via high-end shops—Gucci, Judith Ripka, Burberry, Louis Vuitton, Scoop—usual mall suspects—Banana Republic, Juicy Couture, Kenneth Cole—and clever shopping surprises—a very Willy Wonka candy store, a Starbucks with an ocean view—that terminate in a fountain-and-music-show that occurs every half hour. Restaurants and bars fill the third floor: chic Asian-fusion, retro-fun dining, a big wine bar and bistro, basic seafoodery, a mammoth sports bar, and a nearly cozy Irish pub. 🕘 *2 hr. 1 Atlantic Ocean (btw. Arkansas & Missouri aves.). ☎ 609/345-3100. www.thepiershopsatcaesars.com. Hrs. vary; shops generally open from 11am–8pm.*

3 The Quarter at the Tropicana. Before Caesars had the Pier, the Trop had the Quarter, a vaguely Havana-themed indoor mall with a big Irish pub, even bigger Cuban restaurant and dance club, a little karaoke bar, an IMAX movie theater, and a chic spa. 🕘 *1 hr. 2801 Pacific Ave. (at Iowa Ave.). ☎ 800/843-8767. www.tropicana.net. Hrs. vary.*

4 ★ White House Sub Shop. A local institution, known for its bread (baked across the street at Formica Bros.), cheesesteaks, tuna hoagies, celebrity visits, fast pace, and line out the door. *2301 Arctic Ave. (at Mississippi Ave.). ☎ 609/345-1564. $–$$*

The Quarter at the Tropicana is an indoor mall with a loose Havana theme.

5 Atlantic City Outlets The Walk. A discount strip mall with off-price outlets for Nike, Coach, J. Crew, Ralph Lauren, and the Gap. They're just a couple of blocks away from the Boardwalk (behind Caesars), close to the train station and the bus depot. Shopping is obviously the attraction here, but if you prefer beer to bargains, head to the big brewpub the Tun Tavern. *1 hr. Atlantic Ave. to Bacharach Blvd., Arkansas to Indiana aves. ☎ 609/872-7002. www.acoutlets.com. Daily Jan 2–Mar 8 10am–7pm; Mar 9–May 31 10am–8pm; Jun 1–Sept 10 9am–9pm, Sept 11–Jan 1 10am–8pm.*

6 ★ Absecon Lighthouse. One of A.C. rare seashore attractions is NJ's tallest lighthouse. Climb all 228 steps, watch gulls circle overhead, and see clear to England. Sort of. *1 hr. 31 Rhode Island Ave. (at Pacific Ave.). ☎ 609/449-1360. www.abseconlighthouse.org. Admission $7 adults, $4 children. Sept–June Thurs–Mon 11am–4pm; July–Aug daily 10am–5pm.*

The Borgata is a mix of hotel, spa, and casino.

7 ★★ The Borgata Hotel, Spa and Casino. This golden bayside property most closely resembles what casinos advertise themselves to be: glamorous, flashy, and fun. Decked out in Dale Chihuly (1941–) chandeliers, sequined-dressed nightclub-goers, and restaurants from Michael Mina, Bobby Flay, and Wolfgang Puck, the Borgata attracts its fair share of torpid slots players, but it's got the most high rollers in town, too. The gaming floor seems to be recession-proof, with an overflowing poker room and plenty of blackjack tables (though very few $5-limit ones). Hotel rooms here aren't cheap, but they're pretty and clean and splurge-worthy, as is a day at Immersion, the elevated spa in the Water Club, the newer tower. *2 hrs. 1 Borgata Way (Exit 1 from Expressway). ☎ 888/692-6742 or 609/317-1000. www.theborgata.com. Open 24 hours daily.*

8 ★★★ kids Lucy the Elephant. Before you skip town, head south about 5 miles to see Lucy, a circa-1882, six-story, wooden, "elephantine colossus" folly, now a museum, playground, and great photo-op. *1 hr. 9200 Atlantic Ave. (btw. Decatur St. & Washington Ave.), Margate. ☎ 609/823-6473. www.lucytheelephant.org. Admission $6 adults, $3 children. Mid-June to early Sept Mon–Sat 10am–8pm, Sun 10am–5pm.*

The Savvy Traveler

Before You Go

Government Tourist Offices

Philadelphia Convention and Visitors Bureau (1515 Market St., Ste. 2020; ☎ 800/325-5745 or 215/636-3300; www.philadelphiausa.travel); **Visit Pennsylvania** (☎ 800/847-4872; www.visitpa.com).

The Best Time to Go

Summer is the height of tourism season, especially around historic attractions. Late July through August, be prepared to swelter in line for Independence Hall. (On the other hand, summer is the best time to score a table at a trendy restaurant.) Fall and winter offer the lowest prices on hotel rooms. Spring weather is often peculiar—hot one day, chilly the next—but late May and early June are usually best for garden buffs. Times to avoid: During the University of Pennsylvania's graduation—always mid-May.

Festivals and Special Events

JAN. New Year's Day means the debauched, odd, day-long ***Mummer's Parade*** (☎ 215/336-3040; www.mummers.com) along Broad Street.

FEB. Mid-to-late month, Chinatown pops and sparkles with a ***Chinese New Year*** celebration (☎ 215/923-6767; www.chinesecc.com) on its streets and in its restaurants.

MAR. The ***Philadelphia Flower Show*** (☎ 800/611-5960; www.theflowershow.com) is the largest indoor exhibit of its kind. Go early for the freshest displays. Expect crowds.

APR. For 5 days, 15,000 of the country's best college, high school, and track club runners (and 100,000 spectators) descend upon Franklin Field for the exuberant ***Penn Relays*** (☎ 215/898-6145; www.thepennrelays.com), the country's largest and oldest track-and-field meet.

MAY On a (hopefully) sunny Saturday, some 50,000 celebrants turn out for the **Rittenhouse Row Spring Festival** (www.rittenhouserow.org), a block party gone chic, thanks to dozens of outdoor kiosks offering haute cuisine and sublime shopping.

JUNE Early in the month, bars and breweries host beer-centric events for the ***Philly Beer Week*** (www.phillybeerweek.com) showcasing suds both local and exotic. There's no better place to celebrate ***Flag Day*** (June 14) than Old City's ***Betsy Ross House*** (☎ 215/686/1252; www.betsyrosshouse.org).

JULY The week around Independence Day (July 4) absolutely bustles with a citywide festival called ***Welcome America!*** (☎ 215/683-2200; www.americasbirthday.com), a week of ice cream socials, outdoor movies, and concerts and performances galore, culminating in fireworks over Penn's Landing and the Philadelphia Museum of Art.

AUG. The Reading Terminal Market's weeklong ***Pennsylvania Dutch Festival*** (☎ 215/922-2317; www.readingterminalmarket.org) features quilts, music, crafts, and shoofly pie.

Previous page: Tourists ride Segway i2 Gliders near the Philadelphia Museum of Art.

AVERAGE MONTHLY TEMPERATURES

	JAN	FEB	MAR	APR	MAY	JUNE
High °F/°C	40/4	41/5	50/10	62/17	72/23	81/29
Low °F/°C	26/-3	26/-3	33/1	43/6	53/12	63/17
	JULY	AUG	SEPT	OCT	NOV	DEC
High °F/°C	85/29	83/28	77/25	66/19	54/12	43/6
Low °F/°C	68/20	66/19	60/16	49/9	39/4	29/-2

SEPT. Inspired by the cutting-edge Scottish arts extravaganza of the same name, the ***Philadelphia Live Arts Festival and Philly Fringe Festival*** (☎ 215/413-9006; www.livearts-fringe.org) offers 2 weeks in early September of experimental theater and more in and beyond Old City.

OCT. All manner of fine artists let the public into their workspaces during the two-weekends-long ***Philadelphia Open Studio Tours*** (☎ 215/546-7775; www.philaopenstudios.org).

NOV. ***Philadelphia Museum of Art Craft Show*** (☎ 215/683-2122; www.philamuseum.org) shows off the work of local and international artisans in the Convention Center.

DEC. The biggest, most historic of military sporting events, the ***Army-Navy game*** (☎ 877/TIX-ARMY or 877/US-4-NAVY; www.armynavy.com) is a grand tradition come early December. So is the big ***holiday light and music show***—practically a rite of passage among local kids—at Macy's in the brilliant old John Wanamaker Building (☎ 215/241-9000; www.macys.com).

The Weather

Philadelphia's mid-Atlantic climate produces cold and often gray winters, cool and sometimes rainy springs, hot and typically humid summers, and mild and crisp falls. Just like the seasons in kids' books.

Restaurant and Theater Reservations

Though a few notable BYOB restaurants are first-come, first-served, most larger restaurants accept reservations by phone or via the Internet at Open Table (www.opentable.com). For performances by the Philadelphia Orchestra, the Pennsylvania Ballet, Philadelphia Chamber Music Society, and at the Kimmel Center for the Performing Arts or the Academy of Music, the telephone box office is Ticket Philadelphia (☎ 215/893-1999; www.ticketphiladelphia.org). The city's nonprofit box office Upstages (☎ 215/569-9700) represents a handful of smaller companies and theaters.

Cellphones

AT&T, Sprint, T-Mobile, and Verizon are the largest cellphone providers, offering access throughout the city. Philadelphia International Airport has three Airport Wireless stores (☎ 215/937-1065, 215/937-9620, or 215/365-2755; www.airportwireless.com) selling mobile phones, Palms, PDAs, laptops, and accessories. All-Cell (1528 Walnut St.; ☎ 877/724-2345; www.allcellrentals.com) is one of the nation's largest cellphone rental companies.

Car Rentals

Most major renters maintain offices at Philadelphia International Airport,

Useful Web Sites

www.independencevisitorcenter.com The city's official portal for visitors, also the place to reserve tickets to Independence Hall and for the basics for a short visit.

www.gophila.com A more comprehensive guide to Philadelphia and the surrounding Pennsylvania counties, created by the region's premier promoters—also great for hotel discounts.

www.ivc.org For visitors from abroad and new international residents, the site of the International Visitors Council of Philadelphia is especially useful.

www.phila.gov Straight from local government, this less-than-frequently-updated website has useful info nonetheless.

www.philly.com The ***Philadelphia Inquirer*** and the ***Philadelphia Daily News***, the city's two major newspapers, are the best and fastest sources for local news and events.

www.phillymag.com This monthly magazine offers local insider stories and great editorials on shopping, dining, and events.

and there are a small number of cars available from 30th Street Station and at Center City kiosks. Check out www.breezenet.com—or any number of travel websites—for car-rental discounts. (See p 159 for contact information.)

Getting **There**

By Plane

Philadelphia International Airport (PHL; ☎ 800/745-4283 or 215/937-6927; www.phl.org), is the city's major airport, about 10 miles southwest of Center City. To and from it, a SEPTA train (☎ 215/580-7800; www.septa.com) runs every 30 minutes to town ($7 adults one-way). A taxi in costs about $30, including tip. Smaller Atlantic City International Airport (ACY), in Egg Harbor Township, NJ, is about 1 hour's drive from Philadelphia (☎ 609/645-7895; www.acairport.com), and offers service to many U.S. cities.

By Car

I-95 (not the NJ Tpk.), runs north and south along the city's eastern edge. I-276 (formerly the PA Tpk.) comes in from the north/northeast. I-76 (aka the Schuylkill Expwy.) runs east and west, connecting to Center City via I-676. I-476 (aka the Blue Rte.), connects all of the above via western suburbs, about 15 miles west of town, linking I-276 and I-76 at the north, and I-95 to the south.

By Train

Amtrak (☎ 800/872-7245; www.amtrak.com) runs to 30th Street Station (at Market St.), where you can pick up a cab to your hotel, or connect to subways or regional rail (SEPTA) lines. If you're new to town, it's likely easiest to take a cab, especially if you're traveling in a group.

By Bus

Buses arrive at the Greyhound Bus Terminal (10th and Filbert sts.; ☎ 215-931-4075; www.greyhound.com). Reserve-by-Internet Bolt Buses (www.boltbus.com), travel to and from NYC from 30th Street between Market and Walnut streets, and Megabuses (www.megabus.com) go to and from NYC from 30th Street Station or Independence Mall.

Getting **Around**

On Foot

Center City measures 25 blocks (2 miles) from east to west and 12 blocks (1mile) north to south. A pedestrian should be able to cross town in about an hour and cross Old City in 15 minutes.

By Car

Two-thirds of all visitors to Philadelphia arrive by car. Traffic into town can be congested, especially during rush hours. The majority of Center City's streets are one-way, and some open up to three lanes during rush hour, so pay close attention to street signs.

By Taxi

Base fare for cabs is $2.70 and 30¢ for each additional ⅐ mile. A cross-town trip should cost about $11. Two good operators are Olde City Taxi (☎ 215/338-0838) and Quaker City (☎ 215/728-8000), although hailing from a street corner is usually fastest.

By Bus

May 1 through October 31, purple, daytime-only Phlash buses (☎ 215/636-1666; www.phillyphlash.com) loop to 20 attractions. Fare is $2 per ride; $5 for all-day unlimited ($10 per family). Philadelphia Trolley Works (☎ 215/239-8687; www.phillytour.com) operates double-decker bus and Victorian-style trolley tours with 20 stops; an all-day pass is $25 adults, $8 children.

By Public Transportation

SEPTA (☎ 215/580-7800; www.septa.com) operates all public transit, including buses that run along most major streets and subways that run beneath Market and Broad streets (use the Broad Street Line if you're headed to a sporting event or concert at a stadium in South Philadelphia; it's much faster and cheaper than driving). Fares are $2 cash (exact change required), less if you purchase tokens from a sidewalk kiosk or train station. A $10 one-day Independence Pass is valid for unlimited rides on any SEPTA bus, subway, trolley, or Phlash bus (but not regional rail). A $6 One Day Convenience Pass is valid for eight trips on buses, subways, and trolleys on one day (not valid for regional rail).

Fast **Facts**

APARTMENT RENTALS Try www.craigslist.org or either of the alt weekly newspapers, *Philadelphia Weekly* (www.philadelphiaweekly.com) or *City Paper* (www.citypaper.net).

Philadelphia Neighborhoods

CENTER CITY In other places, this busiest section would be called "downtown." From east to west, the Schuylkill and Delaware rivers bind this easy-to-navigate main city section. South Street and Vine Street bind it to the south and north. Neighborhoods within this area include Old City, Society Hill, Rittenhouse Square, and Washington West.

FAIRMOUNT Also known as the Art Museum area, this neighborhood stretches north from the Benjamin Franklin Parkway to Girard Avenue. Although it's largely residential, Fairmount also includes the Free Library, Rodin Museum, Eastern State Penitentiary, and the Philadelphia Art Museum itself.

OLD CITY Think New York's SoHo, but in the shadow of the Benjamin Franklin Bridge just north of Independence National Historical Park. It's an eclectic blend of 18th-century row houses, 19th-century warehouses, and 20th-century rehabs. This is now the city's hottest neighborhood with chic restaurants, bars, and boutiques set in historic buildings and storefronts.

RITTENHOUSE SQUARE This beautifully landscaped park ringed by elegant condominiums built during the 1930s and historic mansions illustrates the elegance, wealth, and culture of Philadelphia. Now, sleek outdoor cafes and luxury hotels line the park also.

SOCIETY HILL This heart of reclaimed 18th-century Philadelphia is loosely defined by Walnut and Lombard streets and Front and 7th streets. Today, it's a fashionable section of the old city, just south of Independence National Historical Park, where you can stroll among restored Federal, Colonial, and Georgian homes.

SOUTH PHILADELPHIA It's Rocky Balboa–meets–artist lofts and authentic *tacquerias*. Three hundred years of immigration have made South Philadelphia the city's most colorful and ethnically diverse neighborhood, although the overwhelming feel is distinctly Italian (think 1910s Calabria).

SOUTH STREET The street that is the southern border of Society Hill was the city limit in William Penn's day. Quiet by day and cruised by night, it's a colorful spot for casual dining, drinking, shopping, gallery-hopping, and getting pierced (or tattooed). The neighborhood's website is www.southstreet.com.

UNIVERSITY CITY West Philadelphia was farmland until the University of Pennsylvania moved here from 9th and Chestnut streets in the 1870s. Wander through Penn's campus for Ivy League architecture that includes an 1895 college green modeled on Oxford and Cambridge, but with Dutch gables.

AREA CODES In Philadelphia: 215 and 267. In the Pennsylvania suburbs: 610 and 484. In southern New Jersey: 856 and 609.

ATMS Throughout the city, most banks and convenience stores offer 24-hour ATMs, most charging a $2 or more fee per usage if the machine does not belong to your own bank.

BABYSITTING Hotel concierges are your best source.

BANKING HOURS Most banks are open weekdays 6am to 5pm; TD Banknorth (formerly Commerce; www.tdbanknorth.com) is open weekdays 7:30am to 8pm, Saturday 7:30am to 6pm, and Sunday 11am to 4pm.

B&BS Try **Bed & Breakfast Connections of Philadelphia** (☎ 800/448-3619; www.bnbphiladelphia.com) or visit www.bedandbreakfast.com.

BIKE RENTALS **Breakaway Bikes,** 1923 Chestnut St. (☎ 215/568-6002; www.breakawaybikes.com), rents from its shop Monday to Saturday 10am to 7pm, Sunday noon to 5pm, and operates a rental kiosk April to October Saturday 10am to 6pm, Sunday 10am to 4pm at Lloyd Hall, 1 Boathouse Row.

BUSINESS HOURS Most shops and restaurants are open Monday to Saturday 10am to 6 or 7pm, Sunday noon to 6pm. Offices are usually open weekdays 9am to 5pm.

CLIMATE See Weather.

CONCERTS See Theater Tickets.

CONSULATES AND EMBASSIES All are located in Washington, D.C. or New York City. See www.embassy.org/embassies.

DENTISTS See Emergencies.

DOCTORS See Emergencies.

EMBASSIES See Consulates and Embassies.

EMERGENCIES For fire, police, and medical emergencies, dial ☎ **911.** The nonemergency number for the police is ☎ **311.** For poison control, dial ☎ **800/222-1222** or 215/386-2100. For dental emergencies ☎ **866/685-2008** or 215/545-2600 (www.emergencydentist247.com).

EVENT LISTINGS Check out the daily newspapers the *Philadelphia Inquirer* and the *Philadelphia Daily News,* and their joint Web site (www.philly.com). The *Philadelphia Weekly* is available free from corner boxes and publishes on Wednesday (www.philadelphiaweekly.com). The *City Paper* is available free from corner boxes and publishes Thursday (www.citypaper.net). Monthly *Philadelphia* Magazine and its website (www.phillymag.com) are also a great source of info. Greater Philadelphia Cultural Alliance's website, www.phillyfunguide.com, is also a good resource.

FAMILY TRAVEL For family travel info, visit the Greater Philadelphia Tourism Marketing Corporation (www.gophila.com); and don't miss The Philadelphia Pass for family discounts on admission (www.philadelphiapass.com).

GAY & LESBIAN TRAVELERS Center City is welcoming to GLBT residents and visitors. The neighborhoods of Midtown and Washington West, a.k.a., the "gayborhood," have a concentration of gay-owned, -operated, and -friendly businesses. The Philadelphia Gay News (www.epgn.com) is available from sidewalk boxes. For support groups and events, contact the **William Way Community Center,** 1315 Spruce St. (☎ 215/735-2220, www.plgtf.

org). To report antigay violence or discrimination, call the **Philadelphia Lesbian and Gay Task Force Hot Line** (☎ 215/772-2000; www.plgtf.org).

HEALTH CLUBS **Sweat Gym** (www.sweatfitness.com)—with locations Midtown at 1425 Arch St. (☎ 215/546-0303); Rittenhouse at 200 S. 24th St., at Walnut St. (☎ 215/351-0100), and South Street at 700 E. Passyunk Ave., between Bainbridge and Fitzwater streets (☎ 215/627-5600); and elsewhere in the city—offers day passes for $15. **Philadelphia Sports Clubs** (www.mysportsclubs.com)—with locations in Society Hill at 250 S. 5th St., between Locust and Spruce streets (☎ 215/592-8900); and Rittenhouse at 1735 Market St. (☎ 215/564-5424)—offer day passes for $25.

HOLIDAYS Public and observed: January 1 (New Year's Day), third Monday in January (Martin Luther King, Jr. Day), third Monday in February (Washington's Birthday), last Monday in May (Memorial Day), July 4 (Independence Day), first Monday in September (Labor Day), November 11 (Veteran's Day), fourth Thursday in November (Thanksgiving), December 25 (Christmas).

HOSPITALS Philadelphia Children's Hospital, 34th Street and Civic Center Boulevard (☎ 215/590-1000; www.chop.edu); University of Pennsylvania Hospital, 3400 Spruce St. (☎ 215/662-4000; www.pennhealth.com); Pennsylvania Hospital, 8th and Spruce streets (☎ 215/829-3000; www.pennhealth.com/pahosp); Thomas Jefferson University Hospital, 11th and Walnut streets (☎ 215/955-6000; www.jeffersonhospital.org).

INSURANCE Check your existing policies (and credit cards) before purchasing insurance to cover trip cancellation, lost luggage, medical expenses, or car rental. For information on medical coverage, consider Europ Assistance's Worldwide Healthcare Plan, which covers the cost of an accident, repatriation, or death via **Worldwide Assistance Services, Inc.** (☎ 800/777-8710; www.worldwideassistance.com). Canadians should check with provincial health plan offices or call **Health Canada** (☎ 866/225-0709; www.hc-sc.gc.ca). Travelers from the U.K. should carry the **European Health Insurance Card** (EHIC) for treatment abroad (☎ 0845/606-2030; www.ehic.org.uk). For overall travel insurance, get estimates via InsureMyTrip.com. Frommer's generally recommends the following insurers: Access America (☎ 866/807-3982; www.accessamerica.com); Travel Insured International (☎ 800/243-3174; www.travelinsured.com); and Travelex Insurance Services (☎ 888/457-4602; www.travelex-insurance.com). TravelSafe (☎ 888/885-7233; www.travelsafe.com) offers hurricane and "any-reason" coverage. U.K. citizens who make more than one trip abroad yearly should consider an annual policy; check www.moneysupermarket.com to compare prices.

Trip-Cancellation Insurance: Trip-cancellation insurance typically covers you if you have to back out of a trip (due to illness, for example), if your travel supplier goes bankrupt, if there's a natural disaster, or if your government advises against travel to your destination—which isn't much of a worry for Philadelphia. Some plans cover cancellations for any reason. **TravelSafe** (☎ 888/885-7233; www.travelsafe.com) offers both types of coverage. **Expedia** (www.expedia.com) also offers any-reason cancellation coverage for its air-hotel packages. Other recommended insurers include

Hey, Google, did you get my text message?

It's bound to happen: The day you leave this guidebook back at the hotel for an unencumbered stroll through Society Hill, you'll forget the address of the lunch spot you had earmarked. If you're traveling with a mobile device, send a text message to ☎ **46645 (GOOGL)** for a lightning-fast response. For instance, type "fork etc philadelphia" and within 10 seconds you'll receive a text message with the address and phone number. This nifty trick works in a range of search categories: Look up weather ("weather philadelphia"), language translations ("translate goodbye in spanish"), currency conversions ("10 usd in pounds"), movie times ("harry potter 60605"), and more. If your search results are off, be more specific ("lucky strikes bowling chestnut street philadelphia"). For more tips and search options, see www.google.com/intl/en_us/mobile/sms/. Regular text message charges apply.

Access America (☎ 866/807-3982; www.accessamerica.com), **Travel Guard International** (☎ 800/826-4919; www.travelguard.com), **Travel Insured International** (☎ 800/243-3174; www.travel insured.com), and **Travelex Insurance Services** (☎ 888/457-4602; www.travelex-insurance.com).

Lost-Luggage Insurance: If your airline loses your luggage, immediately file a lost-luggage claim at the airport, detailing the luggage contents. Most airlines require that you report delayed, damaged, or lost baggage within 4 hours of arrival. On international flights, baggage coverage is limited to approximately $10 per pound, up to approximately $700 per checked bag. If you plan to check items more valuable than what's covered by the standard liability, see if your homeowner's policy covers your valuables, or get baggage insurance as part of your comprehensive travel-insurance package.

INTERNET Most coffee shops offer free wireless Internet access. **ING Direct Café** at 17th and Walnut streets (☎ 215/731-1410; http://home.ingdirect.com) has computer kiosks, as do branches of the **Free Library of Philadelphia** (☎ 215/686-5322; www.freelibrary.org).

LAUNDROMATS **U-Do-It Laundry & Dry Cleaning** is at 1513 Spruce St. (☎ 215/735-1255; open daily 7am–9pm). **Quick & Clean Coin Laundry** is at 320 S. 10th St., between Spruce and Pine streets (no phone; open daily 8am–8pm).

LIMOS **Dave's Best Limousine** (☎ 215/288-1000; www.daves bestlimoservice.com); **Executive Towncar** (☎ 215/485-7265; www.philly-sedan.com); **Victory Limo** (☎ 215/225-3655; www.victory limo.net).

LOST PROPERTY, CREDIT CARDS For American Express, call ☎ 800/221-7282. For MasterCard, call ☎ 800/307-7309 or 636/722-7111. For Visa, call ☎ 800/847-2911 or 410/581-9994. For other credit cards, call this directory: ☎ 800/555-1212.

LOST PROPERTY, AT THE AIRPORT Check with the Communications Center at the Philadelphia International Airport, Departures Roadway, between Terminals C and D (☎ 215/937-6888; www.phl.org/lostfound.html).

LOST PROPERTY, ON PUBLIC TRANSIT If you've lost an item on a SEPTA bus, subway, or trolley, call ☎ 215/580-7800; on SEPTA Regional Rail, call ☎ 215/580-5740.

MAIL & POSTAGE At press time, domestic postage rates are 28¢ for a postcard, 44¢ for a letter. A letter to Canada or Mexico is 72¢; other international destinations cost 94¢. Find post offices and more rates at www.usps.gov.

ORIENTATION TOURS See Tours.

PARKING On-street parking is notoriously complicated, with zoned neighborhood permits, regulations that change according to the day and hour, and a diminishing number of coin-operated parking meters—as of press time, the city was moving toward a block-by-block payment via automated ticket kiosks. Parking garages abound, but are not cheap: Expect to pay around $24 per day to park.

PASSES Philadelphia Citypass (www.citypass.com) offers admission to six attractions: the Franklin Institute, National Constitution Center, Philadelphia Zoo, Adventure Aquarium, the Academy of Natural Sciences (or Eastern State Penitentiary), and a Philadelphia Trolley Works tour. Admission to all attractions costs $54 adults, $37 children 4 to 12; free children under 4. Tickets are valid 9 days from first usage.

PASSPORTS Virtually every traveler entering the U.S. must show a passport. U.S. and Canadian citizens by land or sea from within the Western Hemisphere may present government-issued proof of citizenship, although a passport is recommended.

PHARMACIES For 24-hour service, go to **CVS,** 1826 Chestnut St., at 19th Street (☎ 215/972-1401; www.cvs.com); and **Rite Aid,** 2301 Walnut St., at 23rd Street (☎ 215/636-9634; www.riteaid.com).

SAFETY Although Center City is generally quite safe, it is not without its muggings and purse-snatchings. Do not leave belongings unattended, especially in a cafe or restaurant, and be especially vigilant during holiday times. Use common city sense and be aware of your surroundings.

SENIOR TRAVELERS A compact downtown, vibrant cultural life, and widely available senior discounts at museums, events, and attractions make Philadelphia attractive to an increasing population of retirees and empty nesters. The Independence Visitors Center publishes a "Seniors on the Go" listing containing dozens of senior benefits and discounts.

SMOKING The city's smoking ban prohibits smoking on public transit and inside restaurants, cafes, hotels and hotel rooms, shops, offices, and the large majority of bars. Smoking is permitted at outside tables and in most public spaces (i.e., on sidewalks, in parks). You must be 18 years old to purchase tobacco products.

SEGWAY TOURS March to November, **iGlide** (☎ 877/454-3381; www.iglidetours.com) offers tours of the Philadelphia Museum of Art area via

Segway i2 Gliders, departing three times a day from Eakins Oval (in front of the Art Museum). Tours are daily at 10am, and 1:30 and 7pm. Daytime tours are 2½ hours and cost $69; evening tours are 1½ hours and cost $49.

SPECTATOR SPORTS All of Philadelphia's professional sports teams play at the stadiums at the south end of Broad Street (SEPTA Broad Street stop: Pattison Ave. station). Early April through early October, the Phillies play baseball at Citizens Bank Park (http://philadelphia.phillies.mlb.com). Mid-September through early January, the Eagles play football at Lincoln Financial Field (www.philadelphiaeagles.com). October through April, the Flyers play ice hockey at the Wachovia Center (http://flyers.nhl.com). Late October through mid-April, the 76ers play basketball at the Wachovia Center (www.nba.com/sixers).

STUDENT TRAVEL There are more colleges and universities in and around Philadelphia than in any other city in the country, so students will find a warm reception from area vendors and sights. A valid student ID will get you reduced rates on cultural sites, accommodations, car rentals, and more. You'll also earn a deep discount at **Apple Hostel** (formerly Bank Street Hostel) 32 S. Bank St. (☎ **877/275-1971**), right in the center of all of Old City nightlife and, oh yes, history.

When in Philadelphia, pick up a copy of student papers such as the *Daily Pennsylvanian* (www.dailypennsylvanian.com) at the Ivy League **University of Pennsylvania,** 34th and Walnut streets (☎ 215/898-5000; www.upenn.edu); *The Temple News* (www.temple-news.com) at **Temple University,** North Broad Street (☎ 215/204-7000; www.temple.edu); or *The Triangle* (www.thetriangle.org) at **Drexel University,** 32nd and Chestnut streets (☎ 215/895-2000; www.drexel.edu).

TAXES At press time, Philadelphia's retail sales tax is 7% on everything except clothing. Tax on liquor is 10%. Tax on hotel stays is 15.5%.

TAXIS See Getting Around, By Taxi.

TELEPHONES Coin-operated telephones are few and far between, but generally can be found at transportation hubs such as train stations or the airport. The cost per local call is 35¢.

TICKETS See box in Performing Arts chapter, p 132.

TIPPING For servers in a restaurant and spa employees, tip 18% to 20% of the bill; taxi drivers 15% to 20% of fare; hotel chamber staff $2 to $3 per day; coat check $1 per checked item; valet parking $1 per ride.

TOILETS Most attractions have facilities, as do restaurants and cafes. The latter often have a "customers only" usage policy.

TOURIST OFFICES The **Independence Visitor Center** is at 1 N. Independence Mall W. (6th and Market sts.), Philadelphia, PA 19106 (☎ 800/537-7676 or 215/965-7676; www.independencevisitorcenter.com). For special advise for international visitors, contact the International Visitors Center of Philadelphia, 1515 Arch St., 12th floor (☎ 215/683-0999; www.ivc.org).

TOURS City-wide, 90-minute tours of 20 attractions via Victorian-style trolley or open-top "Big Bus" are available year round, with passes valid for 24 hours, from **Philadelphia Trolley Company,** 5th and Market streets, (☎ 866/324-4287 or 215/389-8687; www.phillytour.com;

tickets $27 adults, $25 seniors, $10 children 4–12). At the same location, horse-and-buggies gather for tours of Society Hill and Old City; prices start at $30 for 1–4 people; $7 per additional person (buggy seats up to six). Spring through fall, **Ride the Ducks,** 6th and Chestnut streets (☎ 877/887-8225 or 215/227-3825; www.phillyducks.com; tickets $26 adults, $24 seniors, $16 children 3–12) offers lighthearted, 70- to 80-minute tours of the city (and the Delaware River) via land-to-water World War II DUKW amphibious vehicles.

TRAVELERS WITH DISABILITIES Most attractions—although not all National Historic Landmarks—offer ADA-approved access to their facilities. For basic Philadelphia information, contact the **Mayor's Commission on People with Disabilities** (☎ 215/686-2798; www.phila.gov/mcpd). SEPTA buses are lift-equipped, and all major train stations have elevator access. **Art-Reach** (☎ 215/568-2115; www.art-reach.org), a not-for-profit organization, maintains a list of more than 140 area facilities that offer access to persons with disabilities. The **Philadelphia International Airport** hotline for travelers with disabilities is ☎ 215/937-6700 (TTY ☎ 215/937-6755). The Independence Visitor Center publishes *Accessibilities,* a brochure detailing accessible parking spots. The America the Beautiful—National Park and Federal Recreational Lands Pass—Access Pass (formerly the Golden Access Passport) gives visually impaired or permanently disabled persons free lifetime entrance to federal recreation sites administered by the National Park Service.

WEATHER See Climate.

A Brief **History**

EARLY 1600s Europeans first arrive in the Delaware Valley.

1638 Swedish settlers sail up the Delaware River on the *Key of Kalmar* and *Flying Griffin,* and take control of the land along the Schuylkill River.

1681 Charles II of England (1630–1685) signs the charter granting Quaker nobleman William Penn (1644–1718) more than 45,000 square miles of the New World, which offered religious freedom to all within.

1701 Penn issues a charter establishing Philadelphia as a city.

1731 Benjamin Franklin (1706–1790) creates America's first lending library.

1749 Benjamin Franklin creates the University of Pennsylvania.

1751 Benjamin Franklin invents the lightning rod.

1751 Benjamin Franklin and Thomas Bond (1712–1784) create the Colonies' first hospital.

1760 Benjamin Franklin invents the bifocal.

1774 The First Continental Congress petitions King George (1738–1820) for redress of colonists' grievances at Carpenters' Hall.

1775 Delegates from all 13 Colonies meet for the Second Continental Congress, after the American Revolutionary War begins.

1776 The Congress signs the United States Declaration of Independence, turning colonies into states, and separating from England.

1783 The American Revolution ends.

1790 Philadelphia becomes the capital of the new United States of America.

1800 Washington, D.C., becomes the capital of the U.S.

1876 The Centennial Exposition of 1876—the first world's fair—takes place in Fairmount Park and establishes the Philadelphia Museum of Art.

1901–1908 Philadelphia City Hall is the tallest habitable building in the world.

1912 Albert Barnes (1872–1951) meets Pablo Picasso (1881–1973) and Henri Matisse (1869–1954) in Paris, begins to collect art.

1917 Benjamin Franklin Parkway construction begins, creating a future home for the city's most important museums.

1930 A hotdog vendor named Pat Olivieri slaps some steak and cheese on a bun. The cheesesteak is born.

1946 A Penn professor and a lab assistant build ENIAC, the world's first computer.

1970 French chef Georges Perrier opens Le Bec-Fin, starting a Philadelphia restaurant renaissance.

1971 Kenneth Gamble (1943–) and Leon Huff (1942–) found The Sound of Philadelphia, Motown's biggest competitor.

1975 Elton John's (1947–) *Philadelphia Freedom* hits number one on the American pop charts.

1976 *Rocky* hits it big in the box office, then wins the Best Picture Oscar, sealing Philly's rep as hardscrabble.

1980 Philies win the World Series of Baseball.

1985 Mayor Wilson Goode (1938–) authorizes the dropping of a bomb on a home belonging to MOVE, a radical black roots group, killing 11 members of the group and destroying 62 homes.

1991 Future Pennsylvania governor Edward Rendell (1944–) wins the mayor's race and spurs on the rebirth of Center City as a destination for dining, shopping, and bar-hopping.

1999 M. Night Shyamalan (1970–) releases *The Sixth Sense* and puts Philadelphia back on the film-making map.

2008 Phillies win the World Series of Baseball.

Philadelphia's **Architecture**

Like the city itself, Philadelphia's architecture and art scene is a melting pot of schools and styles. Walk down most any Center City street, and you're likely to encounter Art Deco facades, Victorian townhouses, Colonial brick buildings, freshly painted murals, and, above it all, glass and steel skyscrapers. Philadelphia's very first buildings were simple log cabins, which are now all but lost to time. The city's second architectural wave was more enduring:

Seventeenth-century settlers often built their houses of meeting and worship in brick, using a mix of architectural styles from their diverse backgrounds. One such brick edifice is the Old Swedes' Church (see p 23), built around 1700 and still active. The guild-built marriage of Gothic and medieval styles has nods to the then-emerging Georgian aesthetic, featuring alternating Flemish Bond brick patterns.

More examples of Georgian architecture—typified by symmetry and simplicity, paned windows and rectangular transoms—include plainly elegant Christ Church (see p 11), Carpenters' Hall (see p 26), Powel House (see p 55), and Independence Hall (see p 9).

About a half a century later came the next wave of building design, a marriage of classically Greek Palladian and Georgian styles, called Federal. This style dominated important buildings from pre-Revolutionary times until the mid-1800s and can

How to Speak Like a Philadelphian: Ten Terms

1. Philly. Use only if you're a native. Otherwise, it's "Philadelphia."
2. Broad Street. The north-south boulevard bisecting Center City is what would be 14th Street. But never call Broad Street "14th Street." Its new tourist-friendly designation of "Avenue of the Arts" is a little suspicious, too. But "Broad" is good.
3. Second Street. If you're in South Philadelphia, call it "Two Street."
4. Front Street. Really 1st Street. Call it "Front."
5. Schuylkill. Pronounced "Skoo-kill," it's the river that flows by the Philadelphia Museum of Art between Martin Luther King, Jr. and Kelly drives. It's also the name for I-76, the interstate expressway running east-west through the city.
6. Blue Route. I-476, which connects I-95, I-76, and I-276 (the Pennsylvania Tpk.).
7. Passyunk Avenue. Pronounced "Pass-yunk," this one-way avenue runs diagonally south to north from Broad Street to South Street, through South Philadelphia.
8. Sansom Street. Pronounced "San-som," not "Samp-son." Although, if you're going to make a mistake, this is the one to make.
9. The Boulevard. The Roosevelt Boulevard, Route 1 North, is a high-speed thoroughfare running through Northeast Philadelphia, connecting the Schuylkill Expressway (I-76) to I-276 (the Pennsylvania Tpk.), which leads to the New Jersey Turnpike.
10. Cheesesteak. One word. Not "cheese steak." Definitely not "Philly cheese steak."

What Things Cost in Philadelphia

A cup of coffee from La Colombe	\$1.50
Subway, bus, or trolley fare	\$2
A pint of Yards ale at Standard Tap	\$5
Cheesesteak at Pat's King of Steaks	\$7.50
Adult admission to the Philadelphia Museum of Art	\$16
A standing-room-only Phillies ticket	\$18
Taxi ride from airport to Center City, with tip	\$30
Train ride from airport to Center City	\$6
Dinner for two at Ralph's Italian Restaurant	\$59
Average hotel room rate, one night (before tax)	\$138

be found in four-pilastered Library Hall (see p 67) and the Pine Street side of Pennsylvania Hospital (see p 56), in addition to dozens of houses in Society Hill: Look for a front door surrounded by glass panes and topped by an arched window. Another sure sign of a Federal building: The presence of a bald eagle.

The next several decades subtracted the Georgian leanings from Federal architecture and revived the classically Greek. Not surprisingly, this early-19th-century architectural style is called Greek Revival—or, if you prefer, neoclassical. Architects known for this style included artist-turned-architect William Strickland (1788–1854), who designed the heavily columned, dramatically domed Second Bank of the United States; Old City's imposing Merchants' Exchange at 2nd and Walnut streets; and the National Mechanic Bank, 22 S. 3rd St. (btw. Market and Chestnut sts.), now a restaurant and bar. Similarly, architect William Haviland (1792–1852) did some of his most important work in Center City, including the Walnut Street Theater (see p 128), the University of the Arts building at broad and Pine streets, and Eastern State Penitentiary (see p 48).

Frank Furness (1839–1912), another native son, designed distinctively ornamental Victorian Gothic buildings featuring polychromatic masonry (multicolored bricked laid in an icing-type fashion), including the elegant Pennsylvania Academy of the Fine Arts (see p 30) and Fischer Fine Arts Library at the University of Pennsylvania (see p 70). Scotsman John McArthur, Jr. (1823–1890) designed the all-masonry City Hall (see p 20) in Second Empire style.

Philadelphia's earliest skyscrapers would not be considered so by modern standards. At its building in 1925, the Ben Franklin House at on Chestnut Street, between 8th and 9th streets; 30th Street Station (see p 71); and the Franklin Institute (see p 47) were considered tall. The first modern-looking skyscraper was the steel-and-glass PSFS building (now Loews Hotel, see p 139), designed by William Lescaze (1896–1969) and George Howe (1886–1955) in 1932, and considered the world's first International Style building. Native son Louis I. Kahn (1901–1974) served as architect for Richards Medical Library at the University of Pennsylvania, while I.M. Pei (1917–) designed Society Hill T owers (see p 17) and the shining

National Constitution Center (see p 10). In the 1980s, chess-piece-like Liberty One (1650 Market St.) and Liberty Two (1601 Chestnut St.) were the first buildings to rise above the brim of William Penn's hat (atop City Hall). In 2008, cable giant Comcast put its name on the city's tallest building to date, the tech-chocked, USB-stick-looking Comcast Center at 17th Street and JFK Boulevard (see p 63).

Toll-free Numbers & Websites

AIRLINES

AIR CANADA
☎ *888/247-22262 in the U.S. or Canada*
www.aircanada.com

AIR FRANCE
☎ *800/375-8723 in the U.S. or Canada*
☎ *0871/66-33-777 in the U.K.*
www.airfrance.com

AIR JAMAICA
☎ *800/523-5585 in the U.S. or Canada*
☎ *208/570-7999 in the U.K.*
www.airjamaica.com

AIRTRAN AIRWAYS
☎ *800/247-8726*
www.airtran.com

AMERICAN AIRLINES
☎ *800/433-7300 in the U.S. or Canada*
☎ *020/7365-0777 in the U.K.*
www.aa.com

BRITISH AIRWAYS
☎ *800/247-9297 in the U.S. or Canada*
☎ *087/0850-9850 in the U.K.*
www.ba.com

CONTINENTAL AIRLIINES
☎ *800/523-3273 in the U.S. or Canada*
☎ *084/5607-6760 in the U.K.*
www.continental.com

DELTA AIR LINES
☎ *800/221-1212 in the U.S. or Canada*
☎ *084/5600-0950 in the U.K.*
www.delta.com

FRONTIER AIRLINES
☎ *800/432-1359*
www.frontierairlines.com

LUFTHANSA
☎ *800/399-5838 in the U.S.*
☎ *800/563-5954 in Canada*
☎ *087/0837-7747 in the U.K.*
www.lufthansa.com

MIDWEST AIRLINES
☎ *800/452-2022*
www.midwestairlines.com

NORTHWEST AIRLINES
☎ *800/225-2525 in the U.S.*
☎ *870/0507-4074 in the U.K.*
www.nwa.com

SOUTHWEST AIRLINES
☎ *800/435-9792*
www.southwest.com

TURKISH AIRLINES
☎ *90/212-444-0-849*
www.thy.com

UNITED AIRLINES
☎ *800/864-8331 in the U.S. or Canada*
☎ *084/5844-4777 in the U.K.*
www.united.com

US AIRWAYS
☎ *800/428-4322 in the U.S. or Canada*
☎ *084/5600-3300 in the U.K.*
www.usairways.com

USA 3000
☎ *877/872-3000*
www.usa3000.com

CAR-RENTAL AGENCIES

ALAMO
☎ *800/462-5266*
www.alamo.com

AVIS
☎ *800/331-1212 in the U.S.*
☎ *084/4581-8181 in the U.K.*
www.avis.com

BUDGET
☎ *800/527-0700 in the U.S.*
☎ *087/0156-5656 in the U.K.*
☎ *800/268-8900 in Canada*
www.budget.com

DOLLAR
☎ *800/800-4000 in the U.S.*
☎ *800/848-8268 in Canada*
☎ *080/8234-7524 in the U.K.*
www.dollar.com

ENTERPRISE
☎ *800/261-7331 in the U.S.*
☎ *514/355-4028 in Canada*
☎ *012/9360-9090 in the U.K.*
www.enterprise.com

HERTZ
☎ *800/645-3131*
☎ *800/654-3001 for calls from outside North America*
www.hertz.com

NATIONAL
☎ *800/227-7368*
www.nationalcar.com

PAYLESS
☎ *800/729-5377*
www.paylesscarrental.com

THRIFTY
☎ *800/367-2277*
☎ *918/669-2168 for calls from outside North America*
www.thrifty.com

MAJOR HOTEL CHAINS & MOTEL CHAINS

ALOFT
☎ *877/462-5638*
www.starwoodhotels.com

BEST WESTERN INTERNATIONAL
☎ *800/780-7234 in the U.S. or Canada*
☎ *0800/393-130 in the U.K.*
www.bestwestern.com

CLARION HOTELS
☎ *800/252-7466 OR 877/424-6423 in the U.S. or Canada*
☎ *0800/444-444 in the U.K.*
www.clarionhotel.com

COMFORT INNS
☎ *800/228-5150*
☎ *0800/444-444 in the U.K.*
www.comfortinn.com

COURTYARD BY MARRIOTT
☎ *888/236-2427 in the U.S.*
☎ *0800/221-222 in the U.K.*
www.marriott.com/courtyard

CROWNE PLAZA HOTELS
☎ *888/303-1746*
www.ichotelsgroup.com/crowneplaza

DAYS INN
☎ *800/329-7566 in the U.S.*
☎ *0800/280-400 in the U.K.*
www.daysinn.com

DOUBLETREE HOTELS
☎ *800/222-8733 in the U.S. or Canada*
☎ *087/0590-9090 in the U.K.*
www.doubletree.com

ECONO LODGES
☎ *800/552-3666*
www.econolodge.com

EMBASSY SUITES
☎ *800/362-2779*
www.embassysuites.com

FAIRFIELD INN BY MARRIOTT
☎ *800/228-2800 in the U.S. or Canada*
☎ *0800/221-222 in the U.K.*
www.marriott.com/fairfieldinn

FOUR SEASONS
☎ *800/819-5053 in the U.S. or Canada*
☎ *0800/6488-6488 in the U.K.*
www.fourseasons.com

HAMPTON INN
☎ *800/426-4766*
www.hamptoninn.com

HILTON HOTELS
☎ *800/445-8667 in the U.S. or Canada*
☎ *087/0590-9090 in the U.K.*
www.hilton.com

HOWARD JOHNSON
☎ *800/446-4656 in the U.S. or Canada*
www.hojo.com

HYATT
☎ *888/591-1234 in the U.S. or Canada*
☎ *084/5888-1234 in the U.K.*
www.hyatt.com

INTERCONTINENTAL HOTELS & RESORTS
☎ *800/424-6835 in the U.S. or Canada*
☎ *0800/1800-1800 in the U.K.*
www.ichotelsgroup.com

LOEWS HOTELS
☎ *800/235-6397*
www.loewshotels.com

MARRIOTT
☎ *877/236-2427 in the U.S. or Canada*
☎ *0800/21-222 in the U.K.*
www.marriott.com

OMNI HOTELS
☎ *888/444-6664*
www.omnihotels.com

PALOMAR/KIMPTON HOTELS
☎ *800/546-7866*
www.kimptonhotels.com

RADISSON HOTELS & RESORTS
☎ *888/201-1718 in the U.S. or Canada*
☎ *0800/374-411 in the U.K.*
www.radisson.com

RAMADA WORLDWIDE
☎ *888/272-6232 in the U.S. or Canada*
☎ *080/8100-0783 in the U.K.*
www.ramada.com

RED CARPET INNS
☎ *800/251-1962*
www.bookroomsnow.com

RED ROOF INNS
☎ *866/686-4335 in the U.S. or Canada*

☎ *614/601-4075 international*
www.redroof.com

RENAISSANCE HOTELS & RESORTS BY MARRIOTT
☎ *888/236-2427*
www.renaissancehotels.com

RESIDENCE INN BY MARRIOTT
☎ *800/331-3131*
☎ *0800/221-222 in the U.K.*
www.marriott.com/residenceinn

RITZ-CARLTON
☎ *800/542-8680 in the U.S. and Canada*
☎ *0800/234-000 in the U.K.*
www.ritzcarlton.com

RODEWAY INN
☎ *877/424-6423*
www.rodewayinn.com

SHERATON HOTELS & RESORTS
☎ *800/325-3535 in the U.S.*
☎ *800/543-4300 in Canada*
☎ *0800/3253-5353 in the U.K.*
www.starwoodhotels.com/sheraton

SUPER 8 MOTELS
☎ *800/800-8000*
www.super8.com

TRAVELODGE
☎ *800/578-7878*
www.travelodge.com

WESTIN HOTELS & RESORTS
☎ *800/937-8461 in the U.S. or Canada*
☎ *0800/3259-5959 in the U.K.*
www.starwoodhotels.com/westin

WYNDHAM HOTELS & RESORTS
☎ *877/999-3223 in the U.S. or Canada*
☎ *050/6638-4899 in the U.K.*
www.wyndham.com

Index

See also Accommodations and Restaurant indexes, below.

L

M

N

O

P

Photo **Credits**

Notes